THE
SIMPLICITY THAT IS IN CHRIST.

SERMONS

TO THE

WOODLAND CHURCH, PHILADELPHIA.

BY

LEONARD WOOLSEY BACON.

WIPF & STOCK · Eugene, Oregon

Wipf and Stock Publishers
199 W 8th Ave, Suite 3
Eugene, OR 97401

The Simplicity that is in Christ
Sermons to the Woodland Church, Philadelphia
By Bacon, Leonard Woolsey
Softcover ISBN-13: 978-1-7252-9672-5
eBook ISBN-13: 978-1-7252-9673-2
Publication date 1/7/2021
Previously published by Funk & Wagnalls, 1886

This edition is a scanned facsimile of
the original edition published in 1886.

Η ΑΠΛΟΤΗΣ Η ΕΙΣ ΤΟΝ ΧΡΙΣΤΟΝ.—2 Cor. xi. 3.

The Simplicity that is in Christ. (A. V.)

The Simplicity that is toward Christ. (R. V.)

LETTER

DEDICATORY AND INTRODUCTORY.

To the Congregation of the Woodland Church.

My Dear Friends:

I present to you herewith a volume containing some of the sermons which I have preached during the brief time in which it has been my privilege to fulfill among you the duties of a pastor; and with the volume, I beg you to accept the renewed expression of my love, and my willing devotion to your service in the gospel.

* * * * * *

Thus I wrote a few months ago, when I was first preparing this volume for the press. I hoped then that it was to be an aid and reinforcement to my ministry among you. And now that it proves to be rather a memorial of a ministry broken off and ended, I have nothing to change in these words of affection and willing service. "It is in my heart to live and die with you." And if, instead, I seem to be withdrawing from you, it is for your sake that I do it, as I would for your sake far more gladly remain and serve with you.

It is a frequent and good reason for the printing of sermons, that the public interest in them has been proved by a great concourse of hearers. Let us frankly confess that there is no such excuse for this volume. My reason for printing would be just the opposite—that the arguments and persuasions which have been heard with deep attention by a few, might have a wider and more deliberate consideration. In the larger congregation whose attention I would fain engage, I hope to renew the satisfaction of hearing of those who find in these words light upon dark places, and help over hard places, and the pointing out of a plain path where the ways had seemed confused.

Withal, something seemed to be due to those persons who have manifested an eager desire to find something to complain of in my preaching, but have had little or no opportunity of hearing it. It has been my misfortune that, while those who have been constantly attendant on my ministry have seemed generally to approve of it as salutary and good, some of those who know nothing about it should be dissatisfied, not to say aggrieved at it, and much disposed to find fault with it. To such, it seems an act of kindness to offer them some material for their fraternal labors. I am afraid that they will be disappointed in the book; but they may be assured that they were considered in the selection of sermons for it, with an honest purpose of giving them such as they would most enjoy being displeased with.

You who have been of my habitual hearers will recognize the title of this book as indicating a characteristic of the Woodland pulpit. It has been my constant purpose to go back of systems, confessions, traditions, conventional phrases, to "the simplicity that is in Christ." It is away from simplicity that corruption commonly tends, and toward it that good reformation returns. A very common and self-complacent mistake on the part of dogmatists is this: when perplexed, unintelligible or unreasonable statements of doctrine are found to be unacceptable to thoughtful people, to set it down to the charge of "the carnal mind." But in fact, if anything is clearly taught by the history of religious corruption, it is this, that the carnal mind likes its doctrines tough; is not content, in religion, with things easy, direct, simple, intelligible, reasonable; finds no virtue in receiving what is clear, or believing what is proved; finds plain gospel quite insipid without a flavoring of metaphysics or a garnish of tradition. The carnal mind is much addicted to the building of systems, and fertile of material for filling the gaps therein. The carnal mind knows a great deal, and knows it with uncommon positiveness and precision. The carnal mind has found out the Almighty to perfection. Two evil tendencies vex the church in every age: without is agnosticism, and within is hypergnosticism; and either of the twain abets the other.

You will miss some of the sermons for which, since this volume was announced, I have had repeated requests; and you will be at a loss, perhaps, to discover the principle which has governed the selection. But there has been a principle, in favor of which I have been willing to sacrifice your wishes and my own notions of literary value. The book "waits upon teaching." The sermons are chosen rather for their doctrinal contents than for their rhetorical interest; and broken parts of several series have been given, in order that the book may be representative of the course of my preaching.

Since the way of salvation is this, to believe on the Lord Jesus Christ, the essence of the preaching of the gospel is mainly summed up in these two points: 1. What is believing on? 2. Who is the Lord Jesus Christ? and to these two points—"the simplicity that is toward Christ" (to quote the text correctly) and "the simplicity that is in Christ"—the earlier and larger part of the book is devoted.

The three "sermons of Natural Theology," with the four sermons that next follow them, have to do with questions now very widely under discussion.

The last sermon in the volume is of special interest to the Woodland Church; and it gives a means of understanding my views concerning "the church, the communion of saints," to some who have misunderstood them.

One point which I hope to gain by this publication is to discover, through the good offices of my critics, whether or not I am of "the new theology." For it is confidently and sometimes plaintively asserted that there is such a thing as "the new theology;" otherwise we might not have discovered any fact more serious than this, that there are sundry theological writers more or less diverging from each other, and from their predecessors—certainly no novel phenomenon, but one common to every Annus Domini of all the eighteen hundred. If any one could compute the resultant of these diverging forces at any given period, I suppose that would be "the new theology" for that time. If it should appear from such computation that "the new theology" of our time consists mainly in these three tendencies: 1, to concentrate study upon the life and person of Jesus Christ; 2, to accept with a docile mind the teaching of the Bible concerning itself; 3, to subordinate sectarian and provincial theologies to the fellowship of belief in the church universal;—then I would gladly count myself on the side of the new theology,—or count the new theology to be on my side.

LEONARD WOOLSEY BACON.

PHILADELPHIA, *March*, 1886

CONTENTS.

LETTER DEDICATORY AND INTRODUCTORY, ... 1–4

Salutatory and Valedictory. Motives for publishing. Corruptions in religion tend away from simplicity. The heresy of hypergnosticism. Selection of materials for this volume. The author and "the new theology."

THE SIMPLICITY THAT IS TOWARD CHRIST.

SERMON I. THE SIMPLICITY OF REPENTANCE. Acts xx. 21, . 15–23

The two cardinal words of practical Christianity are current in perverted meanings. History of the word *Repentance*. Proposed substitutes for the word. Two forms of false repentance: 1. External reformation; 2. Inward agitation. True repentance, the turning of the mind.

SERMON II. THE SIMPLICITY OF FAITH. Acts xvi. 31, . 24–38

The question What is Faith? one of the open questions of theology.
Four tests of the right meaning of the word.—1. It must be the common, plain sense of the word, as used by common people. 2. It must be a sense applicable to the Scriptural examples of faith. 3. It must describe a voluntary act. 4. It must describe an act which practically involves repentance, love, holiness.

Four false definitions of *Faith*:—1. That it is the assent of the intellect to truth. 2. That it is a peculiar quality or intensity of intellectual assent. 3. That it is a confident assurance of one's personal salvation. 4. That Faith consists of Faith *plus* a certain sequence of experiences.

The true definition: To believe in the Lord Jesus Christ is to trust in him.

CONTENTS.

SERMON III. THE OPEN DOOR OF THE CHURCH. Acts viii. 37, . 39–47

Contrast between the Apostolic and the Modern Church in respect to the Open Door. The point of divergence from apostolic usage. Lessons to be learned from spurious texts.

Those things which God appointed for our Helps, are turned by men into Hindrances. 1. Rites. 2. Experiences. 3. Doctrines.

SERMON IV. THE OUTSIDE CHRISTIAN. John x. 16, ... 48–57

Ecclesiastical jealousy of the largeness of Christ's hospitality.

The Outside Christian an abnormal Christian. Causes of his self-exclusion. 1. Revivalism. 2. Unworthy conceptions of God. 3. Imprudent cautiousness. 4. Unfaithfulness in the church. 5. The multitude of sects. These mingle with baser motives.

What he loses. 1. Strength. 2. Joy. 3. Fellowship. 4. Comfort in the Lord's Supper. The harm he may do. The good he might do.

THE SIMPLICITY THAT IS IN CHRIST.

SERMON V. MAN'S QUESTION ABOUT CHRIST. Matt. viii. 27, . 58–67

The Gospel method of teaching Christ an inductive method; in contrast with the theological method. The return of theology to the method of the gospels.

Christ's perfect manhood being admitted, the question arises how to reconcile to this the facts which seem out of harmony with it.

SERMON VI. CHRIST'S QUESTION TO MEN. Matt. xvi. 15, . . 68–79

The natural way, and the biblical way, of coming to the knowledge of Christ is also the logical way. The authority of apostolic declaration or church definition depends on antecedent admission of the authority of Christ.

The statement of his perfect manhood not sufficient to include all the facts. The series of facts which it leaves out. The question left pending; but in no anxious suspense.

SERMON VII. THE MYSTERY MANIFESTED 1 Tim. iii. 16, . . 80–90

The question on the reading of the text. The meaning of the word *mystery*.

What is the missing fact, or comprehensive statement, which shall reconcile the seeming discordances in Christ's life?

In the apostolic writings, the semblance of discrepancy is rather increased than diminished.

An analogy to the discrepancy in the life of Christ is found in the person of man. This analogy helps us, if not to understand, at least to receive, "the mystery of godliness."

Further than this it is not profitable to go.

CHRIST TEACHING BY MIRACLES.

SERMON VIII. THE PURPOSE OF THE MIRACLES OF HEALING. Mark ii. 10, ... 91–101

Why so many miracles of healing?

I. The obvious answer, that the works of healing had their object in themselves, as conferring happiness and diminishing suffering, is liable to conclusive objections: 1. The deduction from the sum of human misery is insignificant 2. The arbitrary interruption of the general course of human suffering is not in itself desirable.

II. The real answer declared in the text—" That ye may know that the Son of man hath power to forgive"

III. The miracle of healing is a visible exhibition of salvation: 1. How God confers it 2. How man receives it

SERMON IX THE HEALING OF THE PALSIED Luke v. 24, 25, 102–112

The miracle is a parable: 1. Of divine power and love. 2. Of human faith.

Looking at the human aspect of it, we consider: 1. The paralytic's prayer. 2. The answer which he received:—(1) The substance of what he had asked, but not the form (2) A greater thing than he had asked. (3) At last, the identical thing which he had asked.

SERMON X. THE PRAYER OF THE HEATHEN MOTHER. Mark vii 24–30, and Matthew xv 21-28, .   113–122

The story told in these two gospels is the simplest of dramas, having two persons and a chorus The scene of it.

We fix our attention on the person of the heathen woman and note: 1 Her trouble. 2. Her faith, not (1) a superstitious credulity; nor (2) a hesitating experiment. 3. Her reward.

CONTENTS.

SERMON XI. THE HEALING OF THE HEATHEN GIRL. Matthew xv. 23, ... 123–132

We turn our attention now to the other person of the story, the Lord Jesus.

Looking on him as the model of human duty and the expression of the divine nature, we find in this story things amazing and perplexing. What are we to learn from them?

1. The perplexities in the life of Christ are like the perplexities in the government of God.

2. The incident exhibits Christ gazing inexorable, for a time, on human suffering.

3. His apparent unkindness is only apparent.

4. His blessing is already given, while yet the supplicant is unaware of it.

SERMON XII THE GADARENE DEMONIAC. Mark v. 6, . . 133–142

Demoniacal possession in the New Testament. Questions and difficulties.

1. It was not mere lunacy or epilepsy. 2. It was not mere wickedness.

The symptom of a double and discordant consciousness. This is analogous to the inward discord wrought by sin. A dominant passion becomes like a possessing demon. One thus possessed may, at the same time, both seek Christ and repel him.

What hope is there for the soul that is in such a case?

SERMON XIII. THE GOSPEL AMONG THE GADARENES. Mark v. 17, ... 143–153

The report of the swineherds:—1. Concerning the things that had befallen the demoniac. 2. Concerning the swine.

The kingdom of heaven cannot come without inflicting some loss on personal and vested interests:—1 By its institutions 2. By its charities. 3. By its reforms. 4. By its laws of personal morality.

He who is ready to receive the kingdom of heaven, on the whole, notwithstanding all drawbacks, has already entered therein.

SERMON XIV. THE APOSTLE TO THE GADARENES. Mark v. 18, 19, ... 154–163

Perplexing diversity of our Lord's instructions as to making known his works and person,

The settled method of his ministry was to exhibit the facts and let men frame their own conclusions.

The command to the Gadarene demoniac is a solitary exception to our Lord's instructions in like case. A strange paradox, teaching sundry lessons:

1. The path of duty which God has marked out for us may run counter to our best wisdom and our holy desire.

2. Duty is to be preferred above privilege.

3. Duty thus preferred becomes the highest privilege.

HOLIDAY SERMONS.

SERMON XV. THE SIGN OF THE SWADDLING-CLOTHES. *A Christmas Sermon.* Luke ii. 12, . . 164–173

The swaddling of infants as described by J. J. Rousseau.

The *sign* of the Christ was that which was common to him with all the new-born infants in Judea.

The swaddling-clothes are a type of the limitations and hindrances by which Jesus was beset throughout his education and his life.

1. The narrowness of Galilean village life
2. The cramping traditions of the elders.
3. The constraint of the synagogue-discipline.
4. The misappreciation of the disciples.

Jesus is not the product of his age, but its antithesis.

SERMON XVI. THE CHILDREN IN THE TEMPLE. *A Palm-Sunday Sermon. To Children.* Matthew xxi. 9, . . 174–182

The anniversary of the passover-moon. The procession into Jerusalem. The children in the temple.

Two questions:—1. What became of all this crowd of shouting followers during the week? 2. How came it that this beloved Man should be pursued to death by popular clamor?

The witness which the days of the Passion Week bear against those common sins which slew the Lord.

SERMON XVII. THE PETITION OF CERTAIN GREEKS. *An Easter Sermon.* John xii. 20, 21, ... 183–195

Sundry questions that arise on the first reading of the story.

These Greeks were representatives of that great class of "devout persons," who were prepared for the gospel, and by whom the gospel entered in to its triumph in the Roman world. Their petition was an invitation to Jesus to carry the gospel to the Gentiles.

Jesus renounces this, and remains to die; so rising again to draw all men unto him. This is the law of the kingdom of heaven.

SERMONS OF NATURAL THEOLOGY.

SERMON XVIII. CREATION. Genesis i. 1, . . . 196–206

1. The traditionary view of the origin of the world; contrasted with
2. The modern speculative view.
I. The speculative view does not weaken the argument of Natural Theology.
II. It does not conflict with the *religious* teaching of the Scriptures.
III. It corrects traditionary misreadings of Scripture, by compelling us to recognize the work of creation depicted in Genesis, as 1. Protracted. 2 Gradual and methodical. 3. Proceeding by means of material and natural causes.

Science is transfigured in the light of faith. Without faith, its light is as darkness

SERMON XIX. A COROLLARY OF EVOLUTION Eccl. i 13, . 207–218

Evolutionism as a theory of the universe. Its Probabilities. Its Difficulties.

All forces of the universe, according to this theory, are convertible into thought, emotion and volition; and *ex hypothesi* reconvertible.

Corollary: The original form of existence of the universe may have been the form of Infinite Thought, Emotion and Volition—Wisdom, Love and Might —Which is equivalent to saying that "in the beginning God created the heaven and the earth."

SERMON XX. THE NATURAL THEOLOGY OF THE SPLEEN. Colossians i. 16, ... 219–231

The old argument of Natural Theology, from fact to cause, and from the nature of the fact to the nature of the cause, recapitulated;—the argument from the adaptation of an organ to its known function and use.

The Spleen is an organ the use and function of which are unknown, and have been sought for by physiologists for two thousand years.

1. Why suppose that the Spleen has any use?
2. Why suppose that it has an adequate use?
3. Why suppose that it has a beneficent use?

The principles of Natural Theology are presumed in the methods and postulates of science. The unknown testifies of God, like the known.

SERMON ON THE SCRIPTURES.

SERMON XXI. THE SCRIPTURAL DOCTRINE CONCERNING SCRIPTURE. John v. 39, 40, ... 232–248

The Bible a phenomenon to be accounted for. Its influence in the world, described by Theodore Parker.

Whether the power of the Bible is a power *in* the book, or a power *behind* the book is indifferent to our argument. In either case it is divine, and is a divine sanction to the book.

A book divinely sanctioned is presumably divine in all its details.

But this presumption may be disavowed or confirmed by the obvious facts and characteristics of the book. Manifest imperfections in the book are, so far forth, a divine disclaimer of divine responsibility.

1. Do the facts of Scripture disavow a miraculous preservation of the text?
2. Do they disavow a divine freedom from error in facts of science?
3. Do they disavow a divinely perfect exactness of historical statement?
4. Do they disavow an absolute freedom from error in predictions?
5. Do they disclaim absolute freedom from error in moral judgment?

The Bible itself suggests and invites these inquiries, and it alone furnishes the means of answering them.

SERMONS OF THINGS TO COME.

SERMON XXII. RESURRECTION IN CHRIST. 1 John v. 11, . 249–257

The present prevalence of doubt concerning a future life is a new thing in the history of Christendom.

It results from the habitual resting of the hope of the life to come on arguments now found to be fallacious.

The notion of man's *natural* immortality is not grounded in reason, nor in Scripture.

Our hope of resurrection and immortality is in the risen and immortal Christ.

SERMON XXIII. RESURRECTION OF THE UNJUST. Psalm cxxxix. 8, ... 258–266

Old Testament language concerning the life to come.

The Biblical teaching on this subject illustrates two characteristics of the Bible: 1. The progressive method of revelation. 2. "The alternative character of the gospel." The announcement of a resurrection of the unjust proceeds *pari passu* with that of a resurrection of the just.

The doctrine of the Scriptures is given with disdainful disregard, and implied rejection, of the doctrine of natural immortality held by the heathen teachers.

The doctrine of Scripture not less a warning than a promise.

SERMON XXIV. GOD'S EQUITABLE JUSTICE. Luke xii. 47, 48, ... 267–276

Christian doctrine has suffered as much from overstatement as from understatement. Especially the doctrines of sin and punishment. This text declares the gradation of guilt and of punishment The gradations of the guilt of unbelief.—1. In those who have not heard. 2. In those who have not reached an intellectual conviction. 3. In those who, instructed and convinced, refuse to commit themselves to God.

The bearing of this doctrine on the preaching of the gospel.

CHARACTER-SERMONS.

SERMON XXV. JACOB AND ESAU. Romans ix. 13, . . . 277–287

What may we learn from God's loving Jacob and hating Esau?

1. That God's judgment of men is not determined by their natural qualities.
2. What is God's way of salvation?

SERMON XXVI. HEROD PENITENT. Mark vi. 20, . . 288–298

The Herod family.

Herod II. in his better moments   What is his moral condition?

1. In doing many right things, he does nothing right.
2. In such repentance as Herod's there is no stability.

SERMON XXVII. THE FALL AND RISING AGAIN OF SIMON PETER. Matthew xvi. 18, 23,   . . .   299–308

1. The Infirmities and the Fall of Simon as illustrating the magnanimity and patience of Christ.
2. The Worthiness of Simon, and the Promotion of him to the foremost place in the kingdom of heaven, as illustrating the wisdom and redemptive power of Christ

SERMON XXVIII. THE JUDGMENT OF JUDAS ISCARIOT. John xiii. 27,   .   .   309–317

"That thou doest, do quickly." The intent for which Christ spake this.

1. Perhaps to secure privacy from the traitor.
2. Perhaps in utterance of Christ's eagerness to accomplish his sufferings.
3. More obviously, that he might reach the heart and conscience of Judas.

SERMON ON THE INDWELLING GOD.

SERMON XXIX. THE HIGH AND LOFTY ONE, DWELLING WITH THE CONTRITE SPIRIT. Isaiah lvii. 15,   318–328

The apprehension of the infinite illustrated from the analogy of vision.

God enters into the human soul —1 By the Intellect. 2. By the Affections. 3. By Spiritual Communion.

SERMON ON THE CHURCH.

SERMON XXX. CHURCH, SECT AND CONGREGATION. *Preached to the Woodland Church, May* 25, 1884, *on occasion of an invitation to be installed as Pastor.* 1 Timothy iii. 15, ... 329–339

The preacher's unreserved willingness to serve this church so long as his service is needed and desired: and to withdraw at once when his withdrawal is deemed expedient for the church.

Certain reasons for declining to be formally installed :—

1. Installation adds no real and desirable element of permanence to one's ministry.
2. It would be taken to indicate that one allied himself with the emulations and exclusions and propagandisms of a sect.
3. It seems to be exacted, as a condition, that one give assent to certain prescribed questions without giving, at the same time, a full statement of his reservations and qualifications.

THE SIMPLICITY THAT IS IN CHRIST.

I.

THE SIMPLICITY OF REPENTANCE.

Repentance toward God, and faith toward our Lord Jesus —ACTS xx. 21.

HERE are two brief phrases in which, in his touching valedictory to the beloved church of Ephesus, Paul the apostle summed up his three years' preaching among them. He declares that he had kept back nothing that was profitable to them. He takes them to witness that he had not shunned to declare God's whole counsel. But of the matter of his preaching there are no points that he cares to rehearse but these: that he testified the gospel of God's grace; that he proclaimed the reign of God, and that to all men, Jew or Greek, he testified repentance toward God and faith toward our Lord Jesus Christ.

It is something more than a coincidence of language, it is a significant and instructive fact, that the words which sum up thus the preaching of this most advanced apostle, as he looked back thoughtfully on his career in that great city where he had sat in the school of a philosopher instructing inquisitive minds of various race and nationality with such arguments as he has himself recorded in many a profound epistle,—should be the identical words that sum up the preaching of the gospel of the kingdom of God by the apostle's Lord and Master, when he went forth with his simple but startling message to the unlearned peasants of Galilee:

"The time is fulfilled; the kingdom of God is at hand; *repent* and *believe* the gospel."

The two words mark the practical unity of the gospel. There are diversities of ministration. We trace them not only down the divergent streams of church-history; we find them in the words of the earliest promulgators of the kingdom. Paul, James, John, Peter—how unlike each other in temperament, in habit of thought, in habit of expression! How unlike them all was Christ, who "spake as never man spake!" But the preaching of each of them is practically summed up in these same words—"they testified repentance and faith." Begin where they will, this is the point toward which they converge and in which they unite. Whatever the contents of their discourse—prophecy, narrative, exhortation, argument,—everything bears down on this conclusion, that men should repent and believe. These two are the cardinal words of practical Christianity. Everything in the Christian life hinges on them. To them is affixed the promise of salvation. No two words are of such import to all men as these two and their representatives in the various languages. And yet by what Satanic machination has it been brought to pass (for it is impossible to ascribe it to any human design) that these two words have been turned aside from their simple, transparent meaning, and have become current, in the Christian languages, in a perverted sense! The practical corruptions of the religion of Jesus Christ might almost be narrated in the form of a history of the perversion of these two words.

Take the former of these words, *repentance:* it is a question which has been much debated, what word ought to be used in English as the equivalent of the Greek word commonly so translated in the New Testament.* That the word *repentance*

---

* See Dissertation on the proper translation of Μετάνοια, in Campbell on the Gospels. Also, Dr. Chalmers on "The Nature and Seasons of Repentance," published as a tract by the Am. Tract Society.

THE SIMPLICITY OF REPENTANCE.

is not in itself suitable hardly admits of debate. For the idea which this word carries with it is one that is not at all contained in the word which it stands for. The root of the word is the same that we have in *pain* or *pen*-alty. The idea which it carries is that of suffering or sorrow for sin—an idea of which there is not the slightest trace in the word used by our Lord and his apostles. And yet this word *repentance* has, in the principal languages of Europe and America, got itself foisted into the place of one which means something else. And its own meaning has stuck by it in such a way as to cast a shadow over the New Testament.* The instructed preacher will do what he can to bend the word around to the New Testament sense, representing that *Repent* should be taken to mean simply *Change your mind*, but after all he finds that as soon as he lets go of the word it springs back to its proper meaning again.

Accordingly, some scholars have recommended another word. The word *Repent, be sorry*, indicates a passive state of the feelings, they say, whereas the Gospel with its word summons us to an act. The word *repent* represents sorrow as an end, whereas the Scriptures never commend sorrow except as a means to an end. They go on to say (and I do not see how anybody can answer them) that if repentance and godly sorrow had been the same thing, Paul never

---

* A slight aggravation of this mistranslation, which excites much virtuous horror among Protestant readers of the Roman-catholic translation of the New Testament, is the rendering "do penance" for "repent." The history of this rendering is curious, and not specially discreditable. The Latin verb unhappily chosen by Jerome or his predecessors to represent the Greek Μετανοεῖν was an impersonal verb, *pœnitet*, defective in its inflections, for which, in the infinitive and imperative moods, it was necessary to construct the periphrastic form, *agere pœnitentiam;* and this went over naturally enough into the English form "do penance." But the principal mischief was done in the introduction of the word *penitence* or *repentance*, in which Protestants and Roman-catholics have agreed.

would have told the Corinthians that "godly sorrow worketh repentance."*

So they propose to substitute the word *Reform*. "The time is fulfilled; the reign of God is ready to begin; *reform*, and believe the gospel." "The Son of man is come to call sinners to *reformation*." "Godly sorrow worketh reformation unto salvation."† But to this there is an objection of the opposite sort. If the former word relates merely to the inward feelings, this word relates only to the outward act—a change of *form*, not of substance. Christ's word means *Changing your mind*. Sorrow may work this—in which case blessed be sorrow. The goodness of God may lead to it ‡—in which case doubly blessed is God's goodness. In all cases the reform of the outward act is sure to follow after it—works meet for the change of mind. §

The two one-sided notions of the duty to which Christ summons us, that are expressed in these two words, *reform* and *repent*, correspond to two types of religious delusion which many of us have encountered. There is that delusion which is expressed in an outward reformation without any turning of the mind; and that which is expressed in inward agitation of the mind without turning.

1. Of the former it need not be thought strange if we are at a loss for historical examples; for it is the error of a light sort of character such as is apt to fade out of history. He may be a person of amiable qualities, not incapable of perceiving moral distinctions, but looking leniently on his own faults of character, and even for sins, manifest and acknowledged, having no very profound feeling of regret—none that goes to the core of his soul. And yet he has a measure of regret for his sins. He is not without self-respect; and he

* 2 Cor vii. 10.

† See, in addition to former references, sundry remarks by De Quincey, vols. ii. 435; viii. 15, 222. Ed. 1877.

‡ Rom. ii. 4. § Matt. iii. 8.

finds them degrading to his nature. He is sensitive to other peoples' opinion; and he finds that they bring him into contempt. He is ambitious of success; and knows some of his traits and habits to be unprofitable and unpopular. He has an eye on the future; and is convinced that, soon or late, wrong-doing is followed by ill consequence. Or he has come to know that his friends are feeling grieved and anxious about him, and he does not like—good-natured, kindly disposed man—to give trouble to anybody. And so for one reason or another—for his own sake, or his friends' sake, but not in the least for God's sake, or out of any hatred for the sin as sin—he says to himself, and perhaps to others, "I am going to reform; I am going to break off this and that habit, and train myself to overcome this or that trait of character." Perhaps he says, "I mean to make thorough work this time; I'll join the church; you will see a complete change in me." And possibly we do see what looks like it. But as for any substantial change of the man's mind—convictions, feelings, purposes—respecting wickedness or respecting God, there is none, and he does not pretend that there is any. You know what commonly becomes of this fine plan of reformation. It is a plan for hacking away at twigs and branches, leaving the roots in the ground. It is a reformation of the behavior, not of the character. As long as the root is there, the poisonous shoots will keep coming to the surface. What a myriad of examples like this has been furnished during these forty years by the course of the Temperance Reformation! Base, guilty drunkards have been made to feel, not that they were base and guilty—quite the contrary, that they were very unfortunate, the victims of a too generously impulsive temperament, and of some other man's wickedness; that their vices were unprofitable, and ridiculous, in short, that it would pay better every way to reform. So Belial has been cast out by some other devil—by Mammon, perhaps even by Momus—a change which has made a vast difference in the man's social relations and in the comfort of his family, but only an outside difference in the man. And presently the devil that has been cast out to wander in dry places comes back to his old home, and the last state of that man is worse than the first.

2. I have showed you what reformation may mean,—an outward improvement without any turning of the mind. Now observe what repentance may mean,—an inward sorrow without any turning of the mind.

You will find examples enough of it in connection with this same vice of drunkenness. Here is a young man just released from the watchful influences of a Christian home, exposed to the temptations of a great city, and dazzled by the fascinations which evil company, the organized seductions of society, the lures of vicious poetry, have thrown around bacchanalian debauchery. Ah! it was so gay last night! the lights glittered so garishly, and the songs of love and wine rang around so cheerily, and the shouts of laughter welcomed the quick jest, and the wine bubbled in the glass, and the brain swam in a delirious ecstasy. But how is it with him this morning? He has come to himself, on the bed where they laid him last night, drunk. He is surrounded with the evidences of his wicked folly. The filth and vomit of his debauch are on his garments. The sun looks in on him reproachful, and he turns his lack-lustre eye to meet it, and quickly turns away again. He is tormented by a splitting headache, and miserably untoned by the reaction from his fierce excitement. His eye falls on some token from home—the Bible that his father gave him, the photograph of his mother on the wall, the little ornaments and comforts that his sisters wrought for him when he was leaving home—and he thinks of what he used to be, and what he meant and hoped to be—prayed to be, perhaps. And there in his solitary room, he turns himself on his bed toward the wall, and weeps aloud. "Good!" you say; "he repents of his sin. It will all come right after all." Repents! Well, no doubt that is what the word means—he has pain in

THE SIMPLICITY OF REPENTANCE. 21

looking backward. But is this which we see the thing which Christ demands? Wait, and we shall know, perhaps. We will watch for the result the next time that temptation comes to him and sinners entice him, and we will look whether there be signs of the turning of the mind, or whether he goes right on in the path of guilty pleasure that has brought him to this woe, and will bring him to worse woe. Perhaps his life is going to be spent in these alternations of sin and of remorse, as so many a wretched life is spent; with now and then some spasm of reformation, some half-effort of prayer, but on the whole no progress and no hope, the sorrow of this world steadily working death. The capacity of sorrow is growing less, as diseased nerves sometimes ache themselves to death. Or remorse is settling down into sullen despair of doing better; and this *is* death.

We can not but recur to that classical instance of sorrow for sin without repentance from it,—Lord Byron. There is a violent reaction nowadays from the extravagant admiration of the last generation; and it is easy for us to detect the falsehood of many of those wild affectations of his that imposed upon our fathers. But there was no sham about this, that he was miserably unhappy. To apply to him the words which he wrote of another, he was:

> " Th' apostle of affliction, he who threw
> Enchantment over passion, and from woe
> Wrung overwhelming eloquence."

And his misery was because of his wickedness. He felt it; he confessed it.

> " For he through sin's long labyrinth had run."

He was " sore sick at heart." He felt

> " ———— that settled, ceaseless gloom
> The fabled Hebrew wanderer bore,
> That will not look beyond the tomb,
> But cannot look for rest before.

> "Through many a clime 'twas his to go,
>   With many a retrospection curst,
> And all his solace was to know,
>   Whate'er betide, he'd known the worst.
>
> "What is that worst? Nay, do not ask!
>   In pity from the search forbear!
> Smile on, nor venture to unmask
>   Man's heart and view the hell that's there."

This was sorrow for sin. If ever sorrow, by its intensity, could have claimed the promise of forgiveness, surely it was this. But how different from that godly sorrow that worketh a change of mind! For all the while it was working death. Like a sulking child, he grew bitter against himself and morose toward his fellows, and hardened his heart toward God, kicking against the goads that drove him. We contrast this picture with that of another great poet, constituted with a poetic temperament no less susceptible of deep feeling and intense suffering, and no less endowed with the gift of utterance in song. His odes are filled with laments over a personal distress not less profound than that which overflows the stanzas of Childe Harold. For he too, like Byron, had sounded the foulest depths of wickedness and planted in his own bosom the seeds of remorse; and the utterances of his sorrow for sin are among the few supreme lyric poems of the world's literature,—as when he writes—

> "I acknowledge my transgression,
> And my sin is ever before me.
> Hide thy face from my sins,
> And blot out all mine iniquities.
> Create in me a clean heart, O God,
> And renew a right spirit within me.
> O Lord, open thou my lips;
> And my mouth shall show forth thy praise."

Here is sorrow after quite another sort—a godly sort. Here is sorrow that is good for something—sorrow that worketh a change of mind. Here is repentance that looks forward as well as back—not only repentance *from*, but repentance *toward*. This is the turning of the mind about-face, because the kingdom of heaven is at hand—because God is all ready to take up and carry on the government if you will but suffer him and join with him.

Does this explanation of the word already begin to make clearer things in Christian truth and duty that have sometimes perplexed you? Have you sometimes pondered the summons of the Gospel, with its ample promises and its awful alternative, and felt an honest embarrassment over the question how that just Judge who cannot but do right should invite, urge, command us to a state of the emotions that is not to be had by a resolution of the will? Has it seemed strange that God should seem to command that for which human languages sometimes fail to furnish any imperative mood? Have you been tempted to fall back into a passive attitude of mind, alleging yourself incompetent to God's exactions of sorrow, and saying to yourself, "I will wait until, in the sweep of some prevailing religious excitement, the requisite agitation of the feelings shall overtake me"? and thus, with an uneasy sense that you are not right nor doing right, have you rested in the wrong, and yet reassured your conscience in your inaction?

Look now once more, in the light of this day's study, on the word of God in the Scriptures, and this darkness shall begin to be light about you. *Turn about toward God*, not in the reformation of the outward life only, but in the inward purpose of the heart. *Turn your mind to God and trust in Christ* to see you safe. This is repentance toward God and faith toward the Lord Jesus. Is not this a plain way into the kingdom of heaven, by which a little child might enter in —by which you may enter in, if you will but become as a little child?

II.

THE SIMPLICITY OF FAITH.*

Believe on the Lord Jesus Christ and thou shalt be saved.—ACTS xvi. 31.

I INVITE you this morning to the sober study of a grave subject. I am not afraid but that it will be interesting to those who seriously want to know the word of God concerning the salvation of men. To the rest, I think it will be dull. Those who have come to church to be entertained with fine talk will go away disappointed and say, "Ah! he is not the preacher we took him for." I pray for divine grace to be a dull preacher to such, and an interesting and helpful preacher to those who want to learn God's truth and man's duty.

The question which I propose to discuss this morning is this: What is Faith? or, in other words, What is it to believe on the Lord Jesus Christ? For strangely enough it is a question to this day among Christians, among theologians, What is this thing to which is given the promise of eternal salvation? Not that there is any active controversy on the subject. No, alas, that is the pity of it, that there should be diversity of opinion on the meaning of the great cardinal word of practical religion, and no controversy at all. There ought to be controversy. Why isn't there controversy? Where are our professors of

---

* This Sermon, which was too much like a theological treatise to begin with, was presented, for substance, to the Presbyterian Ministers' Association of Philadelphia; and some of the notes and other additions which were more specially suited to that professional audience are here retained.

polemics—of fighting theology? What are such warriors good for, if they are not found at the front when questions like this, so vital, so practical, are still undecided, and plain people may be at a loss to know not only what is true, but even what is orthodox? Don't talk of the blessings of theological peace! What is peace, compared with truth? First pure, *then* peaceable, is the wisdom that cometh from above.

There is not the slightest difficulty in determining the meaning of this word in the New Testament. There are four tests by which the true meaning of it may be proved:

1. The word is not a word peculiar to the Gospel, to carry a new idea, but an old word, in common use already, among those to whom the Gospel was first preached. Now when the Gospel says to plain, common people, in plain common words, Believe on the Lord Jesus Christ and thou shalt be saved, the words are to be taken in their plain common meaning, or the Gospel is a fraud. It won't do to say to people who have accepted the offer and claimed the promise, "Oh, but we were using the words in a technical sense of our own."

2. The act of faith is illustrated by multitudes of instances throughout the Old Testament and the New. The true definition must be one that describes an act that is common to all these believers.

3. To the act of faith, men are exhorted in the Scriptures, with the exhibition of rewards and penalties. Therefore the true definition of it must describe a free act, to which men may be induced by motives, and the neglect of which may be charged as a sin.

4. The act of faith is named in the Scriptures as the indispensable condition, and the sole condition, of salvation. "*Whosoever* believeth shall not perish, but shall have everlasting life." But certain other things are also named in the word of God as indispensable conditions of salvation, such as Repentance, Obedience, Love, Holiness. We can not reconcile this

difficulty, unless our definition of Faith describes an act which practically involves all these others.*

What now are the various definitions of Faith that are offered to us by Christian theologians and preachers; that we may bring them up, one by one, and try them by these tests?

The first and most generally current of these definitions is this: that Faith is the Assent of the Intellect to Truth. Faith in Christ is the holding of Christian truth. Faith in God is to account as true propositions submitted to the judgment on God's authority. This is the definition given by all Roman Catholic writers, and by many Protestant writers. Dr. Chalmers, for instance, admits in faith "nothing more than the intellectual act of believing"—"a simple credence of the truths of revelation"—"just a holding of the things said in the gospel to be true." † Is this the true definition? Let us try it by all the tests.

(1) Is this the natural, common meaning of the word as it stands in the gospel? It does look so, doesn't it? When you believe a thing you hold it to be true. When a man says "I believe the world is round" or "I believe the doctrine of limited atonement," there is no doubt what the words mean. They mean that he holds these things to be true. Suppose he

* As John Owen says: ("On Justification," p. 84. Ed. Presb. Board of Publication) "We allow no faith . . . but what virtually and radically contains in it universal obedience."

† Notes on Hill. Ed. Harpers, 210, 422.

See also *John M. Wilson*, annotation in Ridgley's Body of Divinity, p. 124. Ed. Carters.

Archibald Alexander, Practical Sermons, p. 150. (Presb. Board of Publication)

Archibald Alexander, Rel. Experience, p. 154. (Ed. Pr. Board.)

Ashbel Green, Lectures on the Sh. Catechism vol. II., pp. 295 sqq. (Presb. Board of Pub.)

Pearson on the Creed. London, 1835, p. 16.

Abp. Tillotson, Ser on Heb. xi. 6.

Alex. Carson on the Atonement.

THE SIMPLICITY OF FAITH. 27

says "I believe in the existence of God," he uses a form of speech never found in the Scriptures, but he means by it that he is convinced, in his understanding, that God exists. And when he says "I believe *in* God," "I believe *on* the Lord Jesus Christ"—what does he mean then? That he is convinced of certain propositions—that he holds certain tenets to be true? I think not. I do not believe you will find that phrase "I believe on" or "I believe in" used in any such sense in all the Scriptures, nor in the Greek language of their time. The Scriptures speak of *believing* certain facts or certain truths, but not of *believing in* them.* When the Scriptures speak of Faith *in* God, or of believing *on* the Lord Jesus Christ, it is a different matter, as we shall see as soon as we apply the other tests of a true definition.

(2) Try it by the examples of faith in the Scriptures both Old and New. There is a long roll of the heroes of faith given in Hebrews xi. What are the truths that have been held in common by all those who have been saved by faith, from the

---

* The use of language in the early creeds is significant; and equally significant the later corruption of their text. Calvin remarks with emphasis, *Instit.* IV. i., § 2. " Ideo credere *in Deum* nos testamur, quod et in ipsum ut veracem animus noster se reclinat, et fiducia nostra in ipso acquiescit: quod *in Ecclesiam* non ita conveniret, quemadmodum nec *in remissionem* peccatorum aut carnis resurrectionem. He refers, on this point, to Augustine and other early writers. But then this is one of the points on which Calvin was not much of a Calvinist.

The same point is strongly put in the ancient Waldensian catechism, long before the Reformation.

"A dead faith is to believe that there is a God, and to believe those things which relate to God, and not believe *in* him."

" *Qu.* Dost thou believe in the Holy Catholic Church?

"*Ans.* No; for it is a creature; but I believe there is one."

—*Milner's Church History,* Cent. xiii. ch. 3.

It would be very shocking, did we not make allowance for modern corruptions of language, to hear worthy people talk of *believing in* human depravity, or *believing in* falling from grace, or even *believing in* the devil!

days of righteous Abel until now, and the holding of which is the condition of salvation? One party says it is the doctrine of limited atonement. Another says it is the doctrine of the atonement in general. Another says it is the doctrine of the divinity of Christ. The Athanasian Creed (so called because Athanasius never heard of it) declares that it is a certain scholastic statement of the doctrine of the Trinity, " which if a man believe not, without doubt he shall perish everlastingly."*
The Roman Catholic Church, which always knows its own mind on points of this kind, declares it to be the whole sum of revealed truth. Presbyterian writers are commonly more liberal, and agree to let you off with " certain essential doctrines or fundamental truths," to use the language of Ashbel Green and the Presbyterian Board. And this author then submits a little syllabus of dogmas of his own composition, as being "the special object of saving faith." † But it is constantly observed that when a theologian of this stripe gets on the committee of a Tract Society or an Evangelical Alliance, his dogmatic "object of saving faith" undergoes a visible shrinkage; so that it is difficult to agree upon a single dogma or group of dogmas which a man is saved by holding and lost by rejecting.

The one doctrine that comes nearest to uniting modern Christians as the saving doctrine the acceptance of which is the condition of salvation, is the doctrine of Atonement for Sin by the Vicarious Death of Christ. Observe them as they go through the Bible from chapter to chapter trying to read this in between the lines, and to make out that all the old heroes of faith held this tenet of Christian theology. Adam

---

*That genial theologian, Nathanael Emmons, demonstrated that "it is absolutely necessary to approve of the doctrine of reprobation, in order to be saved"—H B. Smith, Faith and Philosophy, p. 219.

† Lectures on Shorter Catechism, II., 295 sq. So Dr. C. Hodge speaks of "the doctrines which the Scriptures present as the objects of faith." Theology, I, 179.

THE SIMPLICITY OF FAITH. 29

and Eve were dressed in skins—they must have been sacrificing animals as a type of Christ! Abel's offering was accepted and Cain's refused—this must have been because Abel held and Cain denied that without shedding of blood is no remission. Rahab the harlot let down a scarlet thread from her window—scarlet is blood-color, and this was a prefiguring of the Atonement. And so on with Gideon, and Samson, and Barak, with Jephthah, also, and others whom time would fail me to mention. "These all died in faith." Did they all accept the doctrine of Vicarious Atonement—whether general or limited? Or is there any *other* tenet of Christian theology that they agreed in? When we are trying these painful operations on the simple, straightforward stories of the Old Testament (and the New Testament too, for that matter) are we not engaged in putting something into the Scriptures, instead of drawing from them the instruction that is there?* This definition of Faith, then, that it is the Assent of the intellect to Truth, does not correspond with the examples of faith given us in the Bible.

(3) Try it by the third test. Faith is spoken of in the Scriptures as if it were a voluntary duty. Men are entreated, urged to it with the promise of reward; the neglect of it is solemnly charged upon them as a sin. Is "the assent of the intellect to religious truth," of this nature? Do men hold their opinions by an act of the will? Is the balancing judgment brought to a decision upon doubtful questions of truth by offer of reward or threat of punishment? Does the intel-

---

* It is a curious fact which I have observed in the course of theological reading, that just in proportion as a theologian sets out with extreme views touching the infallibility and sufficiency of the Holy Scriptures, he practically shows, before he gets through, how insufficient he finds the Scriptures to be until they are supplemented by an extensive system of his own guess-work. For my part I am very well content with the Bible as it stands.

lect give judgment according to evidence, or is it to be bribed by considerations of expediency? To ask these questions is enough. We need not stop to answer them.

(4) We come to the fourth and final test. Faith, according to the Scripture meaning of it, is something which carries with it Repentance, Obedience, Love, Holiness. For each one of these is named, on the authority of God, as a sufficient condition of salvation, and each one of them as an indispensable condition. The only conceivable explanation of this is that these things always and inevitably go together. Faith in Christ, then, as the Bible uses the word, is something invariably associated with Obedience, Love, Holiness. Is this true of the holding of sound doctrine? Take whatever standard of sound doctrine you choose,—however strict, however liberal, —is it true that every man that has ever held it has been holy, loving, penitent, obedient? And if any such man has been unholy, unloving, impenitent, has he been saved? And if not, is this holding of sound opinions the *faith* to which is given the promise " Whosoever believeth shall not perish, but shall have everlasting life "?

The fact is that you have here the *Roman* definition of Faith. And if you accept the Roman definition of Faith, you would do much better to take with it the Roman doctrine of justification. For man surely is *not* justified by faith alone, if by faith you mean orthodoxy. To hold the Protestant doctrine of Justification with the Roman definition of Faith is putting new wine into old bottles. The wine runs out, and the bottles perish.

II. It is doubtless the feeling how dangerous and demoralizing it may be to announce forgiveness and salvation as promised simply to those who accept certain truths with the intellect, that leads many conscientious preachers to qualify the offer of divine mercy to "whosoever believeth" by cautions and limitations of their own, and to give us a new definition of " saving faith," as being *a peculiar quality or intensity of intellectual assent*, different from ordinary belief. "Whosoever believeth " with *saving faith* "shall have eternal life."*

We need not give a second thought to any such limitations and qualifications as these. No man has a right to interpolate them into the divine promises. This is not the way Christ speaks, not the way the gospels speak, not the way the apostles speak. They take a common word with a plain meaning, and say in all languages " whosoever believeth on him "—" believe and be saved." And for us to amend their words for them, and say that they did not mean them in the common sense in which men use them and understand them, but in a special sense, a theological sense, a spiritual sense, is to accuse them of practicing a fraud on mankind. The difference that the Bible makes between saving faith and other faith is not in the nature of it, but in the object of it.

III. But now here is a third definition which has sometimes found great favor with theologians, and is to this day sometimes urged upon us with great zeal and importunity. It is this, that Faith consists in the undoubting assurance of one's own salvation. Justifying faith is assuredly believing one's own self to be justified. To believe on Christ is to be confidently sure that you yourself are saved by him.†

This definition fails on every test.

(1) It is not in any sense the natural meaning of the words Believe on the Lord Jesus Christ.

---

*Thus that excellent preacher, Dr. J. W. Alexander (Sacrl. Ser. 222) after stating the dogma which he holds to be "the object of saving faith," adds, " the man who believes this, *with a spiritual apprehension of what he believes* is a saved man "

† I have been stoutly assured, by people who thought they knew, that this fantastic and pernicious notion has never been held in the Presbyterian churches; whereas for three generations, and those the most formative in the history of Protestant theology, it was the generally accepted Presbyterian orthodoxy; as may best be seen in Principal Cunningham's essay on "The Reformers and the Doctrine of Assurance,"

32   THE SIMPLICITY THAT IS IN CHRIST.

(2) It does not correspond with the facts in the lives of believers; for some of the most divinely approved examples of faith are the examples of believers who suffered under many misgivings concerning their personal salvation.

(3) The state of mind which it describes is not invariably associated with repentance and holiness. On the contrary it is very common among impious and immoral fanatics.

(4) But when you come to this final test: Is it a free act to which a man may be exhorted as a duty, and for failing in which he may be condemned as for a willful sin, the absurdity and folly of this definition become apparent. To exhort an unbeliever to this sort of faith—to tell him Believe that you are saved, and then you will be saved, is to tell him to believe a lie so as to make it true. And to condemn him for unbelief, under this definition, is to hold him guilty for not believing what the very fact of his condemnation proves to have been false.

This definition represents the gospel as a cruel Sphinx setting insoluble riddles to all passers-by, and devouring them for not furnishing impossible answers.

IV. And here is one more mistaken definition of faith—that faith consists in a succession of states of mind and feeling and action such as constitute what men call "experiencing religion"—that faith means faith and something else. I take this statement from a tract of the American Tract Society: (No. 357.)

"What is it to believe on Christ? It is to feel your need of him; to believe that he is able and willing to save you, and to save you now; and to cast yourself unreservedly on his mercy, and trust in him alone for salvation." That is, to

in "The Reformers and the Theology of the Reformation," p. 119. It is by no means extinct at this day; although it is far less common in this country than in some others, to have people rush at you with the question, "Have you a perfect assurance of your own salvation?"—as if this was the point of duty and the essence of Christian faith.

believe on Christ is first to feel something, and then to believe something, and then to do something, and then—what? Why then—to believe on Christ. Why not say that to begin with and to be done with? Doubtless one does often come to this act of trusting in the Saviour through such successive stages of emotion, and conviction and action. But to confuse these together as parts of the act of trust itself is a misleading, perplexing, mischief-making thing. It is not justified by the plain, common use of words in the Gospel. And when we remember that faith is enjoined on all men as a duty—a voluntary act, to which they are exhorted under force of inducements, and with the alternative of personal guilt,—then the mischief of a bemuddled definition in which the antecedents and incidents of an act are not distinguished from the act itself, becomes apparent. You entreat me to experience certain emotions! You urge me to entertain certain convictions! But you cannot procure a state of the emotions by offering a reward for it. You cannot produce a conviction of the understanding by threats of damnation. What bungling processes of ours are these! How unlike "the wisdom of God to salvation!" When God wants to convince an intellect he does it in the only way in which an intellect was ever yet convinced,—by reason and evidence. When he would move the feelings, he does not order a man to agitate himself, but he brings to bear upon us those appliances of love and sympathy that affect the heart. And when the question is on the free choices of man's will—will he? or will he not?—he throws into the scale the tremendous sanctions of his government, and uses the announcement of infinite reward or infinite loss to sway the free determination which may not be constrained.

Of course the question will be put,—"Since these conditions are constant antecedents of faith, is there any practical harm in including them in the definition of it?"

Well, is there any *good* in it, of any kind? When you

have gone through with your description of these antecedents of faith, you come, in your definition, to the word *trust*, to which all these things are just as necessarily antecedent as they are to faith: so that your definition has tangled up within itself an endless coil of antecedents, through which a logical mind would never get at the thing itself, to all eternity.

And the practical harm of it is this: it perplexes plain minds by a complex definition of a simple act. It encourages men in computing the evidence of their faith by the intensity of their preliminary experiences, rather than by their daily life of faith and acts of faith. It takes off from the unbeliever the burden of guilt for refusing his plain duty, to comfort him with the complacent feeling that he is an unfortunate person, not altogether to blame for not having happened to get hit by a religious experience.

We have reached the true definition at last. *To believe in the Lord Jesus Christ is to trust in him.* It is so simple that words of explanation would only darken it. We may only try this definition by the several tests, and it will answer to every one of them.

(1) It is the natural and obvious meaning of the words as they would be understood by those to whom they were preached. What else could they mean? What is this object of faith— "the Lord Jesus Christ"? It is not a doctrine concerning his person; not a theory of his atonement; not a series of fundamentals in theology; not a system of religious truth; and yet they who misunderstand the first part of this command are compelled to substitute one or another of these things as the object of Christian faith for the Lord Jesus Christ himself.*

---

* I might quote again my favorite theologian, Ashbel Green; or, better, the orthodox Wilson, annotator of Ridgeley. Ridgeley had said that faith was an "act of trust or dependence on him who is its object.' To which Wilson replies: "*The object of faith is* NOT A PERSON, but a proposition or a statement. Trust, on the other hand, has reference

THE SIMPLICITY OF FAITH. 35

(2) The act of Trust in the Lord Jesus Christ does involve in itself, of its own nature, Repentance, Obedience, Holiness, and whatever things beside are demanded in the Scriptures as conditions of salvation. The act of obedience is the act of faith. The life of holiness is the life of faith. It is "*in well-doing*" that we "commit the keeping of our souls to a faithful Creator."* So in the classical instance of faith, it is written of Abraham, father of believers, "he believed in Jehovah,"—not merely he rested on him, but—הֶאֱמִין בַּיהוָה—he built on him. Not merely that he thought probable, or felt certain, that the promise would come true, but that he *ventured himself* upon the Lord. In the great trial of his life, all his three days' journey to Moriah, he rested all his weight on God. As he climbed the hill with Isaac, his faith was not his conviction what God would do, nor his own purpose of what *he* would

---

entirely to a person. The difference between it and faith, in fact, is just that the one has a person and the other has a statement for its object" II, 125 The Wesleyan theologian, Watson, is very sound and judicious on this subject.

There is a very curious illustration of how completely the traditionary theological idea of faith, now so rarely met with outside of the theological systems, had, almost to our own day, occupied the mind of the church to the exclusion of the New Testament idea. Never was an honest sermon so searched for heresies as Albert Barnes's sermon on "The Way of Salvation"; and yet of all its gainsayers, no one thought of objecting to the mistake that lay patent on the surface of it. The preacher, drawing out in ample argument his views of the method of the divine government, of atonement, and of regeneration, exclaims with impassioned earnestness, "Fly to this scheme!" "Commit your eternal interests to this plan!" Upon which Drs. Junkin and Breckenridge reply, with equal earnestness, "Don't do anything of the kind! Don't fly to Mr. Barnes's scheme—to the New England plan! Fly to our scheme—commit yourself to the Scotch system, or the Dutch!"—and never saw that the gospel "Way of Salvation" was, not to commit oneself to anybody's "scheme," but to "commit oneself, in well-doing, to a faithful Creator."

* 1 Peter iv. 19.

do; it was, moment by moment, what he *did*. In his acts was his faith perfected. Having trusted God, he trusted him to the end. In his great surrender, he cast forth upon God's hands the treasure of his heart, the hope of his race, the pledge of God's promise. He flung himself, with his whole weight, on God's faithfulness and love. Herein his faith was made actual. You see, then, that it is by works, by the act of faith, that a man is justified, and not by faith which does not act,—which is *not* faith, except in the sense in which a dead man is a man.

(3) This principle of personal trust in God is the one principle common to all saints from antediluvian Enoch and Abel down to the latest of those who through faith have obtained a good report. In this view, the practical religion of the Old Testament and the New are one and the same. Consult your Cruden's Concordance; in the Old Testament, the word *trust* occurs two hundred and twenty-five times,—it is the synonym of piety and acceptableness with God. In the New Testament it is hardly found at all. In the Old Testament the words *faith* and *believe* are only met with a few times; in the New Testament they occur seven hundred times, and stand as the synonyms of holiness. It is not because God has changed, or that the conditions of his favor have changed; but simply that in our translations we have shifted a word. There is but "one faith;" and "the Catholic faith is this."

(4) The condition of salvation, thus defined, is a voluntary act and therefore a practicable and reasonable demand to be made of any man. Demanding this, God is no longer presented to the world as one who would bribe or terrify the intellect into a partial or biased decision of questions of evidence; nor as one who would extort the instantaneous exercise of involuntary emotions; but only as the stern enforcer, the infinite rewarder, of every man's simple duty toward a faithful Creator.*

---

* There is no point on which the splendid "progress in theology" which has marked the history of the Presbyterian Church during the

THE SIMPLICITY OF FAITH. 37

That is a sharp criticism upon modern preaching, that instead of teaching men that they must "be converted and become as little children," it has taken to teaching little children that they must become converted and become like grown folks. But the criticism loses its cutting edge when the faith which we preach is the child's own faith—the leaning of the weaker on the Stronger, of the foolish on the All-wise, of the sinful on the infinitely Merciful, of the wavering on him that is Faithful and True,—the faith to which the wise and mighty find it hard to bow themselves, but which suffers little children to come unto the Lord, and in the mouths of babes and sucklings doth perfect his praise. Salvation by this faith is a salvation for every one, at all times. When the mind is weak and ill-instructed and cannot "understand all mysteries and all knowledge," it can yet trust, and so be saved. When evil habits have seized and bound one, and imperious passions do so dominate the will as to leave no hope in oneself of successful struggle against them,—when life is shortening up, moment by moment, and the issues of eternity are compressed within the compass of an hour,—when the sick and bewildered brain swims and the intellect staggers in the vain attempt to grasp new thoughts and arguments, then this gospel "Believe on the Lord Jesus Christ and thou shalt be saved"—"Fear not; only believe"—comes

last forty years is more commendable than the point considered in this argument. The view that the act of faith is trust, and the object of faith not dogmas but a person, has grown to be so orthodox that many are surprised to find how lately it ceased to be a heresy. One of the best utterances on the subject is by a man with whom, on some subjects, it was a pleasure to disagree: "Believe, only believe; not opinions, but *on* a personal Saviour; not a creed, but *on* a Christ" [Discourses on Redemption, by Stuart Robinson, p. 341.] For some of the most distinct statements of the truth, in honorable inconsistency with the hurtful errors of earlier publications, see some of the more recent issues of that wisely progressive body, the Presbyterian Board of Publication;—for example, "Plantation Sermons," by A. F. Dickson, p. 82.

to us, to every man, bringing great salvation. Having this promise, in the utmost conscious weakness and ignorance and sinfulness, one can rest confident in the everlasting arms of Him who " is made to us wisdom and righteousness and sanctification." Having this, the frightened soul that is shuddering on the giddy verge of eternity may compose itself to perfect peace, and unperplexed with difficult and painful thoughts may lean the aching head upon the bosom of the Lord,

"And breathe its life out sweetly there."

Thanks be to God for so great salvation, accessible to every creature! How shall we escape if we neglect it?

III.

THE OPEN DOOR OF THE CHURCH.

What doth hinder me?—ACTS viii. 36.

As you read this story—in fact, as you read the whole New Testament—you get the impression that the way into the kingdom of heaven, in the days of our Lord Christ and his apostles, was a very obvious and straightforward way to any who was willing to enter it. It might cost one an inward struggle to consent, but to one consenting, the way of entrance was plain, even if it was not easy. Such an one might find difficulties in himself; but he would have no hindrances put upon him in the name of the Lord—nothing but helps and encouragements. There were trials, self-denials, persecutions, even, incident to entering into the way of life, but no obscurities. How wide open "the happy gates of gospel grace" did seem to stand, in those days, to be sure! Daily they gathered into the church such as should be saved. Daily?—thousands in a day! And what a simple business they seemed to make of it! Not a word said about a judicious deliberation and delay in the case of these new converts! Not a word about preparing them by catechising, or taking them awhile on probation, or about examining them on their religious experience.

"What shall I do to be saved?" asked the jailer of Philippi, at midnight, in the midst of the terrors of the earthquake; and "that same hour of the night" he was baptized, and all his, immediately. Here is this stranger from the upper Nile, reading his Greek translation of Isaiah as he rides, and asking Philip to step up into the chariot and explain it to him.

And right there by the desert road to Gaza, as they come to some roadside stream or fountain, he says, "Here is water; what hinders me from being baptized?"—as if to one who had learned about Jesus Christ and wished to be his disciple and follower, it was the most natural thing in the world. And at once the evangelist seems to answer, "Of course; why not?" He never thinks to say: "Oh, this is very sudden and premature. There are a great many things to be thought of first. It is a very serious and solemn matter; you had better take some time to think about it, and be sure that you know your own mind. How long had you been under conviction before I saw you in the chariot?" Or, "I do not like to assume the responsibility in this case. Let us go on to some place where there is a church that shall decide about your admission. Or at least let us wait for some suitable and appropriate occasion, when this rite of baptism may be performed with due solemnity, and in the presence of witnesses." But no. Right then and there, by the roadside, as if it had been the most natural and matter-of-course thing in the world, he baptized him. And at once they parted. The Ethiopian, now a confessed Christian, going on his desert way to Gaza, rejoicing, and Philip disappearing from his sight and coming to Ashdod.

And when we read the story in the form in which Luke wrote it, dropping a few words that do not belong in it but have been added to it in later copies, our impression is deepened. There is so much to be learned from the occasional interpolations and changes that have been detected in the text of the New Testament! They are not always due to blunder or slip of the pen. Very often indeed they are deliberately meant for improvements;—they indicate wherein the earlier Christians were not quite satisfied with this Scripture as they received it—felt, perhaps, that it was not quite safe as it stood,—thought they could better it by adding a word or two. So when we come to one of these interpolations that have been detected by the astonishing insight of modern criticism, it shows us in a most interesting and emphatic way what it was that the first witnesses of the gospel distinctly refrained from saying, but which some of their followers in the first three or four centuries wished they had said, and thought they ought to have said, and thought it would be no great harm to add or alter a word or two so as to make them say it. These variations and additions (some of which gained such currency that they are actually included in our common English New Testament) point out the spots at which the early church began to diverge from the standard of the apostolic faith, and put us on our guard lest we stray in the same by-path.

Now here we have a specimen of one of these tamperings with the story. The whole of the 37th verse ["And Philip said, If thou believest with all thine heart, thou mayest. And he answered and said, I believe that Jesus Christ is the Son of God"] is an addition not found in the best and most ancient manuscripts of the New Testament. The words were added, perhaps, in order to make the passage correspond with some early ritual of baptism, and with the idea that they would make a much safer sort of Scripture than that which represented Philip as receiving this new convert at once to baptism without asking any questions or exacting any formal profession. Undoubtedly it began very early to be felt, what there is a strong disposition to feel even now, that the exact scriptural practice was rather a lax and incautious and unsafe practice; and so they mended it in their fashion. But the exact story, as it was written by the hand of Luke, was simply this: "As they journeyed along the road, they came to some water. And the eunuch said, Behold water; what hindereth me from being baptized? And he ordered the chariot to halt, and they both went down into the water, both Philip and the eunuch, and he baptized him."

The difference, at this point, between our ways and the ways of the New Testament was deeply impressed on me when, in my boyhood, I was going over the very track of the apostles in company with some of their successors. For never, I believe, have there been truer successors to the apostles, in faith and zeal and all long-suffering, in their daily lives of preaching, and in the very circumstances of their work, than our own missionaries in those same lands of the East. To ride for a day's journey alongside of Eli Smith, or Henry Van Dyke, hearing their discourse with one eager group of listeners after another on the question What shall I do to be saved?— was like the privilege that Luke or Silas had, in attending the missionary journeys of Paul. It was a daily commentary on the book of the Acts of the Apostles. There were the same names, the same scenes, like costumes, languages, manners; and the essence of the work was the same—to make men feel in their consciences that they were sinners, and lead them to turn from all wrong-doing and trust the mercy and love of God in Christ to save them. Thus far it seemed so like; but at one point, how different!—and that was the long delay, hesitation and caution of the missionaries in receiving those who declared themselves ready to go with them as fellow-disciples in Christian faith and obedience. "There, over on the flank of the mountain, is a village where they have expressed a desire to be received into our communion; but we have told them they had better wait a year." "Here is a family in which the grace of God is manifestly working; but we think it advisable to keep them on probation for awhile." "In this town, many have openly received the Gospel, and after careful examination have been gathered into a church; but we do not quite venture to leave them yet, and so one of our missionaries stays with them as a pastor, though he is sorely wanted in the regions beyond, where they have not so much as heard the Gospel." It sounded cautious, prudent, worldly-wise—it sounded everything but scriptural and apostolic. You will not think it strange that I should have come back from that great mission-field to begin my ministry in America, with this contrast deeply, ineffaceably impressed on my mind; and with the solid conviction that the foolishness of God, in the large, wide-open hospitality of his church, is wiser than all the timid precautions and hesitations of the wisest and best of men. This Book of God, this code of holy examples, is a safer standard to go by than any men's church theories or traditions of administration. I love the noble imprudence of Christ's first apostles. I delight in that wise "foolishness of God." And I mistrust, sometimes, that what we account to be our advanced wisdom, in the affairs of the kingdom of heaven, may be quite as justly set down to the account of our diminished faith. When we have learned to renew "the boldness of Peter and John" and Paul, in declaring the simplicity of the Gospel, we may hope to renew their triumphal progress. In this last century of modern missions, if we had had faith and courage to follow the apostolic way and as fast as the seed had sprouted in one field had pushed forward to the regions beyond, already the ends of the earth should have seen God's salvation, and once more it should have been fulfilled which is written in the Psalms:

> "Their line is gone out into all the earth,
> And their words to the ends of the world."

Returning, now, to the personally practical question, What doth hinder me?—What doth hinder you?—from entering into the peace of God and the fellowship of Christian believers, —I beg you to observe that while our Lord himself sets up no hindrance in the way of any willing, consenting, trusting soul, the hindrances which we encounter are very apt to be constructed out of the very material which is meant, by God's goodness, for helps and encouragements. God lays steppingstones over the hard place, and men pull them out of place and set them so high as to make them stumbling-stones; if, indeed, they do not build them square across the way into a barrier. His word points out to us certain simple conditions of forgiveness and peace; and it really seems as if the world, not to say the Church, had received them in the temper of Naaman the Syrian general. "What, wash in Jordan? Will the prophet deal so lightly with my case as that? I'll not go!" "But, my lord, if he had bidden thee do some great thing, wouldst thou not have done it?" We had far rather do some great, difficult, imposing, elaborate thing, and when we look at the simplicity of Christ, we cannot be quite contented with it, and at once set to work to make up something very much finer and more formidable.

Three points on which this tendency has been most strikingly illustrated are these: I. *Rites.* II. *Experiences.* III. *Doctrines.* Each has been meant for a help. Each has been converted into a hindrance.

I. *Rites.* Our Lord, providing for the need which his believing followers would have of some way of declaring their discipleship in visible form, named two ordinances—sacraments we call them (though *he* did not), from an old word meaning an oath of military allegiance. And what were they? The commonest acts of common daily life—the daily bath and the daily meal. The bath, by which one coming to Him signified his putting away, from that time forth, of the sinful, defiling service of the world, and his new, clean life of consecration to the Father, and the Son and the Holy Spirit; and the supper, in which he remembers his Master and Friend, declares his dependence and allegiance, and shows his Lord's death until he come. So simple and so easy that men said "That can't be all: that is not enough." And so to-day, among the majority of Christians, baptism is overlaid with various well-intended ceremonies—with oil, and salt, and spittle, and a stole and a candle, and various incantations and exorcisms, because men want to do some great thing, even though the Lord has only bidden them do a very little and easy thing. And the Lord's evening meal, the eating and drinking in remembrance of him, has been metamorphosed in all our sects, more or less, into an awful mystery from which simple-hearted believers are driven away in terror. Thus the rites which were meant as helps to us, by men's own faults and blunders have been changed into hindrances.

II. And as with Rites, so with *Experiences*. Needless, it should seem, to declare that the experience of other disciples was meant to be a help and encouragement to each one of us in our way into the heavenly kingdom. And so, read aright, it is. Such a lesson it teaches us of the plainness of the way! Looked at in any large and reasonable way, the lesson from the vast diversity in the spiritual history of true and holy Christians is a lesson of unbounded encouragement. It shows us, among these "disciples whom Jesus loves," men and women of the most diversely variant inward temperament and outward surroundings; the story of whose spiritual history, in their coming into conscious discipleship with Christ, is more diversely variant still. And the great and liberal lesson of it is this: that he who is the Way, and the Door to the way, does not care by what path we come up to him, if only we do come. Some come up scourged by sorrows, and some whom the goodnesss of God has led to repentance; some in the calmness of solitary reflection, and some amid the fervid agitations of a prevailing revival; some with a loving obedience that has grown within them from before their earliest memory, and some with revulsions of feeling tearing themselves away from a life of inveterate selfishness and worldliness; yet all received with like welcome by the one Saviour, and sharing alike in the bounteous gifts and graces of the Holy Spirit. How happy the assurance which we *ought* to gather from all this—that the question through what vicissitudes of feeling we are brought to Christ is an unimportant question, so long as the main question, do we come to him, is settled aright. This is part of the comfort that we ought to draw from the large privilege of "the communion of saints."

But see how miserably we abuse it and ourselves, when from the conspicuous and exceptional character in some religious biography, or from the prevailing type of religious personal history in some period of peculiar spiritual exaltation, we select a standard of what we consider to be a normal Christian experience, and begin to judge ourselves thereby, and, what is worse, to judge one another;—to turn God's friendly helps into hindrances—his stepping-stones into stumbling-stones.

III. And as with Rites and Experiences, so with *Doctrines.* Surely the teachings of God's word were meant to lighten our way to him not to darken or perplex it. These teachings were meant as our helps to salvation; but we talk of them sometimes as if they were the hard and rigorous condition of it. And it seems sometimes as if we were bent on making them hard and dark so that we might do "some great thing," some high feat of intellectual toil, or perhaps of the mortification of the intellect, as an appropriate condition of God's great gift. Now God's truth is very plain; it is very easy; and oh, how helpful! What confidence it gives you toward him! As he declares to us the great fact of the reconciliation of the world to himself in Christ, how it wins us to trust in his plain, faithful promise, and to rest in the perfect peace of him whose mind is stayed on God! This is such a plain, easy, happy thing! But is this all? Is this enough? Ought there not to be required something more as a fit condition of so great a gift? —some "sacrifice of the intellect," some believing of things incredible or unintelligible, with which sacrifices God should be well pleased? Be assured, dear friends, that if such be the craving of your "natural heart," it is a demand which will never fail of its supply. The same genius which has enriched Christ's simple outward ordinances with curious ritual traditions, and mystified them with scholastic theories; and which has ordained its elaborate programs of emotion and agitation in religious experience; the same will be ready also with its codes of "fundamental doctrine," labeled "essential to salvation," among which you need not despair of finding things hard enough to satisfy the utmost craving of the soul that would fain find "some great thing" to do, rather than the "easy and light" thing which God requires. But all the while "the foundation standeth sure;" "God's word abideth faithful;" his promises "in Christ Jesus are Yea, and in him Amen;" and " whosoever believeth on the Lord Jesus Christ shall not perish but shall have everlasting life."

IV.

THE OUTSIDE CHRISTIAN.

𝔒ther sheep 𝔍 have, which are not of this fold.—JOHN x. 16.

THIS is a word of indispensable comfort to good men; and yet a word which good men of the very churchly pattern, tending to exalted notions of the organized kingdom of God as they understand it. are reluctant to take in its full and happy meaning, and are disposed to quote very timidly and with cautionary explanations, lest some should get too much comfort from it, and so have their sense of the importance of the Church impaired. In fact, the words of our Lord are pretty safe words, if we would only trust them. We do not better them much with our caveats. There are none of us theologians that are not now and then made aware of this or that divine utterance that is not just what we would have it, and which we do not like to read without qualifying it a little. But after all, the foolishness of God is wiser than any of us. And this enduring word of Christ is much safer than what we, in our anxiety for the dignity of the Church of God, might have put in the place of it.

But those that heard this word did not think so. At once there was a new division and debate among the Jews who were listening to the Master. And we need not go out of our way and imagine malignant motives for the party in opposition. The story is a clear one without any such conjectures. Never were there men who had better reason to consider themselves representatives of the true Church of God than these very people; and when this Galilean openly teaches, perhaps in the

THE OUTSIDE CHRISTIAN. 49

hearing of some of the Gentiles themselves, that there is salvation outside of this true fold, is it not high time for them to protest against such dangerous doctrines? It was just so, a little later, with the Hebrew Christians, when they heard of Peter's baptizing Cornelius, and Paul's preaching to the Gentiles. And in fact, all down through the history of Christianity, it would be amusing, if it were not so pitiful and painful, to see this anxious jealousy on the part of one party of Christians or another, who conceived themselves to represent the visible church, for fear it would be thought that some would be saved from outside of that fold; and to read the awful language in which they denounce the idea that any will be saved from among the untaught heathen, as "pernicious and to be detested."*

And yet, when you look at it calmly, there is no need of any mistake about it—this "pernicious and detestable" thing is the very teaching of Christ himself. In that solemn discourse in the twenty-fifth chapter of Matthew, "all the heathen"† are to stand before the Judge, and those among them who well had loved and served their fellow-men are going to be surprised when they are called forth and placed at the right hand of the Judge, and told that in comforting the poor, the sick, the starving, they unconsciously had been serving the blessed and glorious Saviour whose name they had

---

* See *Westminster Confession*, x. 4. It is sometimes an important duty of the preacher, when by searching he is able to find some point at which to differ from this excellent formulary, to indicate it plainly, and so clear himself of any suspicion of holding that there be two infallible rules of faith. But no humane person should refuse his sympathy to those whose official duty it is to maintain that this document is fallible in general, but infallible in all its particulars, and who have been at times embarrassed, at this and other points, by the necessity of showing that it does not mean what it says.

† Πάντα τὰ ἔθνη, verse 32. Is it quite out of the question that there should be any etymological connection between the Greek word and the English?

4

never known. And Christ's doctrine on this point has not failed to get itself asserted even in the hardest and narrowest times. Says Augustine, "there are wolves within the fold, and there are lambs without." The Roman Church, when it has been severest in declaring that out of its own pale is no salvation, has always had plenty of theological expedients by which honest and pious heretics and heathen could be provided for. And the narrowest sects of Protestantism, who have held that salvation was a peculiar privilege, not only of the fold, but of their own compartment of the fold, have generally relaxed their rigor at the voice of their fellow Christians, however unsound and erratic in doctrine, naming the name of Christ in love and duty and discipleship.

Let us freely take all the comfort that there is in the assurance that Christ has other sheep, outside the fold. It seems sometimes as if our faith would fail without this assurance. The world of men is so great, and the fold is so small, and within the fold are so many who are not of the Lord's own sheep, that we cling to this word of his, spoken in that dreadful age when the world was at its worst, that he has other sheep besides these who are visibly his own; and we wonder whether from among those sordid, foul, depraved communities of which Paul wrote to the Romans, there were not many, even then, who without law were doing the things contained in the law, and who would be surprised in the judgment-day to find themselves justified and saved by the grace of a Saviour whose name they had never heard.

And I think that no one who knows how to compare the different ages of Christian history will doubt that it is quite as true in our days as it was in Augustine's days and in the days of the Lord himself, that "there are lambs and sheep outside of the fold, as well as wolves in sheep's clothing within it." It was a profound and painful impression that was made on me when I began to grow acquainted with my first country parish in Litchfield, Connecticut, and found that some of the truest Christians in all the community, humble, diligent, charitable, believing, devoutly spiritual,—were outside of the communion of the church. One face I remember as if it were photographed before me at this moment—a sad, saintly face, never absent from the Sabbath worship, always before me with such serious earnestness at the school-house prayer-meetings on Chestnut Hill, the face of a woman, as her life declared, "full of faith and of the Holy Ghost," full of love for all Christians, and all Christian work,—and yet never once written down in the number of the disciples, nor gathered with them at the table of communion. And none of my boyish arguments or persuasions could ever overcome her shrinking scruples, mistaken as they were; and I presume that she died in the same meek and trembling faith, and in the same lack of the name and badge of discipleship, the same strange misgiving about counting herself in that number of Christ's followers in which there was not one who followed nearer and more constant than herself.

Do not think, because I speak of this instance which so deeply impressed me as a young pastor, that I judge the outside Christian to be presumably a very exemplary Christian. On the contrary, the outside Christian is an unnatural growth, and commonly a stunted and distorted growth. This saintly woman that I have spoken of would have been twice the saint that she was, for being a happy, openly confessed believer, in the communion of the church. The abnormal position outside, not only tends to defects of character, but grows out of defects—defects of knowledge, or of faith. Such cases as I found in Litchfield among the older people of the congregation seemed to me to have much to do with the succession of great revivals which had characterized the history of the church under the tremendous ministry of old Dr. Lyman Beecher, and under some of his successors. I do not mean that it was revivals that wrought this result, but *revivalism*— the unhappy notion that it was the sole business of the church to have revivals, and that nothing important could be done except by means of revivals, and that the only way into the kingdom of heaven was by being awakened, and convicted and converted in a revival. This is one thing that results in the position of the outside Christian.

And the second is like unto it—the notion that our Master is a very captious Master, not content with simple, honest, straightforward faithfulness in his service, and not the considerate, forgiving Master and Saviour that he declares himself to be—forgiving till seventy times seven times, and wishing that all should be saved; as if there was something more in his requirements than the simple language of them implies,—as if there were some sort of mental reservation in his hearty promises to those who trust him and try to serve him, and as if he were always on the lookout for some pretext for not keeping them.

3. Then, for another reason, the outside Christian shrinks from counting himself among his fellow-Christians because he mistrusts his own stability, and is afraid that if he allows himself to be called by the name of Christ, he may fall, and bring scandal on that name, and so be a harm to others instead of a help. He shrinks from it for Christ's sake, and for other men's sake; withal he shrinks from it for his own soul's sake; for he dreads the sin and peril of presumptuousness, and says to himself "it is not safe for me to indulge myself in a joy and peace that may be delusive, lest I break down in my overconfidence. I must walk cautiously and with constant self-suspicion if I would walk safely. In mistrust of myself is my strength; and self-examination and anxious care will keep me." Poor man! he has never learned "the *joy* of the Lord is thy strength," and "the *peace* of God shall keep your hearts and minds through Jesus Christ."

4. Sometimes the outside Christian stands without because of the unworthy and false disciples that he sees within, and doubts whether it be his duty to go where he will be brought

even into apparent and external fellowship with such.—And forgets his Master's parable of the tares amid the wheat; and forgets that of his Lord's own original church, of the twelve members there was an eight per cent. of treason, and an awful amount of defection under trial.

5. I suspect that there are outside Christians who hesitate on the threshold of the Church of Christ, with the doubt "what church, among so many, ought I to join?"—and do not discover, underneath these surface variations and divisions, that there is really only one church, and that is the Church of Christ, so that he who joins himself to any congregation of believers as a Christian disciple, does thereby declare his love and fellowship, not toward one congregation or one sect, but toward the whole company of believers, both here and elsewhere. If it were implied, in numbering oneself with the communion of a particular congregation of disciples, that one thereby connected himself only with the Methodist sect, or the Presbyterian sect, or the Episcopalian sect, there would be many more outside Christians than now, and I should beg the privilege of being one of them. But when my joining myself to the Christian fellowship of this Woodland Church is practically the declaration of my common faith and hope with the whole communion of Christ's people in the city and the world, and my love to all the brethren—then this reason for standing outside the threshold is taken away. But I suspect that there are those who stand outside and do not see that it *is* taken away.

Observe that these considerations which certainly do work, in one conscientious mind and another, to keep them outside of any visible connection with Christ's Church, are very far from implying any unworthy motive in the mind. But observe, also, how easily they mix with unworthy motives, and furnish a cloak for them. This shrinking mistrust of oneself, how humble and modest it looks!—but it may be the plausible expression of your unwillingness to trust God to keep you.

Your unwillingness to incur the risk of putting scandal on the church in case you should fall into wrong-doing—it seems like a most honorable and unselfish scruple; but under it, may lurk an unwillingness to make it as hard as possible for yourself to go astray,—as you ought to be glad to make it. Your hesitating to join yourself to a church in which there are unworthy members, how easily it may slide into a habit of making self-conceited and complacent comparisons of your own superior scrupulousness with other people's laxity! In fact, this is a temptation that easily besets those who conscientiously separate from the rest—those are two such easy steps, from conscientiousness to self-righteousness, and from self-righteousness to censoriousness.

We have seen, now, how The Outside Christian comes to be outside—sometimes for motives, however mistaken, however mixed, which are not in themselves unworthy of respect. But we are bound, at the same time, to observe that however conscientiously he comes to this position, it is an unhappy and unsafe position to rest in, both for himself and for others.

See what he loses for himself:

1. He loses the immense strength that comes from an openly avowed allegiance to Jesus Christ. When Hedley Vicars, a young officer in a British regiment in the Crimean war, consecrated himself to be a soldier of Jesus Christ, his first act was to set up a Bible, open, in a conspicuous place in his tent, so that every man coming in would be sure to see it. The young fellows of the staff and line would drop in, and seeing it, would chaff him about it. "Yes," Vicars would say, "those are my colors; I propose to stand by them." It brought him some annoyance, at first; but what safety, what exemption from a multitude of temptations such as beset the way of one whose position in the great controversy between God and wickedness is in the least uncertain or indefinite! Of all men, the man of a modest, self-mistrustful mind, conscious of his own instability, is the very last who ought to

excuse himself from the most positive, manifest taking of sides in this great controversy. There are many ways of letting the world know which side he is on; but none so obvious and so effective as that of connecting oneself by distinct act of adhesion with the right party against the wrong. The Outside Christian is in all the more danger, because he will not give this public notice to the temptations of the world to stand off and let him alone.

2. He loses the joy and peace of believing—of believing on God wholly, unreservedly;—for the half-hearted trust in God, which is sincere as far as it goes, but does not go so far as to cut quite free from the world and give up all thought of keeping open the lines of retreat, is not the sort that brings settled joy and peace, but rather draws the soul into turmoil and unrest and controversy with itself. But what Christian can afford, as a mere matter of security, to lose the joy of the Lord, which is his strength; or the peace of God, which keeps the heart and mind; or the hope which is like an anchor, and like a helmet?

3. He loses the fellowship of good Christians—I mean that unreserved full confidence that goes out freely toward those who are unmistakably committed to our own side, and identified with us in our efforts and struggles against sin within us and round about us. And he can not afford to lose it. For if he is a Christian at all, he loves these men and women who are with him in like repentance from sin, and in like precious faith, and in earnest longing for the good kingdom. He needs counsel and society from fellow Christians, and is lonely without it, even though he may not be very clearly conscious what it is that he lacks. He feels weak without it, and he *is* weak, for God never meant us to stand *alone* in our faith and love, but to stand by one another and strengthen each other.

4. The Outside Christian loses the comfort and strength that are given in the Communion of the Lord's Supper. He does not know what it is that he loses; and if we tell him what the

Lord's Supper means to us, he will reply—" Well, I know and feel that already." And yet he does need to come with his fellow-disciples and eat the bread and drink of the cup which shew the Lord's death until he come. He does need the very presence of the Lord as it is made known to the believers in the breaking of the bread. In staying away he is wronging his own soul,—and yet he does not know it.

So much the Outside Christian loses for himself. But think how much, all the time, he may be losing for the cause and the Master that he loves. By just as much as, by his standing outside, he secures the name of Christ from scandal in case of his fall,—by just so much he takes all the honor away from Christ, in case of his faithful and blameless walk. Nay, it is a doubtful question whether every good thing in his life and character will not be used in disparagement of the name of Christ, and to the detriment of his cause—whether his name will not be quoted to show how well a man can live without prayer, without faith, without hope, without God in the world, and how little need there is of any salvation by Christ.

We love this Outside Christian, but we are afraid for him, and we are afraid for the cause of God and of man because of him. If only the Outside Christian would come *inside*, what joy it would be!—joy to us all,—joy and peace to his own heart, and a new invitation and welcome to other hearts still outside. It does seem as if a new advance of the kingdom of God would begin from the hour that these lingerers on the threshold should come within and let the world know, and the church know, that they are wholly and irrevocably on the Lord's side.

And now I know what some of them will be all ready to say—that this is *a very serious matter*, this coming into the fellowship of the church of Christ, and not to be decided on hastily; and so on the pretext that it is a serious matter it will be deferred, and deferred, as it has been in the past.

No, dear friends, whom we love, and whom the Lord loves,

if that is what you mean by a serious matter—an affair to shrink from, and shirk, and postpone—this is no serious affair at all, but a glad and joyful thing that you should come to eagerly as to a festival; as indeed it is a festival. If you would know what is a serious affair indeed, from which you should recoil with a sense of solemn awe and dread, it is this: when the gentle voice of Jesus the Master is heard saying "take my yoke upon you," that you should halt for a moment and seem to listen, and then pass on and give him no answer. This is a very grave and serious responsibility to take. Are you prepared to assume it? And when he shall bid you again to the table of his own remembrance, and in his pierced hands shall reach out to you the broken loaf and the cup of salvation and say, " Do this in remembrance of me,"—for you to turn upon your heel and go your way and make no answer—is not this a pretty serious thing—a responsibility which you are not willing to assume?

V.

MAN'S QUESTION ABOUT CHRIST.

What manner of man is this?—MATT. viii. 27.

This is a sort of question which is very much asked in the gospels, and very much oftener asked than answered. On this occasion, it was asked by the fishermen in the boat with the Lord, as he crossed the stormy little lake of Galilee, and as they saw him make the sea a calm so that the waves of it were still. At another time, it was asked by scribes and learned men, partly amazed and partly shocked that he had said to a paralytic man, "Son, be of good cheer; thy sins are forgiven thee." "Who is this," they asked, "that speaketh blasphemies?" On the Palm Sunday, when the strange procession came marching and shouting down the mountain to escort him into the temple, "the whole city was moved" to ask the question "Who is this?" Sometimes he squarely put the question himself. He perplexed the learned theologians of the temple by asking them, "What think ye of the Christ? Whose son is he?" He demanded of his disciples, "Who do men say that I, the Son of man, am?" And then, "Who say ye that I am?" He puts the question, but he rarely answers it. John the Baptist sends to him from his prison, wondering at the long delay of the coming kingdom, with a tone of something almost like despair in his message, asking, "Art thou he that should come?" But even then the Master answers never a word, but goes forward with his works of grace and might, and bids the messengers "go tell John what you have seen." He does not seem even to wish others to answer for him,

MAN'S QUESTION ABOUT CHRIST. 59

When men know him not, the evil spirits know and fear, saying, "We know thee who thou art;" but he will none of their testimony; he rebukes them into silence, and will not suffer them to say that they know him. And when at last the foremost of his disciples attains to an answer to this question, the Master strictly charges his disciples that they tell no man that thing. As if, perhaps, he preferred that men should keep on questioning until with much asking they should receive, and seeking they should find, and knocking it should be opened to them; rather than they should be spared the pains and trial of the quest and come to the results without going through the processes.

And this method of Christ himself is the method of the New Testament. It begins with a genealogical table, on the first page of Matthew, and goes forward through all the first three gospels with the facts of a marvelous biography which set us wondering and questioning at every page. Not till the church has well learned Christ thus, from hearing the plain facts of the story, does that later gospel of John come to the church declaring wonderful mysteries of godliness, but even then answering not so many questions as it raises for us to answer— or not to answer, as the case may be. It would seem as if the Bible was meant to give us theology in the method in which the creation gives us science—throwing down before us facts in bewildering profusion, and questions that task our utmost powers, and bidding us arrange, classify, theorize, inquire and conclude. Certainly it does invite us, with great welcome, to study into these things into which angels desire to look. But certainly, also, it does not make our salvation or our acceptance with God to turn on the success of our theologizing. We find in these Scriptures (which are in nothing more wonderful and more divine than in the things which they do not contain) no plan of salvation by scholarship, nor of salvation by logic, nor of salvation by orthodoxy, but a plain way of salvation by faith. Take the little gospel of Mark. It is a whole gospel.

It was originally meant to stand alone. It is able to make wise to salvation. But there is not much doctrine in it. In fact, there is not much of anything in it besides a Saviour,— his life and death and resurrection. And we are given to understand that it is safe to trust all our anxieties to him, who careth for us; and that the man who trusteth in him shall never be confounded. Of course to one who has thus trusted in him, knowing him and loving him from the story of his holy and blessed life, the further study of the question "What manner of man is this?" becomes thenceforward one of the most profoundly important and interesting questions that can possibly occupy the thoughts. But thenceforward, also, it can *not* be a life-and-death question. The question of life or death is settled. I know enough of this mighty and gracious one to take him for my teacher, the guide of my conduct, the keeper of my conscience, the forgiver of my sins, my Saviour to eternal life; and what he has offered and undertaken to do, I have confidence in him that somehow he will perform. That is the vital question, and that is settled. And now to these other questions, as they come up, let me address myself with profoundest interest indeed, but without anxiety. It is not a dangerous thing for one who has read this story of Jesus and learned to love him with the affection and gratitude of a disciple, to go on and study the deep things concerning his person and character and the method of his saving work. It is quite safe; and you are safe. Let no man frighten you from the perfect calmness of your delightful study. There are many Christians so unfortunate as to have been brought up to believe those shocking and unchristian statements of the "Athanasian Creed" that "whosoever will be saved it is necessary above all things that he believe," a certain code of scholastic propositions concerning the person of Christ and the Trinity, "which things if a man believe not, without doubt he shall perish everlastingly." One who believes this unscriptural and immoral heresy thereby becomes almost incapable of intelligently believing anything besides. He has forbidden himself to inquire candidly, under peril of damnation; and where a man cannot candidly inquire, he cannot solidly and intelligently believe. He can make believe.

Take this way of Christ and of the Gospels: to begin with plain facts—wonderful facts, but simple and intelligible in themselves—and with asking questions; and contrast this way with the way which theology has commonly followed, and see how much the foolishness of God is wiser than man. For the way of theology has too often been to begin at the other end, with enunciating its dogma, and then to hunt through the Bible for proof-texts with which to support it. It has been in the habit of making much of the epistles, and little of the gospels—much of doctrines about Christ, and little of Christ's own teaching, and of the living Christ himself, who is greater than his teaching.

It has been a most noble advance that the church of our century has made in the knowledge of Christ, since the time when it began to study, according to the method of the Scriptures, to know Christ himself, instead of knowing things about Christ. And we owe this progress to the attacks of heretics and infidels. If it had not been for the powerful and learned labors with which such scholars as Paulus and Strauss in Germany and Renan in France have attacked the gospel history and attempted to discredit the very facts of the life and death of Christ, the church might have been busy to this day, as it was busy fifty years ago and less, pettifogging the old, unfruitful controversies about election and decrees, and theories of atonement, and questions relating to moral government and free-will. It was not by any wisdom of ours, but by stress of this attack upon the credibility of the gospel history, that we were lifted out of the old rut, and turned into that study of the four gospels themselves, and of the life of Jesus Christ among men, which is the characteristic of the Christian scholarship of the present generation. There is nothing so characteristic of our Christian literature in this generation as that it dwells upon this theme—the person of Jesus of Nazareth. What countless multitudes of volumes on this subject are yearly crowding more and more the shelves of our libraries!—and this whole department of literature, now so vastly voluminous, is, we might say, the growth of these last fifty years. It is the fruit of the return of the church to the method of the Bible, by which, taking the story of the facts of the birth, life, teachings, death and resurrection of Jesus of Nazareth, and asking What manner of man is this?—it rises, so far as it is able, from the contemplation of this simple history to the understanding of all mysteries and all knowledge. This is the method by which the church first learned of the glory of its Saviour's person.

And if there be among you any mind that has been stirred up, in the agitation of prevailing controversies and inquiries, to question the habitual or traditionary conceptions of this august person, on which the whole superstructure of the scheme of Christian doctrine has been builded up,—this is the method to which I would bring him back. I would *not* enunciate to him the statements of orthodox opinion, and bid him take those and read the four gospels in the light of them, and see whether he does not find them confirmed thereby. What confidence is a really candid inquirer likely to feel in the result of inquiries so entered upon with a foregone conclusion in the right hand. I would rather he should begin with that chapter of proper names at the beginning of Matthew, and go through the four biographies again as if they were a fresh book; and at the end of it all, put to himself again the old question, What manner of man is this? And if the answer does not readily come, let him read again, and ask again. And if a life-time should be spent in such questioning as this, without reaching a hypothesis that will include all the marvelous facts, it will be a life-time nobly spent. What companionship is this to which the soul is thus addicted! What likeness to the mind of Christ must needs grow in that mind that converses long and lovingly with the life and words and works of Christ! How much to be preferred, the suspense of such a doubter, to the easy-going confidence of one who taking everything for granted, finds no need for ardent and constant contemplation of the mystery of godliness, without controversy great, and who having "never doubted, never half believed!" Be assured, the questionings that bring you and keep you in this personal acquaintance with the Christ of the four gospels are fruitful questionings, indeed.

> In such society as this
>   My weary soul would rest;
> The mind that dwells where Jesus is
>   Must be forever blest.

Now in the course of your studies into the documents of Christ's life (and these are very few and small—these four little pamphlets constitute the whole of them), it is safe to take one thing for granted: It will be with you as with every one who has gone before you in this study, with the exception of some exceptionally coarse minds who have entered upon their work with undisguised malignity of purpose. Setting aside all theological prepossessions, you will be impressed with the beauty and dignity of the life which passes before you in this fourfold picture. It is with a studiously dispassionate pen that one has attempted briefly to sum up the impressions which the story of Jesus makes on those who have read it without accepting the Christian doctrine of his person.* They " see in Jesus a unique and sinless personality, one with whom no other human being can be even distantly compared. . . . He taught but three years, and not continuously even during them. He accepted the most ordinary customs of the teachers of his day. He wore no broad phylacteries like the Pharisees; he was not emaciated with asceticism like the Essenes; he preached the kingdom of God, not as John had done, between

* Canon Farrar, s v. *Jesus.* Encyc. Brit. Ninth edition.

the gloomy precipices of the wilderness, but from the homely platform of the synagogue. . . . He appeared before the people not in the hairy mantle of a prophet, but in the ordinary dress of a Jewish man. . . . He came eating and drinking. He had no human learning; his rank was that of a village carpenter; he checked all political excitement; he directed that respect should be paid to all the recognized rulers, whether heathen or Jewish, and even to the religious teachers of the nation; he was obedient to the Mosaic law; his followers were unlearned and ignorant men chosen from the humblest of the people. Yet he has, as a simple matter of fact, altered the whole current of the stream of history; he closed all the history of the past, and inaugurated all the history of the future; and all the most brilliant and civilized nations of the world worship him as God." The greatest minds, unprejudiced or filled with hostile prejudice, have given concordant testimony. " Kant testifies to his ideal perfection. Hegel saw in him the union of the human and the divine." "Spinoza spoke of him as the truest symbol of heavenly wisdom. The beauty and grandeur of his life overawed even the flippant soul of Voltaire. Between him and whoever else in the world, said Napoleon I. at St. Helena, there is no possible term of comparison. If the life and death of Socrates are those of a sage, said Rousseau, the life and death of Jesus are those of a God. He is, says Strauss, the highest object we can possibly imagine with respect to religion, the being without whose presence in the mind perfect piety is impossible. The Christ of the Gospels, says Renan, is the most beautiful incarnation of God in the most beautiful of forms. His beauty is eternal. His reign will never end. John Stuart Mill spoke of him as a man charged with a special, express and unique commission from God to lead mankind to truth and virtue."

When we find such singular accordance among men so widely differing, extorted, as one might say, by mere power of the subject of which they speak, in spite of hostile feeling and a disposition even scornfully critical, it may safely be presumed that the same traits will make a like impression on yourself. You will find in the story of the gospels, as others have before you, the traits of a man of exceptional and wonderful endowments of intellect, of heroic courage, of dauntless tenacity of principle and purpose, and of a dignity and stainless purity of character and an impassioned love of righteousness which cause him to be thus reckoned incomparable among the human race; at the same time, a man of singular humility and modest forgetfulness of self, who, endowed with every faculty for great achievement, seemed to have escaped "the last infirmity of noble minds," and to be without ambition to achieve anything that the world calls great: who accomplished no stroke of battle or of state, put in operation no organized society, constructed no philosophical or ethical system, left no writing behind him, whom nevertheless subsequent ages and distant nations and races have crowned with that honor which he never sought, accounting his teaching the last authority in ethics, theology and law, his person to be an object worthy of the highest reverence, and the epoch of his birth as the Golden Milestone from which to measure in either direction the paths of history; a man who was, withal, poor, despised and a sufferer, and yet in poverty and suffering most sublime, and in his malefactor's death glorious beyond the power of envy, prejudice and unbelief to behold undazzled; —whose grandeur of intellect, dignity of character, and religious elevation of soul are nevertheless to men's eyes so outshone by his attributes of love and gentleness, wider than the earth and stronger than death, that the former are forgotten in the latter.

And yet remember, while you gaze and wonder and admire, that this is not the object of your present study; that you have opened this volume of the gospels with great and earnest questions that demand an answer. Have a care lest the inquiries which you send out be like those soldiers sent to apprehend Jesus, who before the glory and dignity of his presence go backward and fall to the ground, and have no report to bring back to those that sent them but this: Never man spake like this man. Our duty is inquiry, not eulogy. And if we are faithful in this duty, be assured that here and there, in the miraculously simple and truthful histories from which our conceptions of the character of Christ are drawn, we shall recognize some facts which, to our candid reading, do not seem naturally to fall into harmony with these large general conceptions;—exceptional facts, which make us feel that the person in whom they are found is thus far an unsolved enigma to us, until we are able to discover (if ever we shall discover it) some larger conception of his character and person which shall include these with the rest.

These are the things which will cost us thought and study as we read, taking the four gospels into our hand as if they were a fresh book speaking to us of the life of one of whom we had not known before:—the things in the life of Jesus of Nazareth which are perplexing or inexplicable on any theory of his human character which we are able to frame. These things must be fairly met and considered if we would deal justly by ourselves. We may not leave the difficult facts out of view. We may not strain and garble them into compliance with a preconceived theory. We may not indolently call them "mysterious" and so leave them. We need to know the real Jesus, and not a tradition, or a doctrine, or an imagination.

And when we have gathered the facts we are driven by the necessary instinct of the mind to frame them together. We read the story of Washington, and in the midst of that great, calm, religious career, we come upon an authentic scene of profane violence which startles and pains us. We do not say, "This is contrary to our conception of Washington—we must suppress it." We frame it into our conception of him, and say, "This was a man not constitutionally impassive, but of mighty passions which sometimes broke through his strong habitual self-control." We see him inexorably stern commanding the execution of an amiable young man, and we do not say "he was an inconsequent, incongruous mixture, half humane and half cruel;" we are at no loss to find a principle in his life which reconciles these contradictions.

We deal on this principle not only with living and historic, but even with fictitious characters. How many volumes have been written by inquirers after the unity of Hamlet's character, or Faust's? And is it to be expected that the laws of our intellectual activity are to be suspended when we come to the study of the gospels?

But our only study for this evening is as to ways and methods, not as to results. We part, you and I, as we gathered here, face to face with a great question—"What manner of man is this?" But let me not affect to think it doubtful in what direction this inquiry, diligently pursued, will lead you. I will not predict it in the terms of any scholastic formula or phrase of historic orthodoxy. No man can tell for you what form of statement the truth will take in your mind as you dwell in contemplation on the holy and reverend form of him who is the Truth. But it must be that as you continue gazing upon the glory of his countenance, you shall by and by begin to recognize that beholding it you have beheld a more than human glory—the glory as of the only-begotten of the Father, of him who is full of grace and truth.

VI.

CHRIST'S QUESTION TO MEN.

Who say ye that I am?—MATT. xvi. 15.

THE natural way of satisfying ourselves concerning any person, who and what he is, is to find the authentic facts of his life—what he said and did, and what he did not say nor do,—and to form our judgment upon these.

The biblical way—the evangelical way—of satisfying ourselves concerning the person of Jesus of Nazareth, what manner of man he is, is to take the facts of his life (which we are happy in having ready to our hand in four singularly simple and honest records), and to frame our judgment upon them.

And it does not require much reflection to perceive that the natural way, and the biblical and evangelical way, is, in this case, the only rational and logical way. We think sometimes, to find a short and easy way to the knowledge of who Jesus Christ is by some apostolic declaration or some church definition of dogma. But we are bound to remember, that so long as the person of Jesus Christ is held in doubt, the ground of our confidence in apostolic declarations, or in church definitions, is gone out from under us. What is it that commands our deference to the religious teachings of an apostle but this,—that he is an apostle of Jesus Christ? Wherein consists that authority of the church, the fellowship of believers throughout the world, when we recognize its accordant testimony on any point of doctrine,—but in this, that it is the church of Jesus Christ? Now, when the question is on the authority of Jesus Christ, the Lord of the apostles and the Lord of the church,—that question which was put to him in the temple, "By what authority doest thou these things, and who gave thee this authority?"—it is very obvious, to a logical mind, that this question cannot be decided by quoting from sources whose only authority is what they derive from him. We can only answer this question by turning to the facts of Christ's life themselves, in the only form in which we have access to them—in the four gospels;—in these gospels considered simply as the substantially true and trustworthy histories which most men find them to be from their own internal as well as external evidence. For waiving, for the present, all questions that any may raise as to the supernatural quality of these four books, it is quite enough, for the purpose of the present argument, to assume that they are true and honest. A fair man, reading through Matthew, Mark, Luke and John, whatever his views on inspiration may be, is pretty sure to rest solidly in the conviction that these are fair and singularly straightforward and sincere accounts of a real person—of his life and acts and teachings.

Already, a week ago, we have made a beginning in the study of who this person is. Looking at him as the fourfold picture of his life revolves before us, we find the first impressions of admiration and love which are irresistibly made upon our minds confirmed (as we might say) by the general suffrage of mankind. You have not forgotten that impressive consensus of testimony from men whose distinction in history has been the suspicious and incredulous jealousy with which they have denied and contested every ascription of honor to the person of this man Jesus, but those which are undeniable and incontestable,—with what singular unanimity they agree in declaring him to be *the perfect man*, the type of an ideal humanity,— the sum of every human virtue. We are here on ground so nearly uncontested among all thoughtful and serious readers of the gospels, Christian, unchristian, anti-christian, that we may speak with very little hesitation of the symmetry and harmony of a perfect human character as illustrated in Jesus. And this is the one thing that humanity beside, in all its generations, fails to show us.

I asked a studious artist, once, about the famous Belvedere torso of Hercules—whether, in all his studies of living models chosen for their physical perfection, he had ever met with its counterpart in muscular development; and, as I expected, he told me no. It was not infrequent, he said, to find some parts or members thus exceptionally developed—as in the right arm of a smith, or the thighs of a porter—but never the whole system, as in the torso; besides, he said, you see in the torso the entire muscular system in a state of simultaneous activity, which is hardly true to nature. You can hardly expect to find the whole system in vigor at once. The antagonist muscles, as the extensors and the flexors, can hardly be in tension at the same time. When one set is contracted the other set will be relaxed. We must consider the torso as the fragment of an ideal figure.

So we make our allowances for the *moral* constitution of human nature. Some high qualities of humanity seem hardly compatible in the same subject; and there are what might be called antagonist virtues of which one sort seems to be held in suspense or abeyance when the other is in exercise. We pretty much give up looking to find a whole manhood both strong and symmetrical, and wholly righteous in all virtuous acts, thoughts and feelings, at once. We try to make up such a character by combining in our picture the highest qualities of more than one; and when we have finished, the critics cry out upon our delineation for an impossibility, not resembling any real man or woman that anybody knows.

Now the thing which has moved the unanimous wonder of the cold-blooded and not too friendly critics whom I have quoted to you, is not so much the prodigious development of some astonishing quality in Jesus, as this blending of seeming incompatibles in a perfect manhood. The qualities that seem to pull in opposite directions seem in his person to find their radiating center and focus of convergence. Courage and heroism, profound sagacity of intuition, exquisite sense of right and fitness, are joined with a lofty and severe justice, a greatness and purity of soul which mean and evil motives dared not approach, or approaching found nothing in him. And to all these were united in highest perfection the eminently human virtues—the virtues that characteristically belong to a finite, dependent being, such as great humility, modesty, self-denial, submissiveness to authority, deference to public ordinance even on questionable points, tolerance of personal wrong and injury; insomuch that the epithet which has passed like a surname into common speech is this,—" the meek and lowly Jesus." Joined with these were a reverence before God, a childlike trust in God, and a habitual prayerfulness and obedience toward God, which were like a crown of light on the head of his perfect character, outshining all his other human virtues, and yet by its shining making them all the lovelier.

And now why can we not rest here, with this perfect example of human duty and virtue, and be thankful? What need have we of any further theory of the person of Jesus Christ beside this simple one that he was the perfect and sinless man, who practically realized in his person that which many have aspired after and some have approached? Why is it that men *don't* rest here; and that when very noble Christian scholars and teachers, and men of very lofty and beautiful spirit,—such, for example, as the late Dr. Channing—have set forth this simple, comprehensible statement of the perfect human holiness of Jesus as a sufficient statement, and have commended it to men with every form of persuasive argument, reinforced by the attraction of beautiful and holy living, instead of laying hold of it and clinging fast to it, men seem to scatter from it in one direction or the other? The difficulty with it is that it does not include all the facts. It has the attraction of being very simple; and it is easy to have a simple theory when you leave out of view such facts as do not easily fall in with it. And that there are such facts is felt by the general sense of those who read the story.

For we look again, and lo, this meek, gentle and lowly one, this man so modest, retiring, self-forgetful, claiming nothing for himself, assuming no honors, diligently withdrawing himself from those that are thrust upon him, jealous for nothing but the cause of the wronged and the truth and honor of God, this wiser than the ancients, this hero and martyr of a serene courage and fortitude unmatched in history, is found acting in scenes, manifesting traits, giving utterance to words and sentiments, which are not accounted for by this estimate of his character. That character which seemed most simple and comprehensible for the very reason that it was perfect, is set back under a cloud of mystery and perplexity. There are things in his life that are not like him. And yet men do not say of them that they are blemishes and inconsistencies, for somehow they do not seem such, in him. They only make us think that we have not wholly known him when we have summed up the whole account of him in saying, "he is our perfect fellow man,"—that there is something to be added to this (not deducted from it) before we have a statement which comprehends his whole life and all his deeds and words.

For instance, one of the conspicuous qualities of his soul, obvious to every spectator, admitted by every enemy, is that very common but always noble quality of *courage*. And in his case it is of the finest tone and type. There is no bluster nor defiance in it; it needs not to be nerved by enterprise and great action. It is of that tranquil and serene sort, which in the presence of imminent peril can quietly do nothing when there is nothing to do, and can go forward with words of teaching or works of mercy with an equal mind. I know not whither, in classic history or chivalrous romance, to turn for examples of just such courage. And now holding in mind this model of the supremely heroic man, will you explain— Gethsemane?

Alike characteristic of this Man of men is the spontaneous unforced modesty which is the antithesis both of egotism and of selfishness. No need to cite instances to prove it; we all feel it as we read. It is a common trait and ornament of greatness, especially of great wisdom. And in his case, how content it made him, the Light of the World, to be counselor of the ignorant and outcast, comforter of little children, friend of publicans and sinners. His highest public office was to be reader in a country synagogue, and that office he diligently fulfilled; and when this congregation rejected him, he had no complaint at spending the rest of his days a homeless wanderer without place to lay his head. And yet this same man openly claimed to be greater than Solomon, and older than Abraham, and demanded that all men should look up to him as teacher and Lord.

It was one of the greatest and wisest TEACHERS of mankind, Confucius, who having given to his race a system of moral duties admirably true and complete, modestly paused on the border of religious truth, declaring that of God and the unseen world he had no authority to teach. But this unpresuming carpenter's son declares,—"All things are delivered to me of my Father," and of the profoundest mysteries of religious truth avers,—"We speak that we do know and testify that we have seen."

It was a KING illustrious among the monarchs of England, Canute, surnamed the Great, who in bitter scorn of human greatness bade his courtiers plant his throne upon the beach, and with humble irony commanded the unyielding tide to stay its waves. It was this Galilean, Jesus, surnamed the Meek and Lowly, who confidently trampled on the waves, and in solemn earnest commanded the storm "Be still," and the winds and the waves obeyed him.

SCRIBES and SCHOLARS learned in the sacred law of Moses, and in the books of the inspired prophets, and in the accumulated expositions of generations of grave interpreters, had been wont to teach the people out of the treasures of their lore, and it was their boast and honor that they taught on higher authority than their own—the authority of antiquity and of inspired Scripture. But this man, this Nazarene, the gentlest, most submissive of men, sat on his Galilean hill-top, and denounced the best culture and highest respectability of his age and nation as being blind, extortionate, hypocritical, and cited the language of sacred writ and the words of the ancients, to contradict them with the words, "But *I* say unto you," until the multitudes were astonished at his doctrine because *he* taught them as one having authority, and *not* as the scribes.

Consecrated PRIESTS, called of God as was Aaron, deemed it a high and solemn function to set forth in appointed symbols the great truths of divine forgiveness and the gift of the Holy Spirit. On the great day of the feast, they were wont each year, clad in beautiful and festal garments, to the sound of various instruments of music, to descend the temple hill, and from the living spring of Siloam to dip an urn of water and bring it back, with song and symphony, into the temple, to be mingled with the wine and poured upon the altar and the victim. At such a time, when, at the pouring of the libation, the temple and its courts were filled with solemn silence, harp and trumpet hushed, before bursting forth again with multitude of jubilant voices in Isaiah's song, "With joy will we draw water out of the wells of salvation,"—at such a moment, what rude voice is it that breaks in with a loud cry, to mar the holy stillness? It is the Nazarene, again—the humble and devout, the meek and lowly—who stands forth with Galilean garb and speech, crying out to the multitude, "If any thirst, let him come unto *me* and drink."

The HIGH-PRIEST, being thereto called of God, might, not without shedding of blood for his own sins as well as for the people's, sprinkling himself with these prophetic drops, and hiding his own person behind the fragrant cloud from the censer, venture into the presence of God's earthly glory, and make bare before the mercy-seat the names that were written upon his breastplate; and from this awful presence might nevertheless come forth alive. But this man Jesus, with no priestly lineage, no breastplate nor robe, no censer, no offering for his own sins, and no confession for himself, fears not to enter into the very secret place of God, uttering words which it is not lawful for man to utter; he bids all men to come to the Father through him and they shall in no wise be cast out, —to ask what they will in his name and it shall be given them;—this man, most humble and devoutly reverent, most meek and lowly, most childlike, and dependent, and submissive! What manner of man is this?

There had been divine PROPHETS before the day of Christ, men who had desired to see his day and had not seen it, and many were the signs and mighty works which they had wrought. Men of like passions with ourselves, they had prayed earnestly, and the heaven had become as brass and the earth as dust; they prayed again, and the heaven gave rain and the earth brought forth her fruits. Such an one had gone into the still chamber where lay the body of a dead youth, and shutting the door upon them twain, had stretched himself upon the dead, mouth upon mouth, eye upon eye, hand upon hand, and there with long entreaty prayed to God, and prayed and prayed, until at last the parted life came back, and by faith the woman received her dead raised to life again, and God's were the power and the glory. But who is this, that lays his hand upon the bier and the bearers halt, that speaks his orders to "the dull, cold ear of death," saying "Young man, *I* say unto thee, Arise;" and the wondering dead sits up upon his bier and begins to speak? Behold the man, pressing through the crowd of those who laugh him to scorn, meek, unreviling when reviled, who takes the dead child by the hand, and says (how touching the grateful memory that would not lose the very syllables he spoke, when they wrote down the story in another tongue!)—he says to her *Talitha, cumi,*—damsel, arise; and then (as it perplexes us to read) "straitly charges them that no man should know it."

See him once more. He has lost a friend, he whose foes are so many and whose real friends so few. The sisters of the dead cling to him, when at last, long waited-for, he comes to Bethany, and say, one after the other, "Lord, if thou hadst been here! Lord, if thou hadst been here!" And as he followed with the weeping company along the sad, familiar street of Bethany, and took the path toward the village sepulchres, to go and see where they had laid him, human nature was too strong for the composure of that affectionate, wounded heart, and Jesus wept! And then, declaring, "*I* am the resurrection and the life"—he, this sorrowful, bereaved man, with the tears of his affliction still wet upon his face, looked down into the fetid grave's mouth, and shouted to the four-days dead, "Come forth!"

Holy APOSTLES, made bold by his authority, like prophets who had been aforetime, speaking by the Spirit of God, have declared to those who confess their sins that God is faithful and just to forgive them their sins, and have encouraged the penitent to look to God in faith for pardon. But this man, Jesus, looked on the anxious face of the palsy-stricken, and said to him, "Son, be of good cheer; thy sins be forgiven thee." And when the whisper ran through the shuddering crowd: "Who is this, that forgiveth sins also? Who can forgive sins but God only? This man blasphemeth;"—he answered all their questionings by that which could only provoke to deeper questions still—he bade the palsied Arise and walk,—that they might know that the Son of Man had power on earth to forgive sins.

It is told of blessed SAINTS who preached the story of his life among the heathen, and were attended on, as he had promised them, by signs following, that on one occasion, when in the name of Jesus of Nazareth they had wrought a miracle of healing, the heathen priests, with an impulse of reverent gratitude, brought oxen and garlands to do them honors of divine worship. But they rushed in among the people, with rent garments, with horror dissuading them from such an act. Before the feet of a holy ANGEL, seen in a heavenly vision, a man fell down to worship; but the angel forbade him, saying "See thou do it not. I am thy fellow-servant. Worship God." But the meek and lowly Jesus, who taught supreme love and worship to be due to God alone, saying "him only shalt thou serve"; who taught the equal brotherhood of men, bidding them call no man Master, and himself was not ashamed to call them brethren; and who would not suffer the young man kneeling at his feet to call him good;—he it was who commanded that all men should honor the Son, even as they honor the Father, and in open defiance of the charge of blasphemy for which men were ready to stone him on the spot, asserted boldly, "I and my Father are one."

What manner of man is this?

But the mystery of this strange and unaccountable personality becomes most perplexed, not by the honors which he claims for himself, but by the amazing things which he boldly and unhesitatingly undertakes to do for others—for any who will trust in him—things which to man are impossible. What boldest of the children of men, of the messengers of God, has ever dared to utter such words? "O Israel," they had been wont to cry, "return unto Jehovah thy God!" "Come, and let us return unto the Lord: for he hath torn, and he will heal us; he hath smitten, and he will bind us up." Thither they pointed, to the one true, ever-living God, fountain of life and light, who forgiveth all iniquities and healeth all diseases, and redeemeth the soul from destruction. Is it nothing strange, when the humblest and most filial of the sons of God, a Galilean villager, standing before the throng of his fellow-countrymen, bids them, *not*, Return to God, but "Come unto *me*, and I will give you rest;" when he repeats, "Believe in God, believe also in me;" "I am come that ye might have life;" "I am the door; I am the way; I am the bread that cometh down from heaven; I am the truth; I am the resurrection; I am the life. Whosoever believeth in me shall never die"? What can we make of that strange scene when in the midst of an unnatural darkness resting at noon-day over all the land, two neighbors, in the uttermost paroxysms of dying anguish, descried each other's tortured faces through the gloom, and one said to the other,—himself just writhing as if in the final struggle, his forehead torn with thorns, his brow beaded with the death-sweat, his voice choked with feverish thirst, his head about to drop upon his breast in death—"This day shalt thou be with me in Paradise." Did he seem the man to undertake such a trust and hold forth such promises unauthorized? Would he invite such confidence to disappoint it? And yet what suffering, dying man that was ever born of a woman, could claim to himself the power of giving or withholding everlasting life?

Be not impatient if I leave you still confronted with all that is solemn and beautiful, with all that is deep and perplexing, in this crowning problem of all human history. I would not be eager to bring you to any foregone conclusion of my own. I have no anxiety at all that you should hasten to accept certain ancient scholastic statements that are current under the name of orthodoxy. I would not even hurry you at this hour, to the consideration of those indications which the Holy Scriptures themselves give of the direction in which we are to seek the solution of these contradictions. Why should you not, like the first disciples of Jesus, continue for a time face to face with this wondrous Being, the mystery of piety, who was manifested in the flesh, justified in the spirit, seen of angels, preached among the nations, believed on in the world, received up in glory; and ponder in your own hearts the questions which he puts, and which the world puts: Who do men say that I am? Who say ye that I am? Who is this? What manner of man is this?—or that question which Pilate asked, What shall we do with Jesus who is called the Christ?

And if, while yet you gaze perplexed upon that blessed face, so marred more than any man's, while as yet you have found no solution of these deep wonders in which your mind can rest, if peradventure you see something in Jesus Christ which gives you assurance of his tender and personal love to every human creature, and of a perfect truthfulness and faithfulness which could not betray nor disappoint the confidence of any who trusted him according to his promise—if you should say to yourself, " I do not understand this Jesus, but I love him ; I put my trust in him ; *how* he saves I do not altogether know, but he has promised, and I take his word ; he shall be my teacher, and he my guide, and he my forgiveness, and he my peace with God, and he my salvation forever and ever ; "—then will that peculiar blessing rest on you, the blessing which the risen Lord pronounced on those who have not seen and yet have believed.

VII.

THE MYSTERY MANIFESTED.

Without controversy great is the mystery of godliness; he who was manifested in the flesh, justified in the spirit, seen of angels, preached among the nations, believed on in the world, received up in glory.—1 Tim. iii. 16.

BEFORE entering upon the great subject that is brought before us in this text, some things need to be premised about the language, and (in the strictest sense of the word) about the *letter* of the text.

You have noticed, as I have read the familiar words, that the phrase "*God manifest in the flesh*" is changed, in the Revised New Testament to "he who was manifested in the flesh," for the reason, given in the margin, that the old reading rests on no sufficient evidence. It is a long and agitating controversy the decision of which is thus pronounced. It was a question on the crossing of a *t*. Did a certain Greek letter in an old parchment book in the British Museum have a stroke across it or not. One said, "Yes, I can see it." The next man answered, "No, but what you see is in a darker ink, and was added by some one who wanted to strengthen this text for a proof-text." "Yes," says the first, again, "I acknowledge that the text has been tampered with; but under the dot of black ink, I see a faint stroke in the same ink with the rest of the word." "No," replies the second, "you think you do; but what you see is really a stroke on the opposite side of the parchment, which shows through, and, in fact, has at last corroded through the parchment; and here is Professor Maskelyne, with a very powerful microscope which will settle the matter." And so the matter is settled, not by Professor Maskelyne's microscope only, but by the testimony of other manuscripts, and the laborious collation of all possible proofs. The change of reading, which was resisted by the friends of orthodoxy as if the safety of Christ's church were at stake, has had to be admitted at last; and yet the church still stands fast on the Rock, and is like to stand for all the gates of hell can do against it. It has only lost a proof-text—that is all; and it has gained in the conviction that its knowledge of God and his truth stands in something much clearer and stronger than a proof-text—in the general tenor of Christ's life and of the whole teaching of the holy Scriptures.

Another preliminary point is the proper meaning, in the New Testament, of the word *mystery;* as in this phrase, "the mystery of godliness, without controversy great." There is a modern and popular use of the word, in which it means something inscrutably dark and perplexing—something hopelessly baffling to the powers of the human mind—an insoluble riddle or enigma; and this modern and popular sense of the word is often enough carried back into the Scriptures and applied to the word as found there, in such a way as to hide the meaning of it. It is a very favorite word with some sorts of theologians, who are fond of shortening up an argument, when it begins to be troublesome, by saying of one subject or another, "Oh, that is a mystery!"—as if this word were the end of all questioning. Now it is well to understand that the word in the New Testament has no such sense. It means a thing once hidden, but now brought to light. It means *a new discovery*. It does not at all imply that the matter, when once revealed, is difficult of understanding. It may be a very simple and elementary matter, such as simple minds can easily grasp when it is brought to them. Our Lord did not call around him, for his disciples, a group of twelve acute philosophers; but to the twelve simple and teachable fishermen whom he did call, he said, "To you it is given *to know* the mysteries of the kingdom of God;"—to them, and to us, also, if we are willing to learn. There is nothing in this word, *mystery*, to drive us away with our questions, but everything to encourage us.

We draw near, then, with deep reverence, but without terror, to the great mystery of godliness which is now *manifested* in the flesh, as to a thing which "it is given to us to know." And gazing on those things into which the angels desire to look, we are not afraid to ask what is the meaning of these wondrous contradictions which we have been contemplating in the life of Jesus Christ? We look to find the missing fact, or the comprehensive theory, which will reconcile the opposites and incompatibles which we find in this man. He is the bravest, calmest of heroes and martyrs; and we would know what means that agony and bloody sweat in Gethsemane. He is the humblest of men, in his unobtrusive goodness and preference of others to himself; but he asserts his dignity as higher than Solomon's or Abraham's. He faints with hunger, and is weary, and is overcome with sleep: but restrains the storm by a syllable, and scatters health and vigor about him with the touch of his fingers. He bows with deepest reverence before the majesty of God, continuing all night in prayer,—he declares "I can of myself do nothing;" but he bids others to put their whole trust in himself, saying, "I will give you rest"—"whatsoever you ask, I will do it." He bleeds, he cries aloud in pain, he faints, he dies;—he who by his own authority summoned the dead from the bed, from the bier, from the sepulchre, and who declared "I am the Resurrection and the Life;" "I will give eternal life."

Thus briefly and inadequately I have recalled to your mind that series of contradictions which impresses the mind of the thoughtful reader of the gospels, and grows upon him more and more, the more he studies them. And for help in the solution of the question, "What manner of man is this?" whither can we turn with so much hope as to those who companied with him intimately as his disciples; who thus learned the mind of Christ, who were expressly commissioned by him to give account of him to all the world, and who, according to his promise, were endowed with divine gifts equipping them for this very work? What light do we get on this dark question from these, and from their later-born associate, Paul? Shall we not expect to find in their words some intimation that this personality of Jesus Christ was not a human personality, but was something other and higher, as if, being not man, but being of an order of existence separate from humanity, and far exalted above it, those things which may not be affirmed of any such as we are might be true of him? This seems to have been one of the first conjectures of the earliest Christian speculation—that Jesus Christ was not really a human being.

But in the teachings of these first friends and followers of Christ, we get no light at all in this direction. There is no point on which they are more clear, unanimous and emphatic, than in asserting the very manhood of the Christ. He was "the man, Christ Jesus." He was not of the nature of angels, but of the seed of Abraham; he is touched with the feeling of our infirmities, having been tempted in all points like as we are. In fact, in the Gospel and Epistles of John it seems to be the writer's purpose to controvert at every opportunity that considerable sect of early Christians who tried to solve the perplexing facts about the life and teachings and acts and amazing promises of the Christ by saying that he was not really, in flesh and blood, a man. He was that very thing, says John. Our eyes have seen him, our hands have handled him. I saw the spear thrust into his side when there flowed out blood and water. This is that disciple that testified these things, and we know that his witness is true. Jesus Christ is come in the flesh. He was born of a woman, says Paul,—born under the law. He is our brother, says the writer to the Hebrews; "he is not ashamed to call us brethren."

And yet these same writers who so insist on it that Jesus

Christ is our fellow-man in all the qualities and sympathies of manhood, instead of adding anything to mitigate or explain away those prodigious perplexities and contradictions that appear in the story of his acts and teachings, go on to heap them mountain-high by the most amazing declarations concerning this brother of ours, this fellow-man. To him they ascribe the incommunicable names of God,—quoting as of him the words of ancient Scripture that are spoken of Jehovah. To him they impute the works of God, declaring that of him and through him and to him are all things, and that it is he who upholdeth all things by the word of his power. Of him they predicate the infinite attributes of God; and to him they ascribe the worship which is due to God, saying to him, "Thou art worthy, O Lord, to receive glory and honor," —to him, who is "Lord of lords," "Lord of glory," "Lord of all;" "Lord of the living and the dead;" "Lord of all in heaven and on earth and under the earth."

And yet all this, of a man born of woman; who grew in stature and grew in wisdom; who was flesh and blood; who was seen, felt and handled; who was hungry and thirsty; who was weary and slept; who was distressed and prayed for deliverance; who was bereaved and wept; who was a man of sorrows; who was crucified and cried out in anguish; who was pierced with the spear and bled; who died and was buried! Is this all the light that the Scriptures have to give, upon the great problem of the Gospels—upon the question, "What manner of man is this?" You will reproach me that I have brought you hither in quest of light, and have showed you no light at all, but have led you rather into deeper and deeper shades of darkness. I feel as if, for all the relief I have thus far given to your perplexity, you might rise against me as the mariners did against Columbus, when many days of voyaging had brought them only further out upon the seas, with no glimpse of the sought-for land in sight. And I can only plead for yet a little patience, a little watching of the sea and stars and scanning of the far horizon, as of those who know not how soon some bird of unknown wing, some floating branch from undiscovered forests, some distant point of light piercing the darkness, may give hope of our yet coming into our desired haven.

And meanwhile, even in the midst of the amazing and irreconcilable facts with which we are bewildered, it will not be altogether useless to look about us and make a sort of comparative estimate of the situation.

For it goes a great way with us men, when we have an unexplained phenomenon before us, if we can find some other unexplained phenomenon that is in some respects like it, and put the two into a class together. And if we are so happy as to find a third, so that we are able to say of it, "Oh, it belongs to that class of phenomena!" we consider that it is almost tantamount to an explanation of them all. It is not safe for any of us who live outside of the charmed circle of physical scientists to say what those privileged men do not know today; but it is certain that not many yesterdays ago they did not know much about the nature of electricity; and that when galvanism was discovered, they did not know much about the nature of that: but it was a great comfort to them when they were able to find things in common between them, and between these two and magnetism, and to talk learnedly about all three of them in a group, as "the imponderables." It seemed almost like understanding them. And in fact it was an appreciable step toward understanding them. Now in our studies of the New Testament we have been brought face to face with an incomprehensible group of statements and facts concerning Jesus Christ, which seem like irreconcilable contradictions. Is there anything else like this within the compass of our knowledge and experience? If there is, it will at least help to make our minds tolerant of the suspense while we are waiting for a solution; and may even—who knows?—put us forward toward a real understanding of the hidden thing.

Give me a little time, I beg, to state a case in parallel. I will not abuse your patience.

Of all the realities which make up this universe, and which are capable of being the subjects of human thought and study, there are two classes. Each excludes the other. The two together constitute the universe. Each class has its own set of attributes which are incapable of being applied to the other.

These two classes of realities are the material and the spiritual,—matter and mind.

One characteristic of matter is dimension, in length, breadth and thickness. One characteristic of mind is consciousness. It is impossible that a conscious spirit should have length, breadth and thickness. It is impossible that a mass of matter, so many inches long by so many broad and thick, should think, or wish, or love, or be conscious. Not only these things never are, but in the nature of the case they cannot be. It is a curious thing in the language of the old-fashioned exploded science of the Middle Ages that it used to apply to material objects the expressions, as of love and hate and sympathy, which are appropriate only to spiritual objects. Water came up in the pump, they said, because "nature abhorred a vacuum." Different matters would mingle according to their "affinities," or sympathies. The vapor of anything was its soul or "gas"; and the extract of a drug was its "spirit." The language has a poetical, unreal sound to us; and we see that it never can have been really true, to any one, except in some poetic sort of sense —that the facts of the mental and spiritual are not to be seriously affirmed concerning material things.

The fashion of language in our day has changed. The modern blunder is—not to impute to material things the qualities which belong to mind and spirit—but to talk about spiritual things as if they were material, or were functions of matter; —to talk about mind as if a mind was nothing but so many ounces of white and ash-colored pulp arranged in convolutions; —as if a mind could be dissected and weighed: to talk about thought as if it was the secretion of a gland, disengaging phosphorus: to talk about conscience and affection as if these were functions of the viscera and the excito-motory system, like digestion and assimilation. The old blunder was that of metaphysicians out of their sphere, talking about physics in the terms of mind; the new blunder is that of students of mechanics and physics and chemistry out of their sphere, talking about mental and spiritual things in the terms of matter. This sort of talk is doubtless misleading and confusing; but after all, it cannot permanently confuse the common sense of sensible people. We all know that it is absurd to say that an intellect can weigh fifty-five ounces, or that one hundred and ten cubic inches of white and gray pulp can think, or that a soul can have an upper side and an under side. If there is anything that we know, it is that our knowing is not done by a machine but by a mind;—that soul is not body and that body is not soul. Wise-sounding talk may confuse us for a while; but the common sense of mankind always comes right after a little.

And when I think of myself, I know by that very thinking that I am a thinking being—a soul, which by its nature has none of the properties of matter. And what I know of myself I know of other men who by their thoughts, emotions, affections, are made known to me. They, too, are thinking beings, minds, souls. I can not be mistaken. I say of them, without hesitation, those things which cannot be said, without absurdity, except of spiritual existences. I declare that they are wise, benevolent, prudent, learned; that they are sorrowful, penitent, trustful, prayerful; that they are generous souls, great minds, magnanimous spirits.

And now here is some one who speaks of one of these and says that he is short of stature, and of light weight; that he is of fair complexion, or symmetrical in shape; that he has been wounded, or bruised or burned. Absurd! impossible! You cannot strike or cut a soul. You cannot weigh a spirit, or measure an intellect in feet and inches. It is simply a wild and senseless misuse of words, to talk about the complexion of a mind, as if it could be white or red or swarthy. You cannot mean to say these things of him! And yet he does mean it; and no contradiction will shake him from it; and in fact you admit it yourself. Either what he says is absurd and impossible, or else what you say is absurd and impossible; and yet they are both true. It is true of the same being that he is both benevolent and thoughtful and that he is six feet tall and one hundred and fifty pounds in weight;—that he is invisible and intangible, and that he is of a certain complexion, and has been wounded and maimed. At the same time he is sick and he is sound; he is suffering and he is happy; he is mortal and he is immortal.

You think you can explain this perhaps when you say that these different affirmations are made about two different things—about a body and a soul; and you say that these two things are combined or united in the man. Have you solved the perplexity thereby? Or have you only relieved one impossibility by stating another? For I can easily prove to you by arguments of philosophy which "admit no refutation, and produce no conviction," that the combination of these opposite things which have no quality in common, is not only impossible but inconceivable. There is no explanation of this contradiction, but an explanation which just as much needs to be explained, and is just as inexplicable. The two terms of the contradiction stand there together in your own person, incompatible, irreconcilable,—and both true. And this is the creature, man, this bundle of incompatibilities, this incarnate contradiction, this animated paradox, this unsolved and insoluble problem of creation, this opprobrium of his own philosophy, this riddle unguessed and given up, this solemn sphinx in despair over his own enigmas,—this is the creature who halts before the mystery of godliness, without controversy great, now manifested in the flesh, before which the multitudinous hierarchies of the heavenly host hang silently in suspended flight—cherubim whose lifted wings have overarched the heavenly mercy-seat—seraphs whose unending cry of Holy, holy, holy, is hushed in the unwonted silence that is made in heaven—sons of God, whose voices had mingled in the chorus of the morning-stars when the corner-stone of all the worlds was laid—angelic messengers who in their swift ministries have explored the uttermost of the works of God—all into the wonder of this great mystery desiring to look;—man halts before this same mystery of godliness, with his poor, baffled intellect drooping from the vain effort to comprehend his own existence, and remarks, "I do not understand it." Poor fellow-creatures! dear children of men! who *expected* you to understand it?

And yet these very failures of ours in the study of ourselves, these baffled inquiries, these futile reasonings, are a help wonderfully fit, divinely given as it should seem, to enable us—not, of course, to comprehend, but to *receive*, the mystery of godliness. For just as looking on ourselves we recognize inhering in us contradictory attributes such as it is impossible should belong to the same substance, and yet alike belonging to ourselves; so looking upon Jesus Christ, we recognize new contradictions, the finite things and the infinite, such as it is impossible should co-exist in one, yet co-existing. And just as, admitting the baffling enigma in our own nature, we are accustomed to make a so-called explanation of these impossibles by formulating a new impossibility, that soul and body, spirit and matter, which of their nature cannot be united, nevertheless are united in one person, so that of that person we declare the things which are true of either substance;—so looking upon Him who is very man, concerning whom, nevertheless, are affirmed attributes and acts no less than infinite, men, bewildered by the height, the depth, the length, the breadth, aspiring to know the love that passeth knowledge, have attempted to solve these impossibilities by the statement of a new impossibility, that the Infinite and Absolute and Eternal was united in one being with the finite, the conditioned, the dependent. Of which if any man shall say it is incomprehensible, the answer is yes! And if he shall say it is impossible, the answer is, yes, like the facts of which it is the attempted summary and expression—facts which are impossible, and yet are true.

Further than this I do not care to go. Beyond I trace the course in which theology, ever aspiring to find out the Almighty to perfection, has toiled over its statements concerning "eternal generation" and "kenosis" and "hypostatic union"; I see the ground torn and trampled by sterile and blighting controversies; I count the rejected systems, anathematized as heresies, and their adherents stigmatized and cast out with uncharitable rancor; I see the air made turbid with the dust of unprofitable strife, and cloudy with a mist of unintelligible words; and I do not care to follow in that way. I turn me back to where I see the blessed company of humble saints adoring before the cross, and the host of holy angels gazing thereon as they who into these things desire to look, but are not able; and there I find that which is greater than to have solved all inexplicable questions—I find "the love of Christ, which surpasseth knowledge." I can wait—can wait forever, if need be—for the answer to these unanswerable questions. I am not ashamed to share the bewilderment of God's blessed angels.

VIII.

THE PURPOSE OF CHRIST'S MIRACLES OF HEALING.

That ye may know that the Son of man hath power on earth to forgive sins, (he saith to the sick of the palsy) I say unto thee Arise, take up thy bed, and go unto thy house.—MARK ii. 10.

It is not so easy a matter as it might seem, to explain *the multitude* of the miracles that are narrated or referred to in these gospels which give us all that we know of the life of Jesus the Messiah. There are many difficult questions about the miracles, on which I do not mean to touch at this time; but this concerning *the multitude of them* is a question which adds difficulty to all the rest. The accounts of them make up a large part of the four gospels; and this second gospel of the four, which is a sort of condensed gospel—a gospel in tract form, as one might say, for general circulation among plain people—is made up more largely of detailed accounts of healing than any one of the others. We must remember that the least of these gospels is a whole gospel, that it was meant to be complete in itself, and sufficient. And when it comes to presenting the essence of "the Gospel of Jesus Christ the Son of God," in the least possible space, it is interesting and very astonishing to see what is kept and what is left out. I will venture to say that there is not a minister among us all who in preparing a short gospel in sixteen chapters, would have left out the Sermon on the Mount and the parable of the Prodigal Son, or that would have said "whatever else we leave out, we cannot spare the full detail of these acts of healing." I believe that we should have made room for a good deal more of what we call "fundamental doctrine" by condensing into one chapter a half dozen chapters containing the details of one case after another of the healing of sick people. Why is it that these three brief years of our Lord's ministry should have been so largely consumed in these hundreds, thousands of acts of healing men's bodily ailments and infirmities and even inconveniences? And when it comes to putting the substance of "the gospel of Jesus Christ, the Son of God," into the space of twenty pages, why must a good half of the space, or more, be occupied with telling, over and over again, this story of curing sick men, and feeding hungry men, and raising dead men? Take out these and other miracles, and what have you left of the Gospel of Mark? Well, you have four parables, and some brief memoranda of conversations, and the story of the trial and crucifixion and resurrection. But the miracles are more than half the story; so that evidently, in the mind of the evangelist—shall we not say, in the mind of Christ?—the miracles *were* the gospel, in a very important sense. But in what sense are they the gospel, either for us, or for the men of that time? What was the purpose, and what was the result, of all these mighty works?

It seems very obvious and easy to say that this work of healing had its object and end in itself—that it brought just so much of joy and happiness into the world, and diminished by just so much the gross sum of human misery. It seems a very obvious explanation; but the objections to it are quite as obvious, and are overwhelming.

1. If the one object of Christ's miracles was directly to reduce the sum of human misery, then they were a failure; for their result was inappreciably small and insignificant. I know it does not seem so, as we fix our attention on him from day to day of his brief public life, following him as he "goes about doing good and healing all that are oppressed of the devil, because God is with him,"—as we sit beside him, in the city or the wilderness, and see the countless procession of the wretched draw-

ing near to him, and of the cleansed and healed bounding away, and making the air to ring with praises "to God who had given such power to men." A magnificent display, it seems, of the supreme bounty of God, that when he bringeth his only-begotten into the world, he should send him on such a royal and triumphal progress.

> Where'er he went, affliction fled,
> And sickness reared her fainting head.
> The eye that rolled in irksome night,
> Beheld his face,—for God is light;
> The opening ear, the loosened tongue,
> His precepts heard, his praises sung.
> With bounding steps, the halt and lame,
> To hail their great deliverer came;
> O'er the cold grave he bowed his head,
> He spake the word, and raised the dead.
> Despairing madness, dark and wild,
> In his inspiring presence smiled;
> The storm of horror ceased to roll,
> And reason lightened through the soul.

But, after all, when we consider it with some regard to perspective and proportion, what an atom of comfort is this, beside the huge, mountainous mass of human woe! What a mere drop of solace in an ocean of agony! Think how this earth looks, to him who can look down upon it from the circle of the heavens. Here the little globe is toiling painfully round upon its axis, heaving up into the light, and then bearing down again and burying in the darkness its unspeakable loads of misery crying incessantly toward God. For these many, many centuries, until the hundreds of years begin to be counted up into the thousands, in all the various lands of earth, one generation has been growing up after another, strutting its little hour of pride and folly, feeling the pangs of a myriad of diseases and distresses, and reeling, one after the other, down to death. Men have looked in upon the outer edge of the population that swarms and swelters and ferments within the boundaries of China, and have come back sickened with the sight of such teeming masses of human wretchedness, and at the thought of just such millions in province after province of that great empire, beyond, and yet beyond. Just such masses of human sorrow, only the individuals changed, did Marco Polo find in the same region six hundred years ago. Just such were there, but different men and women, one thousand, two thousand, three thousand years before. Press westward thence, along that historic continent, from peninsula to thronged peninsula—Further India, Hither India, each groaning with its weight of suffering humanity—and pierce to those central plains in which the two great powers of modern civilization are preparing to fight over again the ancient battle for the empire of the East. It seems like an unknown desert to us, as we look over its great expanses on the map; and we do not realize that here was the home of primeval monarchies and of those "cities of old and modern fame, the seat of mightiest empire" whose names fill the sonorous verse of Milton—

> "Of Cambalu, seat of Cathaian Cham,
> And Samarcand by Oxus, Temir's throne."

What visions of ferocious cruelty and of helpless misery come before the mind at the opening of that map of Central Asia, with its seats of barbarian tyranny, bringing up such names of horror as Timur Leng, and Genghis Khan, synonyms of bloody atrocity. It is the hive whence all the nations of the West swarmed forth; and what a bloody cradle of our race it is! Come westward still, along the path of empire. Pause to read the records of atrocious torture written out on the alabaster walls of the Assyrian palaces—unearth the ghastly mummies from Egyptian catacombs—tell the bricks laid with the groans of captives into sepulchral pyramids—tread the prodigious ruins of the Roman baths and palaces, the monuments of Christian persecution—stand within the dreadful walls of the Col-

PURPOSE OF CHRIST'S MIRACLES OF HEALING. 95

iseum, and listen for the fading echoes of the groans of those countless victims over whose dying anguish the gay ladies and dandies of the bloody city laughed and chatted.

What shall I more say? The very sea is full of the secrets of piracy and murder and the fearful slave-trade. All Africa is a continent consecrated to cruelty and mutual hate—an arena for mutual tortures among savage men and savage beasts; and the islands of the sea are full of the habitations of cruelty. O pitiable world, of which the fairest corners are so filled with sordid misery and sickness, and whose soil is mellow everywhere with hopeless graves!

Now in the midst of this broad earth, there is a narrow strip of country, a little patch upon the earth's surface—you can hardly find it on the map of the world, it is so insignificantly small; and in the midst of sixty centuries there is a generation, and in the midst of the generation, three short years, and in the course of those years a little number—a few hundreds of sick and lame and demoniac persons healed, and a few thousands saved for some hours from the inconvenience of hunger, and three or four dead persons recalled to life, only to die again after a few months or years. No, no! if the purpose of our Lord's miracles was directly to lessen the sum of the misery of mankind, they failed. They did not accomplish it in any appreciable degree.

2. But secondly, we are compelled to acknowledge that such an object as that of arbitrarily interrupting the general course of human suffering by miraculous interference not only was not accomplished by the power of Christ, but it ought not to have been accomplished—it would not have been a blessing.

The notion that there was too much pain and suffering in the world—more than was right, more than was best, more than was needed by mankind for their own good;—the notion that God our Father had dealt hardly by his children, and that the Son of God, with a superior love, came down to mitigate the hardship which the Father's too great severity had imposed—

is quite too much like some other of the obsolete notions of a mediæval theology, and quite too much unlike the word of God. For it is not true. God tolerates no pain in the world that can be spared. It was not in revenge or cruelty, but in that justice which is another name for love, that he pronounced on the apostate race the curse of toil and suffering and death. His curse was the best blessing that mankind, sinful, apostate, were capable of receiving. The world had flung itself off the track and was ready to rush down into perdition, and it was time for the engineer to put on the brakes. And just this discipline of enforced labor, of inevitable pain, of prospective death, was the only thing that could hold it back. If the world with sickness and unhappiness and pain and foreboding and fear and death is a lazar house, without these it would have been a Pandemonium.

If the philanthropist, guided by the police, looks into the squalid dens of vice where sin conceives and brings forth death, and turns away sick with the spectacle of suffering,—if the occasional revelations of iniquity in higher life startle us by showing what unseen depths of mental anguish, of tormenting jealousy, of unappeased envying and craving, of self-loathing and despair, are covered by the thin garments of luxury and dissipation,—it is the only comfort that grieved humanity can find, to think that the only thing to be imagined worse than what we see would be a world in which sin could riot unpursued by pain and death; in which no screams of woe, no sights of horror, no fearful lookings-for of wrath, should warn back tempted men from paths of wickedness, and enable good resolution to keep its foothold when it stands in slippery places. If lust might revel in its untiring round of voluptuous uncleanness, with no satiety to mock, and no disease to smite and slay,—if there were no adder's sting at the bottom of the drunkard's cup—if covetousness brought no sordidness of soul and no scorning from one's neighbor—if selfish ambition might go climbing on forever, each day delighting itself with giddier

PURPOSE OF CHRIST'S MIRACLES OF HEALING. 97

heights, with never a pang of conscience for the poor disregarded and the right cast down,—if there were no nights to shut men up face to face with their own thoughts, no murdered sleep to haunt the guilty, no sick days to strike away the pride of human strength, no death, no law of God, no wrath to come; —what a hell this world would be!

No, no! There is no pain that is not needed! It never falls but where God wants that it should fall—God, who does not afflict willingly, nor grieve the children of men. He himself, who sends pain and death, brings healing and resurrection. It did not need the Son of God to do these works of mercy. The Father, like the Son, is this day going to and fro about the earth to lay his fatherly hands upon the sick and give health wherever sickness can be spared, and life wherever life is better than death. His ear and eye—like that of Christ who is the express image of the Father—are ever waiting to catch the first evidence of that resignation and faith which show that affliction has wrought its perfect work and can now be dismissed; and whenever that turning of the heart is seen, the word of God calls back his swift, obedient messenger of sorrow, and his healing work is just as surely accomplished, and just as divinely, whether through the chain of second causes that are guided by his secret providence, or in the splendid blaze of miracles that follows on the words of Christ his Son. It is the same God that worketh all in all. "Verily, verily, the Son can do nothing of himself but what he seeth the Father do; for what things soever *He* doeth, these also doeth the Son likewise." It was not the works of *God* that Jesus came to destroy—not even God's "strange work" in suffering and sickness, but the works of the devil. And it is to this end, this chief and sovereign end, that all these mighty works of healing are directed. He declares it plainly himself. It was "that ye may know"—that *we* may know—"that the Son of Man hath power on earth to forgive sin"—for this—that he saith to the sick of the palsy "Arise, and take up thy bed, and go thy way into thine own house." And men do see it and know it; and the throng breaks forth in grateful songs, glorifying God, and saying We never saw it on this fashion!

But hark! what is this? I hear one dissonant, incisive voice piping its shrill protest above all this chorus of grateful thanksgiving, and saying, "Not so! it does not prove it at all! it is entirely inconclusive! Don't praise God yet, and don't have any hope or confidence in the forgiveness of sins, until you have heard my argument about miracles! This belief of miracles doesn't work into my system at all!" Oh, I thought I knew that voice. It is my friend the philosopher, with his theory of the universe. I know him, and I know his argument about miracles—and a very good argument it is, as far as it goes. It is founded on the uniformity and constancy of natural law, of which, he says, there is a universal and instinctive conviction in the human mind. Very good and sound, and founded on observation of the working of nature and of the mind of man. Now, my philosophic friend, carry your observation of the mind a little further, and see if you don't come to another universal and instinctive conviction—an instinctive belief and expectation that this constancy of natural order, may be, will be, broken in upon, on due occasion. I put this universal instinct against the other universal instinct, and back it with examples, ten to one. Your system has no room for it, I know. Your theory of the universe is contrived on the plan of leaving out of view those facts of the human soul that do not work in easily with the rest. It is a beautiful theory, and it is a pity that facts should interfere with it. But here the facts are—the instinctive expectation of mankind—the expectation that has given rise to all the monstrous superstitions of the world, that when God shall interfere to break the dreadful chain of moral causes that binds penalty to sin, he will give sign and token of the same by breaking also the chain of physical cause and effect that holds the creation groaning under bondage to bodily pain and weakness.

When he sendeth his only-begotten into the world he will find some way to signalize him to the wretched, the poor, the hungry, the sick, the palsied, the sinful and unhappy of every land and language and century, as God's authorized commissioner.

There was one hopeful and prophetic soul that had trusted that it had been Jesus who should redeem Israel—who should proclaim liberty to the captive, the opening of the prison-doors to them that were bound. But still he languished in a tyrant's dungeon, and saw no sign of coming deliverance, no ray of hope. So he sent messengers to look for him whom he had baptized though needing no cleansing, and to put the question plainly:—Art thou he that should come, or must we still wait and wait and look for another? And now what answer of comfort, what words of instruction, what doctrine making wise to salvation, will not the Saviour send to suffering John the Baptist? He answers him never a word; but while the expectant messengers are waiting for their reply, he—what?—he goes right on and works miracles of healing. "In that same hour he cures many of their infirmities and plagues and of evil spirits; and unto many that are blind he gives sight;"—and then says to the messengers, "There! that's your gospel! go take that to John."—And to "that same hour" depressed and desponding souls in every age look back and know the token, and say: "It is he that was to come! I know him, the Christ of God." Somehow, these miracles, that look so unphilosophical to certain critics, do seem to be the sort of badge of a divine commission that men generally ask for and expect to see produced on the part of one who comes as a representative of God. And for my part I find it not at all strange that God should conduct this matter with regard to the instinctive wants and cravings of plain men in general, as much as with regard to the refined and possibly sophisticated scruples of a few.

Glance back a moment, now, at the course of our study thus far, as we have asked ourselves, and asked the word of God, what was the object and meaning of our Lord's wonderful works of healing. We find 1, That the object was not, by miraculous intervention, to drive pain, and sickness, and death, or any considerable amount of it, out of the world. This was not accomplished by them—it ought not to have been accomplished. 2. Christ's power to heal the body was meant (so he expressly declares) as a sign and token of his power to save the whole man, body and soul. "That ye may know that the Son of Man hath power on earth to forgive sin,"—*therefore* "he saith to the sick of the palsy, Arise and walk."

But this is hardly sufficient, after all, to account for the *multitude* of these miracles—that the great bulk of this gospel should be made up of miracles and almost nothing else. It does not look like the wisdom of God to salvation that his commissioner should spend the main part of his time in merely proving his commission. And so our mere veneration for the wisdom of God in Christ commands us to look deeper into these works of healing, to find their whole meaning; and we do not look in vain. For,—

3. Christ's works of healing set before us the way of salvation—the way in which he gives it, the way in which we are to receive it. The miracles are parables—not the less parables for being also facts. "The kingdom of heaven is likened unto them." And as our Lord in his spoken parables did sometimes give full explanation of one that it might serve us as a model for explaining the rest,—so did he also in these parables wrought visibly in action. As it is said in Matthew (viii. 16), "He cast out the evil spirits with his word, and healed all them that were sick, that it might be fulfilled which was spoken by Isaiah the prophet, "Himself took our infirmities and bare our sicknesses."

In particular, this story of the paralytic let down from the roof is so told as to be a key to the understanding of all the miracles, and a key of the whole gospel unlocking to us the method of salvation. It shows us the Holy One of God manifested to destroy the works of the devil—not first pain and sorrow and then sin; but first sin, and then the pain, sorrow, death that sin has wrought. He saith not first Arise and walk, and then Thy sin be forgiven thee; but first to the sinner Be forgiven, and then to the sick of the palsy Arise and take up thy bed and go unto thine house.

Not in vain the Scripture saith "the *last* enemy that shall be destroyed is death." While sin remains, death cannot be spared. The wretched world hath need of him. But by and by the great work of the Redeemer shall be complete, and that mysterious scene, the consummation of all the ages, shadowed forth in words of awful majesty, shall be enacted at last, and the Son shall stand before the throne of the Everlasting Father, to surrender up his august commission. He shall point to the great multitude of every land and age, of every kindred and tongue and tribe, and say: " Behold me and the children whom thou hast given me—all whom thou gavest me I have kept." He shall bring sin and Satan in chains, and make a show of them openly, conquered, captive. Sorrow and sighing he shall have subdued and made to flee away. And now, at last, the last enemy, the king of terrors, long ago disarmed of dart and spear, robbed of his dreadful sting, which is sin, despoiled of all power to hurt believing souls,—the last enemy shall be dragged forth to his ignominious execution.

Then how the universe shall shake to the vibrations of that great chorus, " The kingdoms of this world are become the kingdom of our Lord and of his Christ;"—" and the Son shall deliver up the kingdom to God, even the Father; and God shall be all in all!"

IX.

THE HEALING OF THE PALSIED.

That ye may know that the Son of man hath power on earth to forgive sins (he said unto him that was palsied) I say unto thee Arise, and take up thy couch, and go unto thy house. And immediately he rose up before them, and took up that whereon he lay, and departed to his house glorifying God.—LUKE v. 24, 25.

WE spent our last Sunday evening in studying the purpose of those mighty works of healing in which the time and human powers of endurance of our Lord Jesus Christ, in his earthly ministry, were so largely consumed. What was his object in them? What relation did they bear to his great work of saving the world?

It could not have been to diminish, by direct interference, the gross sum of human suffering. For, in the first place, if this was their object, they were a failure; the deduction they made from the mass of human misery was insignificant. And, in the second place, this would not have been a right or worthy object. Pain and misery are not in the world for nothing; they are here for a purpose,—for a good, a merciful, a divine purpose. The Son of God is not more merciful than his Father, and not less wise. The works that he doeth are those that he seeth his Father do—none other. He comes to take away men's troubles and pains, when these can be spared, not before; and just such works as this "his Father worketh hitherto."

And in this very story of the healing of a paralytic, we find the key of his purpose in these mighty works. "*That ye may know that the Son of man hath power on earth to forgive*

THE HEALING OF THE PALSIED. 103

sins,"—for this purpose it is that "he saith to the sick of the palsy Arise and walk." Having this key of the meaning of our Lord's works of mercy, we can follow him through the long succession of them, as he "goes about doing good and healing all that are oppressed of the devil," and can find in them all, not only the sign and proof of his power to save from sin, but the example and illustration of his way of saving. Here we see the two antagonists confronted. In Jesus Christ we see God manifest in the flesh; and in the maladies and visible infirmities of men, we see sin manifest in the flesh. In the infinite diversity of these—palsies, blindness, leprosies, epileptic convulsions, demoniac madness—we have set before us, in no dark parable, the Protean phases of human sin. We hear the authoritative word of absolution, cleansing, healing. We witness the act of faith by which he who asks receives. These mighty works are a continual parable, in which the whole life of Christ sets before us the kingdom of heaven.

I shall count largely on your own thoughtfulness in following up this clue which the very words of Christ give us to the instruction to be found in his works of healing; and because there is so much in this story, so many accessory figures in the scene, all having vital relation to it, we will, for this hour of study, fix our attention on one of the two central figures, and on only two or three of the lessons out of the many that we can learn from this. We will consider, 1. The Paralytic's Prayer; and, 2. The Answer that he received.

But we shall not be able to understand this figure in the foreground, unless we make some study of the accessories of the picture in the gospels.

This incident comes near the beginning of our Lord's work. It is a time of wonder, questioning, excitement in all Palestine, and especially in the region about the Lake of Galilee. The rumor is running to and fro that a new prophet has appeared, one Jesus, or Joshua, a young man from Nazareth. Wonderful things are told of him. His works of healing exceed all that have been recorded of them of old time; even the fables of the heathen have hardly dared feign such marvels as are authentically vouched for by eye-witnesses of the works of this Jesus,—and his deeds are not so wonderful as his life and teaching. We do not need to transport ourselves to a distant land and age to imagine the result. It was then what it would be now. These first two pages of Mark's gospel record the universal amazement that prevailed through all that region. Everywhere they were gathering up their sick folk out of all towns and villages, to go and find the great Healer. And when the crowds beheld the healing of the deaf, the blind, the crippled, the feverish, the lunatic, the demoniac, "they were all amazed." They broke out into shouts and songs of "Glory to God." Against his express desire, they "spread his fame abroad through all that region," every man who had seen the wonder being filled with irrepressible desire to tell it to his neighbors; and some of those who were healed could not reconcile their gratitude with their obedience, but being "straitly charged to tell no man," "went out and published it much, and blazed abroad the matter." But there is a more wonderful thing in the story than any of these—a thing which touches men with a more awful and solemn reverence, and meets a deeper and more hopeless craving of humanity. Not only does he heal bodily ailments with a touch, and calm and restore the diseased intellect with words of power, but he comes to souls bowed under burdens of conscious sin, and subdues even this malady, the most obstinate and afflictive, when once it has become deep-seated—the most unyielding to any human arts, arguments or persuasions—by the authority with which he declares, "Son, thy sins be forgiven thee." There is no stint to his gifts, no price set upon them. None ask but they receive; none seek but find. Of course, he is beset by crowds without number or intermission. The whole city gathers about his door. He rises long before daylight and goes out into a solitary place to pray: but all men are seeking him, and his

THE HEALING OF THE PALSIED. 105

disciples go out to find him and bring him back, and go with him from town to town, preaching and healing. Finally, " he can no more openly enter into the town, but is without in desert places; and they come to him from every quarter."

When the wilderness is no longer a protection to him, he comes back quietly to the town again—his own town, Capernaum. But he cannot be hid. " It is noised that he is in the house." At once, there is a rush. The house fills up, and the long, narrow entrance and the street in front of the door are choked with the crowd. And it is not altogether a common crowd, either. There begin to be some distinguished men in these multitudes. All the way from Jerusalem have come learned men, scribes and lawyers, to inquire diligently and critically, as their duty is, into the claims of the new prophet. Doubtless such great men would have privileged places; and all through the court, and chambers, and narrow entrance-passage, the multitude, sick and well, pressed and jostled and crowded. Thus and then it was that there came four men to the outskirts of the crowd, each holding up the corner of a mattress on which was lying a sick man, helpless from paralysis. What was to be done? The house was full. They could not get near the door, for the crowd; much less force their way with such a burden, through the packed vestibule, through the dense throng in the central court, to the place where, surrounded by the learned scholars in the law from Jerusalem, the young Prophet stood and taught as one having authority.

Now, before we go further with the story, it is necessary for you to get an idea of the peculiar structure of an Eastern house of the better class. It is built solid around a central court, from which all the rooms receive their light and air. On the street, you see nothing but a dead wall, pierced by a single door opening into a long narrow archway that leads into the court. When you have come into the court, you look about you at the doors and windows of every room in the house, of both storeys. But immediately opposite the archway by which you come in, there is one room that reaches up through both storeys to the very roof, and is completely open, without any wall at all, toward the court. The floor of this room is three or four feet higher than the pavement of the court, and this is the chief reception-room of the house. Observe that this elevated floor is a platform from which you can see all over the court, and into all the windows of the house. On such a platform, I have no doubt, our Lord was standing or sitting as he taught the throng in the house at Capernaum.

There is sometimes one other access to the house beside the street-door and archway. Often, an outside staircase leads up to the flat roof, which is the customary place of retirement for the family, the place of devotion, in summer nights the sleeping-place. This suggested to the sick man's friends an expedient. They lifted him tenderly up the staircase, and laid him down on the roof. Just over the reception-platform on which the Prophet stood they took away course after course of the overlapping tiles, and then with cords attached to the corners of his mattress, they let down the helpless, trembling creature, until the scribes from Jerusalem and Galilee, and other dignitaries who occupied foremost places, were compelled to fall back before the new-comer, and this poor bundle of wretched humanity lay in the midst of them at the feet of Jesus, a type of the impotence of sin to heal itself—an illustration of Prayer and of How prayer is answered.

Consider, 1. *The paralytic's prayer.* It was a wonderful prayer —so brief, so comprehensive, so affecting, so complete; stating the whole case, setting it forth in every particular, detailing every symptom of the malady, urging every argument of sympathy, calling for exactly the comfort and help that were required;—such was the prayer offered by the sick of the palsy, as his couch with its half-dead burden dropped on the ground at the feet of the Christ.

What then did he say? Not one word! The silence which this strange intruder brought with him into the school of

Christ was broken only by the voice of the Son of man himself—"Son, be of good cheer; thy sins are forgiven thee." He had told his story well. There was a dead and leaden limb hanging to a half lifeless trunk. There was a hand shaking with the helpless tremor of the nerves that could do little more than tremble. There were the lips druling and mowing, and the tongue lolling with a look like idiocy within the gate of speech, and the eyes, last refuge of the blockaded intellect, looking with longings that cannot be uttered toward him who is the Life. And now do you ask what did he say? Rather, what did he leave unsaid? Just by lying there before the Lord, without a gesture or a word, he had declared his desires, with submission and faith, to his Saviour. Let the disobedient tongue deny its office if it will; let the quivering hands hang down, which he would fain lift in supplication; let the feeble knees refuse to bow;—they cannot hinder him of his approach to the Saviour. The trustful soul has got the victory over the body of this death, and through this tattered vail of flesh he who made the heart hath read the prayer that is written on its fleshly tablets.

It was an unspoken prayer, but not a prayer unuttered or unexpressed, otherwise it would not have been a prayer at all. I know what the hymn says:—"Prayer is the soul's sincere desire, uttered, or unexpressed . . . Prayer is the burden of a sigh, the falling of a tear;" and it is good poetry, and may be truth or falsehood according to the sense in which you take it. It is easy to take this overflow of a Christian poet's heart, and use it, in a sense which the writer of it would have abhorred, as a sentimental apology for never praying. "Prayer is *the offering up* of our desires to God;" the Westminster theologians, not always right, are wholly right in this. A desire never offered up, a lazy longing never addressed to the Giver of good, is a prayer, in the same sense in which a man's lounging through the corridors of the Capitol wishing he had some of the public money, is a petition to Congress. There were plenty of paralytics in Galilee, at that very hour, each one with "a heart's sincere desire" that he had his youth and strength back again, but who never came to Christ to ask for it, and went palsied down into their graves. There were blind men, in the days of Christ, as benighted and needy of all things as Bartimæus and his nameless friend near Jericho, but who never had the courage of faith to cry out for mercy to the Son of David. There were lepers wallowing in hopeless uncleanness and misery, with longing recollections of the days when their ulcerated limbs had been fair and healthy as the flesh of a little child, but who never ventured to say "Lord, make me clean." There were friends, sincere and true, watching by many a hopeless invalid in Galilee and wishing they might see him as in months past, who made no effort to bring their charge to the feet of Christ, or, if any effort, one that was discouraged by hindrances, and utterly dismayed when they saw the crowd about the door. Not to such as these did the great blessing come; but to those in whom the "sincere desire," working together with the consciousness of their own utter helplessness, and with some little mustard-seed of faith in the Son of God, moved them to the very act and deed of presenting, even though it were in eloquent pathetic speechlessness, their requests to Christ, with faith.

I find, in the very nature of this sick man's malady, some instructive indications as to what is the prayer of faith, and what is faith that gives prevailing power to prayer. It is not without significance that so large a proportion of our Lord's miracles of healing were wrought on the *blind*, and the *palsied* —the sufferers from those two forms of human infirmity which most discipline one to a sense of his own helplessness and need, and most educate him in the habit of confiding in the strength and wisdom and faithfulness of another. Not when I look on the hills of Nazareth, or the blue waves of Galilee, or the ancient olives on the hillside by the brook Kidron, am I more reminded of the very person of the Lord Christ, than when I watch the blind man confiding with absolute trust in the hand that leads him, or the palsied resting on the strong arm that supports him, and remember that it was just such helpless, just such trustful ones as these, whose confiding faith won his love and commanded his noblest works of mercy. And as I meditate of blindness and palsy, I better understand the darkness and impotency of sin, and what is that faith by which we should commit ourselves to the infinite wisdom, love and power of God.

2. Observe now the *Answer* which the palsied man received to his prayer. And if it seemed at first, to any, that he had uttered no prayer at all, such will surely think at first that he received no answer at all. Very commonly this is true, in the gospels, of our Lord's response to those who come to him. "Jesus *answered* and said," we read; but the answer has no obvious relevancy to what was asked. Nicodemus says to him, "Rabbi, we know that thou art a teacher come from God." Jesus *answered* and said, "Except a man be born again, he cannot see the kingdom of God." He answers, not the words, but what lay in the heart, behind the words. In such wise he answers the prayer of the palsied—a prayer that says, plainer than any words can say it, "Lord that I might be healed." It seems no answer at all,—" Son, be of good cheer; thy sins are forgiven thee." There seems to be some untold story here. There is more than palsy—there is sin; if not an anxious face, at least a troubled conscience. And there is a keen diagnosis on the part of the great Healer, going deeper than the surface symptoms, reaching to the inmost roots of the trouble. And his answer is given accordingly. Observe in it,—

(1.) That the paralytic received *the substance*, though not the form, of what he had asked, to his entire satisfaction. He received an answer as completely satisfactory to himself, as Paul received when, praying mightily, again and again, that the thorn in his flesh might be removed, he got for answer "My grace is sufficient for thee;" and thereupon "was glad, and gloried." Did the features of the paralytic, think you, betray to the gazing and murmuring scribes some sign of disappointment or discontent, when those majestic words were spoken down to him—"Thy sins be forgiven thee"? Is it ever those who cry mightily to God, who are found complaining that he is slack concerning his promises? And if not, then who are you that are finding fault?—making bold to come between the saint and his Saviour, to complain that the covenant is not fully performed? If Christ is satisfied, and the suppliant soul is satisfied, who are we that we should interfere to measure the prayer against the answer, and remonstrate with the Lord that his ways are unequal?

Nay, I take you all to witness,—

(2.) That this petitioner received *more* than the equivalent of what he had asked, by as much as it is a greater thing to suffer and be happy and joyful in the midst of suffering, than it is not to suffer at all. Three Hebrew youths, faithful to God their Saviour, were shuddering at the prospect of the furnace heated seven-fold and roaring like the mouth of hell to devour them. Think you they did not pray earnestly that the flame might be quenched, or the power of their enemies be palsied, that so they might not be cast into that place of torment? And was God's ear heavy, or his arm too short? Nay, how much greater than what they asked was the thing which they received! It had been a light thing not to be cast into the fiery furnace, compared with the joy and glory of walking through the flames unhurt beside the Son of God, "glorifying God in the fires." Daniel prayed and trusted that the God he served continually would deliver him;—and looked, perhaps, to see the plots of his enemies unvailed, and himself saved from entering the lions' den. But how much greater the answer than the prayer! How sweeter far the night passed with the savage beasts beside the angel of the

Lord, than the sentried security of Darius's palace! We do not need to go, for such examples, to the banks of the Euphrates and the Chebar. We may find them here by the Schuylkill and the Delaware, to-day. Here, many a sick man has implored the Lord for health and strength, and won a blessing greater than he asked, in learning—

> "how sublime a thing it is
> To suffer and be strong."

Many a bankrupt man, that had struggled, with anxious calculations and many an earnest petition, for deliverance from accumulating troubles, and seemed to find no answer from God, has been rewarded at last with the heavenly gift of grace to step majestically down from wealth to poverty, and has found a joy in low estate beyond what wealth could ever give. O mothers, that have bowed with strong crying, and prayer that could not brook denial, over some cradle filled with pitiful moaning and wailing of the little one most dear to you, and have watched the inexorable symptoms grow from worse to worse, while prayer seemed vain, and hope went out in blank despair—have you no testimony to give, how the peace of God, and a possession greater than of sons and daughters, came down into your heart—an answer as much greater than the prayer as the Giver is greater than his gifts?

(3.) But now observe, finally, that when he had received the equivalent of his prayer, to his full content; and when he had received "exceeding abundantly above what he had asked;" at last, this palsied man was given the identical thing which he had asked. Not for *his* sake—no, he did not ask it now. He was of good cheer—his sins were forgiven him. So far as appears, he was full of exceeding peace and content, craving nothing more, but wholly satisfied, the rest of his appointed time, to lie, a helpless infant in the everlasting arms. No, it was not for *his* sake, but "that *ye* may know that the Son of man hath power on earth to forgive sins, *therefore* he saith to the sick of the palsy, Arise and walk."

For now the palsy had accomplished its work, and could be spared. It had brought the sufferer and laid him low and helpless at the feet of Jesus to receive the forgiveness of his sins, and what more could it do for him? The time was come, at last, when it might be dismissed, but not till now. And Christ is not so unkind as to give healing so long as suffering is still needed. He is not less merciful than the Father, as he is not more merciful. Would you dare to ask that your grief, your pain, your burden should be taken away before its work was done? Could you bring your mind to wish that all these past hours, and days, and weeks, and weary months of suffering should have been in vain, in vain; and that God should call back these stern but kindly servants of his, while yet their mission was incomplete, and bid them Let him alone! sorrow is wasted on him! he is joined to his idols; let him alone? But now, the sick of the palsy is forgiven and at peace. The sickness has well fulfilled its painful but beneficent ministry, and he who is Lord over all the powers of life and death, that saith to this one Come, and he cometh, and to another Go, and he goeth, may call away this sad-faced angel, and send him back to where, before the throne, they "stand and wait" for some new bidding upon messages of love.

And he saith to the sick of the palsy, Arise, and take up thy couch, and go unto thine house.

X.

THE PRAYER OF THE HEATHEN MOTHER.

Now the woman was a Greek, a Syrophoenician by race; and she besought him that he would cast forth the demon out of her daughter.—Mark vii. 26. [Cf. Matth. xv. 21-28.]

I TRUST that you understand and approve the reasons which bring me back, again and again, to the study of one and another of the miracles of Jesus of Nazareth. I am looking to find in them, plainly set forth, by word and act, the way of salvation. Nothing less than this, I have before argued with you, could have been the object of this ministry of miraculous healing, than to exhibit the Saviour in the act of saving—to exhibit the lost in the act of being saved; to illustrate God's power and mercy and how he applies it—to illustrate man's need and sinfulness, and how man's faith lays hold of and receives God's help. The gospels are so made as if men, slow of understanding, had said, "If only we could see God save a man, if we could see a man coming to God in faith and receiving salvation from sin, then we should be able to understand these things better than by many definitions and explanations;" and as if God had made reply: "Ye can not see my face; no man hath seen God at any time; God is a Spirit. But this is my beloved Son, in whom I am well pleased. In him I am manifest in the flesh. Know him, and you will know the Father also. Neither can any man see sin, but only the manifestations and results of sin. For sin is a spiritual malady, whose end is death. But here are these bodily maladies that are in the world because of sin, and which are, in some sense, sin manifest in the flesh. And if you would know how men with the invisible burden of guilt on the conscience, and of indwelling corruption in the soul, may come to the unseen God, and be forgiven and renewed and saved,—look here upon God manifested visibly in the person of Jesus Christ, and upon these representatives of humanity, with what simplicity they bring their various woes to him, and are made perfectly well." Thus we do see the Lord, as it is written, "bearing our sicknesses, and carrying our diseases;" and with infinite variety of circumstance and character, like the Protean shapes of ugliness which sin assumes when it is working death, we see coming up before him, sometimes singly, sometimes in throngs, now with their own faith, and again borne or led by the pitiful and believing prayers of friends or parents, the palsies, the blindnesses, the leprosies, the deformities, the lunacies, the sorrows and bereavements of men. And in each variation of character and act and circumstance that is set before us we find some new illustration of God's forgiving love and holiness, and of human ignorance and impotency and need, or human faith and prayer.

Let us look at this touching story of the Canaanitish woman and see whether it has not something to teach us. It is the simplest of dramas—with only two persons in the scene, and a group of disciples, like a sort of chorus, interposing a single exclamation that helps bring out the meaning of the story. But it is very dramatic, and all the more so for being so obviously and simply true.

But to take the full force of the story we must try and bring before our minds the scene in which it is set.

Our Lord had just come out from one of those sharp collisions with the narrowness, formalism, jealousy and sectarianism of the religious people of his time, that were so painful to him, and so disheartening. I cannot but think that, being such as he was, one such harsh encounter, compelling him to solemn, stern words of rebuke and denunciation, must have

THE PRAYER OF THE HEATHEN MOTHER.

been more exhausting to him than weeks of healing and teaching; so that it seems intelligible enough that when it was over he should say to his twelve followers, "Come, let us get away from this and rest awhile;—let us seek out some place where we are unknown, and hide ourselves from the scourge of tongues." Whither can they go? He cannot walk in Judea, for there the Jews are seeking to kill him. If he stays in these Galilean towns, he is beset by delegations of scribes and Pharisees that have come on from Judea on purpose to ensnare him in his talk, and his Galilean neighbors are ready enough to take up a reproach against him. He can find no rest in the wilderness, for they come to him thither from every quarter, so that the desert places become populous with sick and hungry crowds that are as sheep without a shepherd. There is one refuge for the wearied-out, exhausted Man of Sorrows. Toward the North, where the cliffs of Lebanon rise bolder and loftier and crowd closer down upon the sea, is the narrow strip of sea-coast memorable in history as the earliest home of maritime commerce, and of the splendid wealth that resulted from it, as well as of the luxury and corruption, the disasters and overthrows, that followed in their turn—the land of Tyre and Sidon, otherwise called *Phœnicia*. In those lands of the East, men speak of centuries as we speak of decades. Fifteen hundred years before Christ, Tyre was a great and famous town—mentioned in the book of Joshua—and Sidon, a day's walk to the north of it, was older yet. Six hundred years before Christ, following hard after the prophecies of Ezekiel to fulfill them, Nebuchadnezzar the Great came marching down the coast with his Chaldeans, and destroyed it after a siege of thirteen years' duration. It would not stay destroyed. That little rocky island lying off the cliffs of the inhospitable coast has been one of the points of earth predestinated for the abode of man. Three hundred years before Christ, Alexander the Great, marching his Macedonian phalanxes down this narrow coast line, found Tyre lying across his path to India. On its island of rock it seemed to defy him, until, after seven months of vain siege, he gathered up the ruins of the former city that cumbered the shore and tumbled them into the sea, and over that isthmus marched over and took the town and destroyed it again. Since that, to this day, Tyre is a peninsula, and no more an island.

But now, in the days of Christ, the city was growing up a third time. And the relics of its splendor at the period in question are visible to the traveler to-day. You see the traces of that magnificent enterprise that marked the palmy days of the Roman Empire. They sent to Egypt for the numberless granite columns that decorated the quays and breakwaters— you can see them now lying in piles under the blue, tideless Mediterranean waters. They sent to the Grecian islands for sculptured marbles. They decorated the neighboring hillsides with the villas of Greek and Roman merchants, with statues and fountains and tesselated pavements. And not least "on every high hill and under every green tree" they set up again the shrines and temples of that utterly corrupt and licentious idolatry that had polluted not only this Canaanitish race itself, from the beginning, but all the races that came into relation with it. Its pestilent wickedness continued, as God had foretold, to be a thorn and a snare to the chosen people itself. Tyre, destroyed again and again by God's judgments, was heathen Tyre still; and its people were true descendants of Sidon, son of accursed Canaan.

The glory of Tyre is departed now. I spent a night there more than thirty years ago. We looked out of our windows in the morning, and saw the ground strown with ruins, in the midst of which was a long, massive double column of polished Egyptian granite, lying prostrate, that is the relic of a famous Christian Church built here, three hundred years after Christ, by the Emperor Constantine, of which the historian Eusebius preached the dedication sermon. These fragments, and the massive ruins of the harbor covered by the tumbling waves,

THE PRAYER OF THE HEATHEN MOTHER.

and here and there a sculptured stone or a lonely column, are all that remain of the princely city. The hovels of poor fishermen occupy the sites of palaces and temples; and the munitions of her rocks are a place for the drying of nets.

It was to the edge of the territory belonging to this rich, corrupt, heathen city—a most uncongenial neighborhood, that the Man of Sorrows, just because it might be presumed that nobody wanted him, nobody cared for him there, had come for the rest which he could not find anywhere in his own country.

And just here, on the only occasion in the whole course of our Lord's public ministry when he set foot beyond the narrow boundaries of his own little province, there comes out of her house to find him this heathen woman of an alien race, and the little incident ensues which we have just been reading out of the two gospels of Matthew and Mark. I want to hold your attention fixed this morning on a single figure—that of this distressed, supplicating, persevering woman, calling your notice to her *trouble*, her *faith* and how it showed itself, and her *success and reward*.

This woman—not a Jewish woman living over the border, but "a Syrophœnician by race," descended from the old accursed Canaanitish stock whom the Jews hated, and who (of course) hated the Jews back again;—this woman—not a convert bearing witness to the true God amid surrounding idolatry, but "a Greek," that is a heathen still in her religion;—this woman has a dreadful burden of distress which she wants, for some reason, to bring to this man Jesus Christ, and to no one else. Who was she, rich or poor, in low station or in high, of fair repute or of evil? We do not know—we do not care—the questions are of no importance to the object of the story. Here was a broken-hearted mother with a frantic, raving child. That is a sort of case which is a good deal alike the world over, no matter where you find it, high or low.

The case is one of those (the world is full of them) in which distress comes upon one through the malady of another. The immediate sufferer may be half unconscious of his calamity, or half indifferent to it. Perhaps it is the very nature of the malady that it benumbs the sensibilities, and extinguishes both fear and hope in a prevailing torpor or apathy of the mind. It is no infrequent sight, to those whose duties often call them to sick rooms, to see the patient stunned by the terrific blow of a malignant disease, wearing his life away in unconscious pangs. And it is a most pitiful thing to stand in the chamber of such a sickness, where there is nothing to be done, and see compassionate and broken-hearted friends hanging about the sick-bed, feeling that they must do something. But it is not the unconscious patient that we pity; it is the crushed and despairing friends. We see the same thing in this cry of the Canaanite woman: "Have mercy on *me*, O Lord, Son of David! *my daughter* is sore vexed with an evil spirit"—"Pity on *me;*" not the tossed and torn demoniac child, whose power of suffering is blunted already by her malady; who is sinking under the power of it; whom death will mercifully relieve by and by;—no, not on her, but on this heart-broken mother, whose agony of mind is worse than tearing and rending of body, and who cannot be comforted unless the child is cured. The case is one out of a multitude in which the immediate sufferer is brought to Christ not by his own prayer but by the prayer of others. Sometimes it is a paralytic borne of four; or it is a convulsive child brought in the arms of a weeping father, or it is even a dead child or servant, on which his healing or reanimating power is invoked by the intercessions of another. Have you ever seen anything like this in the symptoms of this raging pestilence of sin? Have you ever known the patient fascinated by its illusions, or crazed with its mad delirium, or hardened into apathetic indifference, or inactive in the helpless torpor of despair, so that if anything is to be done in his behalf, it must needs be done by others? And do you find no encouragement, in such stories as this of the Syrophœnician woman, to believe that those who seem to be past the power of praying for themselves may be taken up in the arms of natural affection and brought to where the Lord may lay his hands upon them and heal them? Each bond of social influence, each tie of natural affection, may be a means that God shall use to bring them within the circle of the attractions of the cross, "drawing them with the cords of love, with the bands of a man." O doubly blessed such an affliction, which brings to Christ not one alone but two—preparing the sufferer to receive the grace, and teaching the sympathizer how to pray for it! Learn by this story of the Canaanite to bring not yourself only, but your friends and your children to the feet of Christ. This natural affection with which you yearn for the happiness of others may not be holiness itself—even the publicans possess it, and the very brutes display it nobly; but it is the forerunner of it. It is the messenger that goes before in the path of the Holy Spirit, to turn the hearts of the fathers to their children, and the hearts of the children to their fathers, lest God come and smite the earth with a curse.

2. Observe, now, secondly, this woman's faith, of what sort it was, that so drew the loving approval of the Lord, and won his tardy but abundant blessing. To begin with, it was no superstitious or credulous reliance on she knew not what or whom. Mark by what name she called this stranger faring his way among these alien mountains, and seeking only for seclusion and repose. "Thou son of David," she cried, " have mercy on me!" What was the son of David, or of any other Hebrew king, to her, a Tyrian and a Gentile? Plainly there had come to her,—we cannot tell how, but we can imagine many different ways,—some notion of the divine promises of a Saviour, and some proofs that they were fulfilled in this Jesus. She was not believing on him of whom she had not heard, nor believing without reason or evidence. God never asks one to believe thus. Her faith was not a superstitious credulity. But neither, on the other hand, was it a hesitating experiment, as of one who should say, " Let us try this new

healer,—he can't do harm and he may do good; there is nothing else to try." This is not faith; this is unbelief—distrust. You can tell it, no matter in what reverent language it may try to disguise itself, by its failing and giving up. Faith holds on. It has decided into whose hands it will commit itself, and there it stays. Faith is humble. It is itself a confession of weakness and need, and is not to be cast down nor discouraged by having the weakness and the need set before it. Tell it "You are poor and unworthy," and it is ready with the reply "Therefore I come for help and forgiveness and acceptance." Such tests as these are the trial of your faith,—more precious than the fiery trial of gold that perisheth. That flame which burns away the distrustful attempt to make a doubting experiment of Christ, makes the true faith that commits itself to God without one reserve, to shine out like the drop of pure gold at the bottom of the crucible.

Christ tried the faith of this heathen woman by these two tests, and it was perfect and entire, wanting nothing. She is content to be not only a suppliant, and not only, for the time, an unsuccessful suppliant, but (what is hardest for pride to bear) a neglected, slighted suppliant. What but a perfect faith could have sustained her under the *silence* of Christ? If he had but rebuked her, or argued with her, there would have been something for the mind to lay hold of and react against. But to follow him step by step as he walked on with his disciples talking with them on other subjects, as if he neither heard nor cared for her crying, this was the last crucial test of her perseverance in faith. If the Lord had been angry with her, it would have been easier to bear.

Which of us would not have turned back and given up under the discouragement of such a silence? But still she followed on and cried out, "Have mercy on me, O Lord, Son of David!" he all the time answering her never a word, until the disciples, sturdy fishermen, of no melting mood, could bear it no longer, and begged him not to protract the woman's dis-

THE PRAYER OF THE HEATHEN MOTHER. 121

tress and theirs. But even after this intercession, he had nothing to say to the woman, but kept on his way, merely remarking to his disciples that his mission was to Jews, not to Gentiles.

And through all these discouragements, she grows only the more importunate and persevering. The more this Saviour seems to repel her, the more it seems to her that she cannot be repelled—that she must cling to him. And now when it appears as if he had pronounced sentence against her and the case were closed, and he were departing from her, she cannot let him go. She throws herself in his path with acts of reverence; she cries out still, "Lord, help me! Lord, help me!" However it has come to her, there is no mistaking it, in her is the spirit of faith. She is not trying an experiment. Her heart is fixed. "She believes and therefore speaks." Faith like hers does not need to be taught to pray. Its "native speech" is prayer. It does not need to be cautioned not to faint. It has no thought of giving up. It will keep on calling until the Lord hears and answers. Cavils, objections, difficulties are of no account with it. No matter who may rebuke it that it should hold its peace; so much the more will it cry, "Have mercy upon me, thou Son of David." Tell it that the Lord has no need that we tell him anything; that it is vain to argue with him who knoweth all things. So much the more will it fill its mouth with arguments, and order its cause before him. Thus has it ever been with the great examples of believing prayer. Thus Abraham reasoned with the Lord concerning the guilty city. Thus Jacob strove with the angel, saying, "I will not let thee go." Thus Moses stood face to face with the Lord, and pleaded with him for the honor of his name and the safety of his people, as a man pleadeth with his friend. Thus Hezekiah, when the word had come to him, "Thou shalt die and not live," turned his face to the wall and argued with God for his life. And thus this heathen mother not only followed the Lord with strong crying and tears, but when, at last, she knew the words which he would answer her, and understood what he would say unto her, she put forth all the efforts of her intellect to meet his words. Her prayer was the effort of her whole self, body, mind and spirit—the clinging of her hands, the outcry of her affections, the strenuous endeavor of her intellect in the quick wit of her rejoinder.

Jesus answered and said, "It is not meet to take children's bread and cast it to dogs." And she said, "Truth, Lord; yet the dogs eat of the crumbs that fall from their master's table."

We shall come, by and by, to study the other personage in this dialogue, and shall have difficulties enough to solve concerning the strange words and stranger silence of our Lord. But it remains now only to add to the account of this heathen woman's earnest affection, her bitter trouble, her faith prevailing above all discouragement, her perseverance in prayer,— the story of her reward:

Then Jesus answered and said unto her, "O woman, great is thy faith; be it unto thee even as thou wilt." And her daughter was made whole from that very hour.

XI.

THE HEALING OF THE HEATHEN GIRL.

For this saying go thy way; the demon is gone out of thy daughter.—
Mark vii. 29.

It is a twofold, rather, I ought to say, a manifold revelation, this that comes to us in studying the successive pictures, crowded into the scanty canvas of the four gospels, of Jesus Christ the Healer, surrounded with the objects of his compassion and power. We fix our attention on the chief and central figure, and find the continually changing expression, in the terms of human nature and human language, of the eternal and unchangeable power and love of God. We look about upon the multitude of the sick folk, and of those who bring them, and find not only, in this vast diversity of bodily maladies the types of spiritual disease; but in the various actions and words with which men come or are brought to the manifest and visible Christ, the exemplifications of that faith and prayer with which we may bring our various needs to the Father "whom not having seen we love."

Looking thus steadfastly (in the last Sunday evening's sermon) on the face of that sorrowful woman of an alien race, of a foreign home, of a heathen religion, who besought the Son of David so instantly in behalf of her daughter "sore vexed with an evil spirit," we found personal, practical instruction, I am bold to say, for each one of us: 1. In her example of *intercessory prayer*, which seems to be represented, as indeed it well may be, as peculiarly acceptable and dear to God forasmuch as it is not the bringing of our own immediate griefs and troubles and wants to him, but the bringing of another's griefs and wants, which we thus make our own. In nothing do we come nearer to the fellowship of Christ, than when, like him, we thus "take the infirmities and bear the sicknesses" of others, rather than our own. 2. We note the character of her faith in Jesus, not unintelligent nor irrational, but founded on some knowledge, however it had come to her, of who and what he was;—an unreserved and entire and exclusive faith;—therefore a tenacious and persevering faith which having nowhere else to go will stay beside the Lord until there comes some sign from him that he has heard. 3. We are instructed by the manner of her prayer, which is not only importunate and persevering, but argumentative, as if she would exhibit reasons that should move the mind of the Lord, and contest with him the objections to her petition. And, 4, we find the note of the divine approval placed upon this faith and prayer, in the Lord's mighty work of healing, and in that tender word of his, uttered after his long silence and discouragement of her—that word "O woman, great is thy faith, be it unto thee even as thou wilt!"

And now, having studied this example of human faith accepting and laying hold of salvation, we turn our attention to the other figure in this touching scene,—the Lord and Giver of salvation, and look to find in his acts and words a visible and practical revelation of God in his dealing with suffering and ruined men.

For we look always to the life and words of Christ for a double teaching:—first, as the model of perfect human excellence; and then, as the expression of the divine character—to use an apostle's words, as the visible "image of the invisible God." (Col. i. 15.) And how in the same person we can find this twofold teaching—how we are to distinguish when he is the model and exemplar of perfect human excellence, and when he is setting forth the attributes of the infinite Father, may sometimes be a perplexing question to us; at least it has often been a perplexity to me, until I came to understand that Jesus Christ is never more the revelation and manifestation of God, than when

THE HEALING OF THE HEATHEN GIRL.

he is most the example of perfect and holy manhood, which is the very image and portraiture of the divine nature in which it is partaker. So that we have not to go through the gospels, as some have been wont to do, sifting, sorting and separating, saying, "Here it is the divine nature that speaks, and there again it is the human nature," but shall find, wherever we see the Lord, and hear him, that we have before us at once the perfect model for our imitation, and the expression of the mind of our heavenly Father, who is also his Father.

Now looking thus on Jesus Christ, first, as the model of our duty, and secondly as the expression of the divine nature, we find, as soon as we come to study his part in the story of the Syrophœnician woman, things which amaze us, at least, if they do not even painfully trouble and perplex us. And if they are perplexing to us as believers and disciples of his, I do not know that they are any less perplexing—perhaps they are even more so—to unbelievers. For on the very lowest view that intelligent unbelief takes, now-a-days, of the character of Jesus, allowing the utmost latitude for supposing fault and inconsistency and failure, instead of being thereby nearer to an explanation of his strange dealing on this occasion, we should be further away from it than ever.

Here is a man of whom the very least that can be said, his enemies themselves being judges, is that he is pre-eminently kind, sympathetic and merciful. His ruling trait, as it is expressed by the author of *Ecce Homo* (who is as far as need be from being an implicit and uncritical believer) is an "enthusiasm of humanity." It is an inadequate characterization, but it is certainly a just one, as far as it goes. He is a lover not only of mankind, but of men and women and children, each of them, as he meets them individually; and that is a greater thing than to be a friend of the race. His sympathy stops at no boundary line of race or creed or condition. He is made a martyr to the universal largeness of his humanity. The one tenet which most provokes the spirit of national and sectarian bigotry to plot and compass his death is that of universal charity and hope—the same tenet which provoked persecution upon his earliest disciples after his departure. Everywhere men recognize this in his looks, his words, his actions, and are emboldened, whoever they may be, to make him their friend. The most dejected, depressed and outcast pluck up heart to come to him, and never come in vain. The most alienated from the commonwealth of Israel—the commanders of the enslaving armies, the collectors of the detested tribute, even the Samaritans, most scorned and hated of the outside races—were sure of words and acts of kindness from him, if from none other.

And now see him here followed by a distressed and weeping woman that cries after him for help. The least he could do, one would say, was to give her his sympathy. The comfort of a kind word would cost him nothing. But he does not grant even so much as this. He does not even condescend to notice her. She addresses him in the most respectful terms. She follows him with the humblest entreaties. But he does not turn his head to look at her. He walks on in complete disregard of her, as if she was not there, until at last his friends, a company of rough fishermen from the lake, can no longer bear to hear her heart-breaking sobs and complaints, and beg him to put an end to them. But (still without speaking to *her* at all, or paying any attention to her) he gives them a forbidding answer, to the effect that this case does not come within the scope of his mission. And when she resolutely will not be refused, but comes and throws herself down in his path, and turns up before him that sad, sad face of hers, imploring him, "Lord, help me!" he does not even speak gently to her,—"My good woman, I am very sorry for you, but you must not ask me to do this." He does not even slip quietly aside and leave her. He actually seems to spurn her with insult: "It is not fit to take the children's bread and cast it to dogs." How stinging the comparison, we do not readily conceive. To us, the word *dog* is not exclusively a term of opprobrium; not seldom it is a symbol of loyal affection and fidelity. Not so in the East, where the dog is never spoken of with respect. Remember if you can, any place in the Bible in which the word is used otherwise than contemptuously. In those lands, the dog is not the friend and companion of man. He is not the faithful dog, or the intelligent and affectionate dog. He is looked upon as a mean, treacherous brute, suffered to run wild in the streets of a town for the service he may do as a public scavenger; or if kept about the house, only tolerated there for reasons of convenience. If the phrase had been "it is not fit to take the children's bread and throw it out to the pigs," it would not carry to our minds a stronger impression of disgust and repulsion than this word *dog* did to the woman of Canaan. It carried with it all the contempt which a Hebrew, and especially a Hebrew of the royal pedigree of David, might be supposed to feel for the unclean heathen about him.

How is this to be accounted for? Is there anything in the character of Christ that will explain it? Men have done such things as this before and since, doubtless. But not *such* men. If some men had done it,—seeming to scorn the agony of a heart-broken woman, protracting her distress in long suspense, meeting her humble entreaties with words of repulsion and contempt,—you would say that it needed no explanation at all—that it was perfectly intelligible from what you had known of them; and when you had said this you would feel that you had spoken their utmost condemnation. There are other men of whom if such a thing should be reported, you would say, first, that you did not believe it; and then, if the fact was shown to be unmistakable, you would say that it was something inexplicable, and unless some way could be found of accounting for it, you might very reasonably begin to suspect that there had been some attack of mental disorder such as impels the patient to the exact opposite of his habitual disposition.

But what can we do with *this* case—so extreme, so perplexing? There are two ways of dealing with the discrepancies and other difficulties which we encounter in the gospels. One is to soften down and explain away the difficulty so as to diminish it to the lowest terms, and then blink the remainder. The other is, to take the facts just as they are given to us, and learn from them whatever lesson God means that they shall teach. And this is the way which I mean always to follow.

Here we have an incident in the life of Christ, which is surely not in accordance with the common course of his actions; and no amount of explaining away will suffice to make it seem so. It comes into a small class of the exceptional actions of his life—if we may call those a *class* which have very little in common except this, that they are exceptional and out of the common course of his doings. Such, for instance, are the cursing of the fig-tree, the scourging of the traders from the temple, the terrible denunciations and threatenings against the Pharisees. There is something to be learned from each one of these, concerning Christ, concerning man, concerning God. What is it that we are to learn, in this case?

1. It is something worth learning, in the first place, that the difficulties which perplex us in the life and work of Jesus Christ are very like some of the difficulties that beset our understanding of the acts and government of the heavenly Father. So tender and loving God must be, and we are assured that he is;—assured by his dealing toward ourselves and toward all creatures, assured by the common praises of his people, by the voice of his word, by the testimony of his Son. All his works praise him and his saints bless him.. His fatherly providence extends to every least event. The sparrow does not fall without his care. And yet what unspeakable distresses fill the world, and fill the life of every human creature—distresses which, nevertheless, the word, the silent will of God, might in a moment make to cease! God is the hearer of prayer—nothing in all his word more explicitly declared,

THE HEALING OF THE HEATHEN GIRL.

more gratefully believed; and yet throughout his word the constant refrain of his people's complaints in every age is this: "How long, O Lord, how long? let it repent thee concerning thy servants." "O my God, I cry in the daytime but thou hearest not, and in the night season and am not silent. Why hast thou forsaken me? why art thou so far from helping me?" Alas! "when I cry and shout he shutteth out my prayer." How often these ancient words are the utterances of our own sorrowful experience—the voices of our deep despair! It is worth something to us in those hours of long delay and hope deferred, when we cry and shout, and yet God seems so deaf, so dumb,—to find that when men bring their entreaties to the most mighty, most compassionate of all the sons of men, it may sometimes be that he, with all his quick love, shall long delay to hear, and when he speaks, shall seem only to repel. And when we stand in studious wonder, again, before this contradiction in the life of Jesus, even the darkness of it seems to shine as the day, when we reflect how like it is to the darkness that is round about the eternal Father. "O mystery of godliness," we cry, "without controversy great, that is manifested in the flesh!"

2. We learn from this incident in the life of Jesus, what some have failed to learn, that his love and compassion are not such but that he is capable of looking with unbending fortitude on human misery, whenever there is a sufficient reason for it. His tenderness and loving-kindness toward every form of human distress do not proceed from this, that he has not the nerve to bear the sight of suffering. How the grandeur of his character is dishonored by those who conceive of the great love wherewith he loves, as a matter of nervous susceptibility; and who find him to be made up of no qualities but those of mildness and gentleness, the subject of irresistible impulses of pity which are balanced by none of the sterner virtues of justice and holy indignation, "the hate of hate and scorn of scorn,"— as if he were one whom the cry of distress or the sight of blood

would break down in a moment, and whose voice had no tones in it but those of entreaty and benediction! Ah! they thought not so, who slank away before his righteous anger and his uplifted whip, from the courts of his Father's house. They knew better, who cowered and gnashed their teeth under his denunciations of meanness and hypocrisy and oppression. She knew better, who followed him with entreaties and bitter wailings along the base of those Phœnician cliffs, pleading the anguish of her heart, and the writhing and torment of her demoniac daughter, before his dumb lips and unrelenting features. Any people with the New Testament in their hands ought to know better. But how common a thing it is that when a minister of Christ speaks in the very tone and spirit of his Master in rebuke of wickedness, there are wise editors and other critics to rebuke him by the example of "the meek and lowly Jesus." How often, when he hurls indignant rebuke, the threatening of God and the scorn of honest men, at those who despise the poor and needy, he is cautioned to remember that Christ's kingdom is not of this world! And when he repeats with awe the solemn words with which Jesus himself describes the wrath of God against sin, there are those who are ready to object that Christ's own words are not quite Christian.

It is well worth remarking that we have in this story a lively example of the sort of nervous-sympathetic tenderness that hastens to relieve distress because it cannot bear to see it or hear it; but it is found not in Christ, but in his disciples. They are all for helping and healing. "Dispose of her case and let her go," [ἀπόλυσον αὐτήν] they say, "for she crieth after us." It was only Christ, the infinitely loving and merciful, who held out sternly and unrelentingly. Selfishness was in a hurry to help; love was steady and severe in refusing. How like this difference between the selfish, tender-hearted disciples and the stern but loving Christ, is to the difference between man and God! It is the wholly noble and incorrupt things in man that are features of the image of God; and the weakness of nerve that breaks down uncontrolled in presence of pain, the sentimental and impulsive charity that gives to relieve its own feelings,—these are not of that class. The surgery that cuts boldly, that can burn with escharotics and torture with moxas,—the military rigor that can fire upon a mob with ball cartridges, so saving many lives by the righteous sacrifice of a few,—the magisterial virtue which resolves to hang when weeping sentimentality is whining Pardon,—these are of a divine nature. "Feed the poor tramp; I cannot bear to see him suffer," cries the impulsiveness which is more Christian than the Christ. "No!" answers Christianity itself; "don't feed him; starve him. I can bear it as long as he can. If a man will not work, neither let him eat."

3. It is a point which has already been adverted to incidentally, but which I wish to emphasize to all your minds, that as we read this story it is clear all along that Christ's apparent unkindness to the afflicted woman was apparent only. All the time his true love and tender interest toward her had been glowing under that stern, impassive countenance. He did not hate and scorn her as a heathen dog. He loved her all the more for cherishing, in her Gentile darkness, such faith as he had not found, no, not in Israel. And at last, if there seems a sudden change between them, it is not that she has *radically* changed toward him, nor that he has really changed toward her. Her faith had grown the stronger and the clearer by that sore trial of her faith—more precious than of gold that perisheth. Her faith had been manifested, not only to others, but to her own heart. And now, at last, it is full time that *his love* be manifested. And how like a torrent long pent up it pours forth toward her in the words, "O woman, great is thy faith! Be it unto thee even as thou wilt!" What manner of man is this? How like he is to God, who chasteneth whom he loveth, and scourgeth every son whom he receiveth!

4. Finally, learn from the way of the Lord's working in this act of healing, that which is often true of the way of God with

his children—that they may be heard and accepted and answered and blessed, before they know it. Here was this woman, waiting and crying and entreating at the feet of Jesus, hoping, doubtless, to see him heal in such wise as she had known or heard of his having done before. She looked for some visible or audible sign of healing,—that he should come under her roof, that he should stretch forth his hand and lay it upon the child, or at least that he should speak some word of command or exorcism to the evil spirit, calling it to come forth. But nothing like this did she hear; only this word: "Go thy way, the demon is gone out of thy daughter." It must have been an overwhelming surprise to her; and yet we may almost say that such surprises are characteristic of our Lord's ways of salvation,—so frequent are the parallels in the history of his works of healing, so frequent in the experience of penitent souls. The importunate, believing prayer has been uttered, and as she lingers upon her knees, longing to see the power of God put forth to fulfill it, she finds that already it has been done unto her even as she would. So, many a penitent soul has poured out his believing prayer to God, his health and salvation, entreating the renewing Spirit to be sent for his quickening and rescue and for the casting down of the dominant power of evil, and has waited, and wondered to hear no rush as of a mighty wind, to see no vision, to feel no convulsive rending, and no influx of celestial joy, such as others have told of in their experience of conversion;—and all the while if he had had ears to hear the calm word of God, he might have been glad in the assurance that the very prayer he uttered was the witness to him from the saving Spirit, and might have laid to his heart the benediction, "Go in peace, thy sins are forgiven thee."

XII.

THE GADARENE DEMONIAC.

And when he saw Jesus from afar, he ran and worshiped him; and crying out with a loud voice, he saith, "What have I to do with thee, Jesus, thou Son of the Most High God? I adjure thee by God, torment me not."
—MARK v. 6.

WE are not permitted, in the contemplation of this story of one possessed with a legion of unclean spirits, to avoid speaking of the somewhat difficult question, What was the nature of the so-called "demonism" of the New Testament?

Part of the difficulty in the case is wholly unnecessary, having been created by a misuse of words in the old translation, which (not at all to the credit of the company of Revisers) is perpetuated in the new. It is nowhere said in the New Testament, concerning any one, that he was possessed of the devil. In one passage only (Acts x. 38), mention is made of the healing of "all that were *oppressed* of the devil." But in all other like passages there is no mention made of "the devil," but of "unclean spirits" or "demons." The two words are used with absolute distinctness throughout the books of the New Testament. There is *the devil*, that is to say, the accuser, or the calumniator, used always in the singular number and with the definite article, of a ruling spirit of malignant wickedness, "the ruler of the darkness of this world." And then there is frequent mention of *dæmons*, or spiritual beings capable of coming into relation with men. The word is common enough in other Greek authors, as applied either to good or to evil influences. But in the New Testament it is used rarely if at all in any but a bad sense, as equivalent to "evil spirits," or "unclean spirits." The confusion between these two words is a needless confusion, from which we should have been saved if the counsels of the American scholars had prevailed in the revision of the English New Testament; this word *demon* and its derivatives would not then have been translated as if they pertained to the devil and to things diabolical.

A *second* point of difficulty that troubles some people is that this describing of a malady as if it were the infestation of some living thing that had entered into the person seems so like the relic of a barbarous and superstitious pathology, which ascribes all sicknesses to such a cause. To which we may make either of two answers: (1.) That if this description of certain maladies as wrought by evil spirits is a survival of the superstitious notion that all maladies were so caused, it may be a survival of just so much in that notion as was true and ought to survive. Or, (2.) That if barbarism and superstition used to allege that all human diseases are produced by the agency of living beings invisible to the ordinary sight entering into the patient, then barbarism and superstition are in pretty good company, considering that the very latest word of the most advanced pathological science comes out at precisely the same point.

And here is a *third* difficulty, which is suggested in the question Why are there no cases of demonism in our own times?—a question to which, as before, there are two answers: (1.) That it is not certain that there are no such cases now. There are many to insist, with a very formidable array of evidence in favor of their claim, that cases of possession by spirits, clean or unclean, are peculiarly frequent in these days. (2.) If no cases just like what are described in the gospels are recognized in modern pathology, this is no more than might be expected from analogy. Some of the diseases most clearly defined in early history do not appear in any modern treatise on the Theory and Practice of Medicine, and cannot be identified, by the description, with diseases now known; and on the other hand some of the most formidable diseases that now scourge the human race are known to have had a modern origin. It is one of the commonest maxims of medical science, quoted sometimes to cover its own change of front, that the type of diseases changes from age to age. For my part, I find it nothing unlikely that in an age like that of the coming of our Lord, when a decisive conflict was impending between the kingdom of evil and the kingdom of heaven, these maladies that involve the mind and soul, and indicate the presence of some mischievous spiritual agency, should be found to take on a character of peculiar malignity.

The four evangelists give themselves very little concern about pathology and diagnosis, although one of them was a physician. But taking the gospels as an honest and not unintelligent record of the phenomena, we make out two points very clearly concerning this demonism: 1. It was not mere lunacy or epilepsy, for these diseases are recognized and clearly distinguished from the work of the evil spirits. There are patients in whom the work of the infesting spirit produces symptoms like epilepsy; and other patients in whom it produces symptoms of dumbness; and there are still other manifestations; but beneath these symptoms they detect indications, which the sufferer himself confirms, of something different from the mere physical diseases of like symptoms, by which these cases were surrounded. 2. As this demonism was not mere disease, so, on the other hand, it was not mere wickedness—the willful giving up of one's self to the instigation of the devil;—a mistake to which we are inclined by the unhappy mistranslation of which I have spoken. It is always spoken of and dealt with as an involuntary affliction, looked upon by the Lord with pity rather than censure. Neither is it treated as if it were, in any special sense, a visitation for sin. Doubtless these sufferers were sinners; and doubtless their sufferings stood in some relation to their sins; but it was not *this* relation, that they were "sinners above all others."

The truth seems to be this: that sin, unbelief, ungodliness, opened the way for this awful curse, and that when the alien spirit had taken hold of body and mind and will, it had the power of plaguing with various disorders—with wild, moping, melancholic madness, or with epileptic convulsions, or blindness, or dumbness. Both the disciples and the evangelists, and even the popular apprehension of the Jews, distinguished clearly between such of these maladies as were merely physical, and such as were inflicted by malign spirits.

The startling and unearthly fact, in the words and actions of the demoniac, is the presence in him of a double consciousness and will. You hear now his own voice in pitiful complaint and supplication, and now the fierce cry of the demon, speaking with his organs and claiming to represent his person. He does not know himself. He is torn with discordant desires, and tossed to and fro between conflicting passions. Physicians who have studied the horrible symptoms of *delirium tremens* describe the sort of double consciousness that sometimes characterizes its wretched victims, in terms which remind us of this demonism described by the evangelists.

Here, in the story of the maniac at Gergesa, you find an example of it. The wretched madman, whose malady has defied all remedies and all restraints, who, with the superhuman strength of madness, breaks all fetters and chains, and tears the garments from his body, has fled away into the sepulchral caves, to be the companion of jackals and hyenas. At night they hear his howls with horror in the town, mingling with the cry of those obscene beasts. As one who is at discord with himself, he turns fiercely, not only on his own kind, making the lake road impassable by reason of men's terror of him, but also on himself, hating his own flesh, and mangling his body with stones.

It is another sign of this unappeasable discord within him that as the shallop bearing Jesus, the Caster-out of demons, nears the shore, he rushes down to the water's edge, as if craving de-

THE GADARENE DEMONIAC.

liverance,—and the next moment, when the command "Come out of him" has gone forth from the lips that have just rebuked the wind and the waves, he cries out: "I beseech thee, torment me not." Then, when Jesus asks him: "What is thy name?" his consciousness becomes inextricably entangled again, and he answers, as not knowing which is himself and which is the host of infesting spirits: "*My* name is Legion, for *we* are many."

As to the spirits themselves, we get some hints of their ways here and elsewhere in the New Testament. They are represented as wandering uneasy and restless until they can find lodgment in some human body and soul, if may be; if not there, then anywhere, even in a swine's carcass—some living organism of which they can take possession, and there work their malignant will. The unclean spirit beds itself luxuriously in the consciousness and thoughts and members of its victim, and loathes to be dispossessed. Like certain noxious tropical insects, it sinks its feelers and tentacles into the flesh, so that to tear it away is like tearing the flesh away from itself. To leave it there is torture, and to remove it is worse torture; so that the patient rushes to the surgeon, and when the surgeon puts forth his hand to heal him, it is as if victim and tormentor shrank away together, crying: "Let me alone! I beseech thee, torment me not!"

Now is it any dark parable to you, that I should need explain how like this is to the possession which sin takes of the mind?—how evil thoughts and passions and purposes for which the soul was not made, but which are alien to its divine constitution in God's image, do root themselves like a morbid growth into its very substance, till the soul, bewildered at the unnatural conflict within itself, cries out against the power of sin, craving to be delivered, and then, when the Deliverer comes near, cries out again, with a loud voice: "What have I to do with thee, Jesus, Son of God most high? I beseech thee, torment me not!"

We have the story of just such an inward conflict told by the apostle Paul out of his own experience. Even Paul seems sometimes of doubtful consciousness, as if hesitating which of the antagonists in this interior struggle is himself, and which is the invader from without. Sometimes it seems to him that it is the malign influence that is himself, he willfully "fulfilling the desires of the flesh and of the mind," into whom God enters with the power of a new life, so that thenceforth it is "not he that lives, but Christ that lives in him." But in that almost tragical seventh chapter to the Romans, where he recounts the struggle, he says it was not he that did or consented to the wrong,—his real self was his better self, that revolted from the power of sin. "That which I do I know not; not what I would, do I practise; what I hate, I do. But if I do what I would not, I consent unto the law that it is good. So now it is no more I that do it, but sin which dwelleth in me. . . . I delight in the law of God, after the inward man; but I see a different law in my members, warring against the law of my mind, and bringing me into captivity to the law of sin which is in my members."

Have you no like experience which has showed you how the power of sin so twists itself in with the roots of your life and seems to make part of yourself? Every life that is more than half a life feels the impulse of motive forces, the strongest of which become dominant, and tend to become domineering—"master-passions" we call them. Just in proportion as we rise above the torpor of a vegetable existence, we feel these forces working, throbbing, driving within us, like the motive power in an engine. And when these forces are burned out or extinguished, we do not call it life, but suspended animation. It is a pitiful sight to see a man, with the powers and faculties of a man, become inert and useless for lack of motive—like a disused locomotive rusting on a side-track, or a steamboat that has exhausted her fuel, and is drifting with wind and current. His passion for money, for pleasure, for notoriety, is satiated, or is exhausted, and there is no headway left by which to steer him, except the half-spent momentum of old habits. He keeps up a show of pretending to live, and does a little, in a languid way, of what live men do earnestly and for a purpose. He reads the newspapers a little, and has a little taste for literature or art, but not much. He talks politics a little, and bets a little on horses or candidates, and smokes—well, he smokes a good deal, and gives all his mind to it. But he does nothing with strong interest and has no distinct purpose or object in life. The inspiring, impelling passions of life are to him a mere memory. Now these passions of life which when extinguished leave the man so inert and flaccid, when given free play, without control of law or duty, become to the soul a dear necessity from which it does not know how to part. To rend them away is like tearing the life out of the life. Such is the organization of man, that the passions which impel the mind after certain objects become dearer than the objects themselves. The desire is a greater matter to us than the thing desired. You do not read human nature aright unless you apprehend this. You suppose that it is a craving for more money that keeps men up to their work long after they have money enough? You might as well suppose that the motive which leads a company of English country gentlemen on a toilsome break-neck chase all day long after a poor, worthless brute was their insatiable appetite for fox-meat. It is a most unjust mistake to suppose that the motive which pushes on the business-man in the eager pursuit of money, long after all his reasonable needs are provided for, is the mere sordid love of *having*. It is not this so much as the love of *getting*; and not so much the love of getting, as the love of successfully pursuing and achieving. He must have something to do, and to do with his might. He needs a purpose in life, even though it be an inadequate and unworthy purpose; and so this passionate eagerness of pursuit, after that which in his heart he knows is not worth pursuing, fills his mind with busy thoughts and plans, and makes him company for his solitude, and entertainment for his weariness, and puts a mainspring into his life. It grows to inordinate strength, perhaps; it overshadows his nobler feelings; its morbid enlargement draws away the real strength of his soul; it becomes his master passion,—his besetting sin. But the more it overgrows itself, the more it hurts him, the more it saps his life, the more he feels that he cannot part with it. It has come to be identified with himself; if that were gone there would be nothing left. Take away that fiery, domineering passion, and put nothing in place of it, and what a useless and flaccid creature he has become! life not worth living, nor the world worth living in!

It is not always so. You have known men the cutting off of whose business career did not turn out to be the end of them. There was too much of them—too large and complete a manhood—to be destroyed by a single stroke. They were *men* as well as business-men; and when the business was gone there was a man left. And you have known the other kind, nerveless, extinguished, dead before his time, for lack of a motive power. It is not only failure that produces such. Success can do it as well. The man has reached the figure at which he always said he would retire, and so he buys him land and builds him a country-seat, and retires, with nothing to do; until by and by the spirit that seemed cast out finds its old lodging standing vacant, no new interest or passion to occupy it, and comes back sevenfold stronger, and hurries its victim back into Wall Street or Third Street as a speculator.

I need not multiply illustrations. The same thing may be true in politics, or in any form of literary or professional competition—that men become enamored of their own passions. The more the master-passion becomes aggrandized by use, the more one loves to feed and cherish it. And when it becomes intensified to exorbitant energy, driving the man along with accelerating speed in a course of selfishness, men wonder at the momentum of such a career, and falsely think that it is the inordinate passion, the sin, of the man, that makes his life so like a mighty torrent; just as if, watching the growth of some exhausting tumor that is drawing off into itself the forces of the system, they should say to each other concerning the patient "See what health and vigor! how he gains in weight!"—when, all the time it is not himself that is gaining, but his false self, his own worst enemy, that is so flourishing, while the *man* is wasting day by day.

But after all, although these inordinate passions, rooted and growing like a parasite in the substance of a man, are not the man himself, it is almost as if they were, when the question arises, How shall they be eradicated? Such a strange condition of the mind it is, when the capacity of loving the thing we abhor, and clinging to that we long to be rid of, is developed. We are fascinated with horrors. We throng the theatres to break our hearts over agonizing tragedies—so do we learn to love intense bitterness of agitation. I do believe that there have been those who in their craving for intense emotion have loved to cherish and aggravate within themselves the torments of a guilty conscience. One can hardly read the full story of Lord Byron's life without recognizing him as a morbid amateur of remorse, raging against God and man and against his own soul, ever plunging into new depths of sin, and reveling in new acts and expressions of self-torment. "He was ever in the tombs, crying and cutting himself with stones."

Now it is the nature of your sin that it has so imbedded and rooted itself in you that although it is not of your proper constitution, it has nevertheless identified itself with you to that degree that "when you would do good, evil is present with you." It has planted itself in these natural passions, innocent in themselves, but grown to inordinate dimensions of selfishness until they crowd God from his throne and leave him no room in the heart. For there is no room for God in any heart that does not yield him the supreme place. When that place is denied him, what can he do but depart? And then sin leaps into the vacant seat and rules. And though the soul winces under its cruel lash, nevertheless the tyrant keeps his place by the victim's own consent; and when the Liberator comes near. preaching deliverance to the captive, the opening of the prison-doors to them that are bound, the victim rushes to welcome him, and then in a moment the victim and the possessing demons cry out together, "Let us alone! I beseech thee torment me not!"

What help is there for the soul that is in such a plight—the will, the motives, the desires, the active faculties, all that should co-operate in the effort of self-healing, themselves implicated in the disease, so that even when deliverance is brought nigh, it will none of it, but warns the Saviour away? It will, and yet it will not. The consciousness of need and danger are of no avail; even faith and prayer bring no help, for there is no prayer but with a reservation—let not the double-minded man think that he shall receive anything from the Lord. So Augustine prayed, "Save me, O Lord, save me;—but not now."

O helpless man, the hope for you is that God will be to you better than your prayers, will do for you exceeding abundantly above that you ask;—that when you pray, "Save me, but not now," he will answer, "Now is the accepted time; now is the day of salvation, look unto me now and be saved." Be not afraid to come near your Lord and Saviour, even though the sin that is in you, the evil thoughts, the demoniac passions, cry out against your prayers and say, "Let us alone! torment us not! depart from us! what have we to do with thee, Jesus, Son of the most high God!" Doubt not that the compassionate Lord will be more ready to hear this craving of your better nature than the clamor of a legion of evil spirits, and that if you will but suffer him, he will deliver you from your worse self; he will command the inward discord of your mind to cease, and make the storm a calm; and you, even though it be not without sore rendings from the retreating fiend, shall at last sit peaceful at the feet of your Redeemer, clothed and in your right mind.

XIII.

THE GOSPEL AMONG THE GADARENES.

And they began to beseech him to depart from their borders.—MARK v. 17.

This verse concludes the brief history of Christ's doings among the Gadarenes; for the next verse tells how he took them at their word and went aboard the boat to return to his own city. The four verses, 14–17, are a complete chapter by themselves. They tell the whole story of Christ's coming to a people, the attesting of his divine mission, the impression on the people's minds, their rejection of him, his withdrawal from them. It is the history of *The Gospel among the Gadarenes*.

The scene of this whole story lies somewhere on the eastern shore of the little lake—the pond, as we should call it in America—of Galilee. I have never visited that shore; except at favorable times, or under the protection of a guard, it is not safe to visit it, on account of the plundering and murdering Arabs that infest it. But from the western shore,—from the city of Tiberias, and the lovely little valley of Gennesareth,—I have looked across the four or five miles' breadth of blue water, and seen the green treeless and houseless shores sloping down to the water's edge, breaking here and there into bluffs of rock, in the face of which one may descry the openings of caves that have been hollowed out for sepulchres. Somewhere along that shore this strange event took place; but exactly where has been for fifteen hundred years one of the doubtful questions in Biblical geography. It was "in the country of the Gadarenes," but plainly not at or near Gadara, for that was six miles southeast from the lower end of the lake. It is a famous old ruin, to this day, and in the days of its glory was the splendid metropolis of all that region. But as for any such place as Gergesa, or Gerasa, in the neighborhood of the lake, it was as undiscoverable as Capernaum or Chorazin on the western side, until, a few years ago, my venerable missionary friend and former traveling companion, Dr. Thomson, exploring that desolate shore, stopped beside a little heap of ruined buildings, and asked the Arab peasant who was with him what was the name of that place. He answered that it was called *Khersh;* and as soon as he heard the syllable, Dr. Thomson recognized that it must be Gergesa, and that this was "the country of the Gergesenes." He looked up the lake shore, and there, in the bluff hill-side, were the mouths of such rock-hewn tombs as the demoniacs might have had their dwelling in, and from which they might have come rushing down to the beach to meet the approaching boat. Just about this place, too, the flat by the waterside grows very narrow, the steep hills crowding closer to the lake, so that, as he observed the lay of the land, he felt that he could fix on the very hillside on which the great herd of two thousand swine was feeding, and the very steep down which they rushed into the sea. All which, and a hundred other most lively and interesting illustrations of the Scriptures, are they not written in Dr. Thomson's two delightful volumes entitled "The Land and the Book"?

Wherever it was, on the east side of the lake, that the wonder took place, the frightened keepers of the swine would not have had far to go to find people to tell it to. It is lonely enough there now—among all the crowded heaps of ruin no inhabitant left except the wandering gangs of thieving Arabs. But the ruins show how dense a population once swarmed on this as on the other side of the sea. Into some one of the ten cities that gave the name of *Decapolis* to that region, there rushed some of the panic-stricken peasants who had been tending swine, and told what had happened down by the water-side. "That horrible, naked maniac, possessed with demons, that lives

THE GOSPEL AMONG THE GADARENES. 145

in the tombs—you know him!" Oh, yes, they all knew him! He was the terror of all the neighborhood. They had not dared to travel by that road for fear of him. But what has he been doing now? "Why, he is cured! He is as quiet, and gentle, and reasonable as any man. And the fury and madness that were in him seem to have gone from him into the great herd of swine, so that these went plunging down the bluff into the lake, and we have lost them." Naturally, all the city turned out, as Matthew says; and, as Mark and Luke add, not only all the city, but a great crowd of the country-folk, to look into this strange story of the swineherds. The men must have run far, in their fright, so that the crowd that returned with them had a good distance to come. For by the time they arrive on the scene, this naked wretch has been got into decent garments, and they find him in the midst of the little group of the disciples, sitting at the feet of the great Teacher, "clothed, and in his right mind." It was a great work that had been done, and a great talk they had over it; and the two themes over which these Decapolitans talked with their neighbors who had witnessed the affair were these: 1. "Concerning the things which had befallen him that had been possessed of demons;" and 2. "Concerning the swine."

Without overstraining the story, to make it teach us more than it means, we may find good matter of reflection in this double subject of the inquiries of the Gadarene people, which seems to have been the double occasion of their fear (for we are twice assured that "they were afraid") and of their entreaty to Jesus to depart out of their country.

1. You may be at a loss, perhaps, to see any good reason why the healing of the wretched man possessed of demons should have been an occasion of terror to the people of the neighborhood. It might seem more reasonable that they should have found it rather an immense *relief* to their fears, when the frightful creature that had been the terror of that part of the country, whose horrible frenzies had made the road that led by

his cave impassable, so that they took long circuits to avoid him, was found by them sitting as quiet as a good child, at the feet of Jesus, trying to learn something of God and truth and duty, and of who this wonderful Saviour was—this destroyer of the works of the devil. You might naturally enough think that, being evidently a timid and fearful sort of folk, they would have been so thankful for the relief as to gather at once about the Son of God with a petition that he would never leave them, but stay on their side of the lake and make it his home, lest the demoniac madness should return to their fellow-citizen, or should break out in some of the rest of them. What good reason could they find, in all that they had heard, for sending Jesus out from their borders?

What *good* reason? Ah, but this is asking too much—to look for a good reason for a wrong action. The most that you can expect to find, in such a case, is an actual reason. It is the very nature of sin to be unreasonable. Its reasons are no reasons. We may look for the motives of it; and for the excuses for it. But in giving *reasons* for wrong conduct, we cannot go much further than to show that it is like the conduct of human nature in general under like circumstances. And we do not pretend to justify human nature.

Why should Adam and Eve be afraid when they heard the voice of the Lord God in the garden? Why should Moses be afraid and hide his face when the Lord spoke to him out of the burning bush and said "I am the God of thy father"? Why should Isaiah, when he saw the Lord sitting on a throne high and lifted up, cry out "Woe is me, for I am undone, for my eyes have seen the King, the Lord of hosts"? Why should John, when in spirit he beheld the heavenly vision of the Son of Man, fall at his feet as one dead? Why, when Peter saw the revelation of the power of God in the person of the Christ, should he cry out, "Depart from me, for I am a sinful man, O Lord"? Know this, and you will know why the crowd of the Gadarenes, when they saw by what power it was that their demoniac neighbor had been restored to health and reason, should one and all be struck with terror, and begin to beg the Healer not to stay so near them. It is in human nature, somehow, account for it as you may, that men do not like to come quite so near to God. It is not only that they shrink from the manifestation of the divine anger—that would be intelligible enough; but men do not like such close dealings with God anyway. In fact anything that brings them close face to face with the powers of the unseen world is a thing that men in general shrink from. A supposed supernatural appearance—a ghost—no matter whether it comes on an evil or on a benignant errand, frightens them; they want to get away and hide as soon as they may. And this is still more true with regard to every near manifestation of the Almighty God. Even when God seems winning us to hold converse with him, and by every persuasive word, every reassuring symbol, would draw us into his confidence—as when he says to Moses, "I am thy father's God," and shows him, for his comfort, how all that dazzling glory hurts not and consumes not—even then we hide our faces, and are afraid to listen to his voice. The Christ may come to us only in works of benignant healing. In most gracious and merciful ways, we may behold the wonderful power of God revealed in Jesus. But so long as it is manifestly *God*, holy and just, that is revealed in him, we shrink away. We are afraid. It is our instinctive impulse to cry out, like Simon Peter, "Depart from me, for I am a sinful man, O Lord." Or confusedly, in panic, not clearly confessing to our own hearts what we do, we in our secret thoughts beseech him to depart out of our coasts.

You do not think that this is so with you? Do not be too sure. Perhaps you would know your own heart better at this point, if you had had some wide observation of the working of other hearts, or long experience in trying to persuade them. It is the one labor of the ministry of the gospel to persuade men to come near enough to God to know him—to look Christ in the face long enough to know him. Dr. H. A. Boardman of this city wrote a little book entitled "The Great Question;" and when you looked within to see what "the great question" was, you found it nothing but this—"Will you *consider the subject* of personal religion?" And why should not any man—every man—say *yes* to this Great Question? But they will not. The complaint of the old prophet is the complaint of the modern preacher—"My people will not consider." Christ comes to them with his word of hope, "Repent ye, and believe the gospel," and they will not purposely affront him and rebuff him; but they find it irksome that he should come so near, he, the Son of God, and look them in the face so earnestly with those "eyes like a flame of fire." He comes for nothing but blessing, to help men free of the torment of their infesting sin. But not even thus is he welcome. He cannot be so near us, holy, harmless, undefiled, without being a reproach to us. We see our secret sins in the light of his countenance. It becomes intolerable. Our lips frame words of welcome, and praise; but our hearts are all the time silently pleading with him to "let us alone," and depart out of our coasts, even though we would shrink from putting such a thought into words. We feel easier with a legion of malignant demons near us, than with one faithful and merciful and holy Saviour.

2. The second topic of consultation among the city-folk and country-folk of the country of the Gadarenes, was this:— "concerning the swine."

I do believe (to do these people justice) that if we could have been there, and could have charged them to the face with having deliberately rejected Christ—willfully driven away the great Healer, simply on account of their interest in pork raising, they would indignantly and sincerely have repelled the imputation, and have suggested a number of other reasons by which they supposed they were actuated, instead of the one which really affected and decided their minds.

It is not the way men act, to ponder the question of religious duty in all its aspects, and finally, with conscious, selfish wickedness to confront God or his messenger with the announcement, "I see what is right and what is wrong, but the right is going to be prejudicial to me in the way of business, and I reject it. I will do wrong instead of right. Evil shall be my good." I know something of how human selfishness expresses itself now-a-days, and I do not believe it was so very different then. I do not believe they said explicitly to each other, "This is a great and divine work of mercy. God himself is manifest here destroying the works of the devil, and delivering our fellow-man from bondage to unclean spirits; surely the kingdom of God is come nigh unto us.—But then, on the other hand, see what it costs;—two thousand head of pork is a great deal to lose,—and we will not have God's kingdom." I do not believe they *said* this; I do not believe they distinctly *thought* it; but they *did* it.

And you, beware how you put yourself under the same condemnation. For you need not expect that the gospel of salvation will ever come to you without bringing along with it some conditions of loss and self-denial. It has the promise, indeed, of the life that now is, as well as of that which is to come; and gloriously it fulfills this promise, whether to society or to the individual. The gravest embarrassments to the progress of the kingdom of heaven grow out of the constancy and generosity with which its promise of this life is fulfilled. The fact has been compressed into an elegant Latin proverb, by a famous Englishman of two centuries ago, in something like this shape: "Religion has given birth to riches, and the mother has been devoured by her offspring."* In the long run, on the large scale, on the general average, the blessings of *this* life do so steadily flow toward the godly, that it is as much as the Church can do—it is a great deal *more* than the

---

* *Religio peperit divitias, et mater devorata est a prole.*—LORD FALKLAND.

Church can do—to keep herself clear of those who seek godliness for gain. But the gospel, that brings with it such gain, never comes without inflicting some immediate loss, personal or public.

In its *institutions*, it brings, for instance, the observance of a Sabbath rest; and this, in itself, is a basis of national wealth to the nations that accept it. You are not half aware how much you owe in money for the weekly rest from labor. I remember, when passing through France more than thirty years ago, reading in the French newspapers the report of the debate in the Legislative Body on the bill for the Observance of the Lord's Day, that had been brought in by the illustrious Count de Montalembert. It was met by the economists with the objection that France could not afford to lose so much time out of her productive industry; and the objection was answered on the spot with the undeniable fact that those two countries whose industries were most productive and prosperous were the very ones in which the Sabbath rest was most scrupulously observed—England and the United States. No doubt about it; but then, to begin with, it was going to cost a clear sacrifice of one-seventh out of the working time, and that was too much; and so poor France toils on without her Sabbath, still.

Thus it is with the institutions of the kingdom of heaven— they are a blessing for both worlds; but then they *cost*.

So it is also with the *charities* of the church. You do not have to wait for the light of heaven to show you that it is more blessed to give than to receive. To every one that has learned to give, as God giveth, " with simplicity," this blessing comes, and stays beside him day by day and night by night. *It pays* to give—to give by method, and system,—to make a business of giving. It pays cash dividends in this present life; for to make a systematic business of giving puts a balance-wheel of system into all one's business; so that there is clear logic in that text of Psalm cxii., " A good man sheweth favor and lendeth; **he** *will guide his affairs with discretion.*" It pays, in this respect, to have the kingdom of heaven come; but it costs. It is an income-tax of ten per cent. to you, and blessed is he whosoever is not offended thereat. Blessed is he, who, when the Saviour of mankind draws near with healing for the wretched and the sinful, does not begin to reckon up how many head of swine of his may be endangered thereby.

It is exactly so with the *social reforms* of the Gospel. Not one of the social vices at which they strike, but entrenches itself in vested interests, so that even honest and good citizens find, to their own surprise, that they are indirectly involved in them. You cannot cut out these cancers without cutting into sound flesh. If the secret vice that burrows out of sight in this city, coming to the surface only now and then in some festering and fetid sore, should be exterminated to-morrow, there are very few of you that would not indirectly experience some incidental inconvenience in your business.

There is a legion of demons raging through this community, seizing upon some of the choicest of the young men and transforming them to the likeness of fiends or of brutes; invading the homes of the people to leave behind them a trace like that of a destroying angel; damaging the wealth of society more than if an annual fire were to go sweeping from street to street. And now when some inbreathing of Christian earnestness and sympathy, some gift of a wonder-working faith, makes us strong to say to these tormenting demons, "We command you in the name of Jesus Christ that ye come out and depart,"—when one by one the broken wrecks of manhood begin to take back once more the faculties of reason, and the fashion of their countenance is altered, and their very raiment changes from unwholesome rags to neatness and comfort, and they seek the company of Christian disciples and the assemblies where they meet their Lord, and thus sit at the feet of Jesus clothed and in their right mind, and the constant, consuming waste of mind and property begins to be stayed;—how many are there who, as they look with admiration at the change, will bethink them of the effect it is likely to have on the courses of business, and be tempted to break in upon the songs of those who give glory to God, with the exclamation, "My swine, O my swine!"

It is so with *the personal morality* of the gospel. It will interfere with your plans, break up your arrangements, frustrate your schemes, in business, in politics, in society, in the conduct of life. That petty fraud—that adulteration or misrepresentation, so common that no one thinks of it—that smart, lying advertisement that you have got in your desk ready for the press,—those keen little tricks or disingenuous compliances in politics that are to carry the caucus or the election and put you into office or keep you there—those shams and deceits, that neglect of homely duties and of wearying charities, by which you are studying to gain social position and pleasure—how these herds of unclean things, the soilure and blemish of your lives, will have to rush off into the sea, if the Holy Christ is to come to you and live with you. Are you ready to let them go, or will you rather come and pray the Lord to depart out of your neighborhood?

My dear fellow-Christian, if, at one word from you, you knew that the mighty power of God, quickening, solemnizing, purifying, would descend upon this people, and that multitudes would turn from death unto eternal life, are you sure that you would speak it? How many of your plans—your innocent plans, perhaps—would be quite discomposed by it?—the parties you were going to give or to attend—the merry amusements that you meant to set on foot for the season,—your affectionate calculations on the social enjoyment and success of your children—these might have to wait and stand aside, if there should begin to be a very great and prevailing religious earnestness; and are you quite sure that if, at one word from you, the Lord would draw near, mighty to save, you would sincerely speak it, saying out of your heart, "Yea; Lord, even so, come quickly"?—or while your lips were saying, "Come, Lord Jesus," would your heart be "praying him to depart out of these coasts"? Remember, that it is on what the heart prays, not on what the lips say, that the Lord is looking.

And when the question is, my friend, on your own personal conversion, is there not, perhaps, light to be gotten from this story of the Gospel among the Gadarenes on some of the perplexities that have troubled your mind, and been too difficult for your best counselors? It is an old story, this which you tell me—how you have struggled with that besetting power of sin that has seemed to possess you like a demon—how you have longed to be converted—how, whenever there was a revival of religion you have hoped that you would be a subject of it, but how it never has come so; and how you wonder that God should leave you thus, when you are all ready, and willing, and anxious to be converted. But *are* you willing, wholly, unreservedly? Are there no worldly vanities cherished in your heart which you do not mean to let go?—no selfish ambitions that you have been hiding in your bosom, afraid lest God should see them if he came too near?—no stye of swinish pleasures which you have meant, and still mean, to reserve when the Caster-out of demons comes to dispossess you of unclean spirits? Nothing of these? Are you all ready, with a whole heart, to be Christ's disciple now? Then listen to me this one word: *You are Christ's disciple now;* and the very next thing for you to do is to profess his name, and join yourself to the company of his people.

XIV.

THE APOSTLE TO THE GADARENES.

As he was entering into the boat, he that had been possessed with demons besought him that he might be with him. And he suffered him not, but saith unto him, "Go to thy house unto thy friends, and tell them how great things the Lord hath done for thee, and how he had mercy on thee."
—MARK v. 18, 19.

CAN any one explain the reason and significance of the varying instructions which our Lord gave to those whom he had healed, and to his disciples generally, on the subject of making known his works and his character? They are a perplexity to me. In some cases I can understand the reason, for it is declared on the face of the record. In some other cases I can make a conjecture which satisfies me in part. And in some, it is difficult to make even a satisfactory guess. On the whole, the matter is a puzzle. I wish you would examine it and see what light you can get upon it.

It is not difficult to understand his silencing the unclean spirits whom he cast out, with a rebuke, forbidding them to say that they knew him, or to testify that he was the Christ (Mark i. 34). He wanted no dealings with the kingdom of Satan except as an enemy, and would give no excuse for the blasphemers who declared that he cast out demons by Beelzebub their prince. Therefore he abhorred and repudiated all such endorsements, as Paul and Silas did afterward when the Pythoness at Philippi followed them day after day, crying, "These men are the servants of the most high God, which show unto us the way of salvation!"

Then there are certain cases in which the injunction not to

report a certain miracle seems to be closely connected with the account of dangerous plots against the life of the Lord, as in the third chapter of Mark and the twelfth chapter of Matthew, as if it was simply a just precaution for personal safety. And in this latter passage (Matt. xii.) there is that striking quotation from Isaiah—" he healed them all; and charged them that they should not make him known; that it might be fulfilled which was spoken by Isaiah the prophet: . . . . 'he shall not strive nor cry, neither shall any man hear his voice in the streets;' "—as if this was an expression of that calmness, meekness, absence of egotism or ambition which marked the mind which was in Jesus Christ.

Then there was the command to the three disciples, as they came down from the mount of transfiguration, that they should "tell the vision to no man, until the Son of man should be risen from the dead"; and that more impressive injunction, following upon the solemn declaration of Peter, Thou art the Christ, the Son of the Living God, in which he "straitly charged them that they should tell no man that he was Jesus, the Christ." Perhaps this, too, had something to do with those growing conspiracies against his life which he forewarned them, at that very time, were soon to be successful. But I cannot help the impression that it was part of the settled method of his mission that men should see his works and life, and form their own conclusions as to his person, rather than to have the proposition *Jesus is the Christ* put before them in the first place, and then miracles and gracious words quoted to prove it. This seems to have been the spirit of his answer to the messengers of John the Baptist when they brought the question, Art thou He that should come? He answered them never a word; but told them to look and see, and then go and tell John and let him judge for himself. And it would really seem, to-day, that if that was the thought of our Lord, the Church has at last, after eighteen hundred years of contrary practice—teaching a dogma about Christ and then citing his life to prove it—gone back to its

156 THE SIMPLICITY THAT IS IN CHRIST.

Master's own method, and given all its powers to the telling and illustrating of the facts of his life. Observe how very rarely the Saviour volunteered to tell any one that he was the Christ. He told the Samaritan woman; he told one poor excommunicated blind man; whom else did he tell it to, except in answer to question?

But how do you explain his charge to the two blind men in Galilee, when he had healed them—to "see that no man should know it"? or that command to the household of Jairus the centurion, after the raising of his daughter,—in almost the same terms? But mainly, how do you explain that such injunctions were his *general custom* so far as he gave any directions at all to those whom he had healed of their diseases?

This story of the man from whom he cast out the legion of demons is really, so far as I have found, the one solitary exception to this custom. Other men, filled with a grateful and inexpressible longing to tell of the Lord's miraculous mercy toward them, he strictly charges to be quiet and let no man know about it. In this only instance, one who is beseeching to be allowed to get into the little boat just pushing from the shore, that he may be near his Lord and Saviour and follow him meekly and silently as a learner, is repelled and sent away with the command to go on a mission and preach the story of his marvelous cure among his kindred and to his father's house! Can you tell me the reason why the rest should be forbidden to tell of the loving-kindness of the Lord, and why this man should be forbidden to do anything else?

Why is it all? There are a dozen charges to conceal the gospel, to one charge to proclaim it; and yet I have heard this one text exhorted and preached upon a score of times, to where I have heard the others once,—if even they are ever preached upon at all. I leave the question for your own meditation and study; and now, in the moments that remain, let us study this solitary case by itself for our own instruction.

Take the scene once more into mind. It is changed since

THE APOSTLE TO THE GADARENES. 157

last we looked upon it. First, we saw the strange meeting between the great Healer, and the fierce demoniac who rushed down to encounter him as he neared the shore. Then we had sketched before us the group on the hillside—the Healer of sicknesses and Caster-out of demons standing in the midst with his disciples; at his feet, sitting as a learner, clothed and in his right mind, looking up with wondering awe, and calm, peaceful gratitude, at his Deliverer's face, the frantic creature of a few hours before, whose hideous cries and feats of desperate madness had been the horror of the whole country; and the crowd that had rushed out from the towns of that densely-peopled region and were standing terrified yet angry, beseeching Jesus to leave their borders. And this group has now broken up. There, away up the hillside, the angry crowd are lingering yet. They have carried their point, and the Saviour whom they have rejected has turned to leave them;—it is so easy to be rid of Jesus if you will. Downward he goes in sorrow to the beach where the little shallop lies rocking in the sands, and timidly in the rear comes this new disciple with only one humble petition—" that he might be with him."

Among the greatest wonders of Christian art are to be reckoned the things it has *not* done nor attempted—the incomparable subjects it has neglected. Who, for example, ever saw a picture of the young man with great possessions going away sorrowful, followed by that pitying look of tenderness and yet of disappointment, on the face of the Saviour who "looking upon him loved him"? And what painter has ever attempted to set before us this scene of true human interest—the man dispossessed of the demons rushing down into the water as the little boat is pushing off, begging them to put back for him, that he may be with Jesus; and the Healer standing up and looking back with face so full of tenderness, but with inexorably forbidding word and gesture, saying, "Nay, not so; but go to thy friends and thy father's house, and tell them how great things the Lord hath done for thee and how he had mercy on thee." And I seem to read upon the features so lately distorted with demoniac passion the bewildered wonder of his disappointment, as the boat recedes from his vainly outstretched hands, and the dear face of Jesus fades into the distance, and he stands there, deserted of the Saviour, and so lonely! How strange a thing it is! Here the Great Teacher goes about the land bidding men leave all and follow him, and stretches forth his hands to a gainsaying people that make light of his call and go their way, some to their farms and some to their merchandise; but now there comes to him one who would fain be his follower, and him he casts away from his presence, and escapes to the other side of the sea. So many he has charged to hold their peace and tell no man of his wonderful works of mercy; and here is one who asks nothing better than to follow him everywhere, and gaze in grateful silence on the face of his Benefactor,—and this one he bids go back to his friends and publish abroad the story of his deliverance! These are strange doings on the part of Christ— perplexing things. They do not seem to be natural, according to the ordinary courses of human conduct. They are not like the way men act in like circumstances. *What are they like?* Ah, my dear friends, these strange acts of Jesus Christ—unaccountable, perplexing, bewildering—are they not marvelously like the acts of God—his strange acts, and like his work—his strange work? If Jesus never did anything that troubled us to understand, and worried us, and drove us, at last, to the sheer act of trust that it must needs be right since *he* did it— how unlike he would be to the Father!

But just here things do look perplexing enough to this poor man! "Go home to thy friends!" "But, Lord, I have no friend but thee. I have been an outcast now these many years,—a dweller in unclean sepulchres, abhorred of men. What have men done for me but bind me in chains and fetters of iron? But 'thy hand hath loosed my bonds of pain, and bound me with thy love!' Let me be with thee where thou art!" But still from that most gracious One comes still the inexorable, "Go back—back to thy friends and thy father's house—go tell them what the Lord hath done for thee!" "What? I, Lord?—I, so disused to rational speech? whose lips and tongue were but now the organs of demoniac blasphemy?—I, just rallying from the rending of the exorcised fiends? I, surrounded by a hostile people that have just warned away my Lord and Saviour from their coasts?—And can I hope that they will hear my words, who turn a deaf and rebellious ear to thee? Nay, Lord, I entreat thee let me be with thee, there sitting at thy feet clothed and in my right mind, that men may look and point at me and glorify my Lord, my Saviour! Let *them* go, whose zeal to tell of thee even thy interdict cannot repress,—there be many such—send them! But let me be near thee, be with thee, and gaze, and love, and be silent, and adore!"

Was ever a stronger argument of prayer? And yet the little boat moves off, and Christ departs, and the grateful believer is left alone to do the work for which he seems so insufficient and unfit! How like Christ's dealing is to his Father's!

To translate the story into the terms of our daily life, it shows us,

1. That the path of duty which Christ has marked out for us may be the opposite of that which we naturally think, and ardently desire. All our natural aptitudes, as we estimate them—all our tastes and preferences, yes, our purest and highest religious aspirations, may draw us toward a certain line of conduct, while on the other hand the manifest indications of God's word and providence inexorably close up that way and wave us off in another direction.

A noble and unselfish impulse, a sacred ambition, may stir you to join yourself to the company of Christian ministers, and it looks like a duty so high as to be paramount to every other. But there thrusts itself in the way some petty but importunate call of humble and private duty, some obligation to kindred or a father's house, which, with eye fixed on the hope of great and signal usefulness, you try to push aside as a temptation of the devil; but it will not be thrust aside. You say to yourself that a man must be willing to leave father and mother and children and business for the gospel's sake—but God finds some way of admonishing you that a man must also be willing to stay by them for the gospel's sake, when he is called thereto, and answers the fine texts with which you try to excuse yourself from humble and irksome duty, with other texts,—how he that provideth not for his own household is worse than an infidel,—and how he makes void the law of God who says to his father or mother *Corban*—I have consecrated to religious uses the time and labor that might have gone to your support;—and so God shuts up your favorite path of service and makes plain before your feet a very humble and obscure little by-way for you to walk in.

There is many a man with a ready facility of speech, and an enthusiasm burning to utter itself, never so happy as when he is overflowing with earnest talk, who is overwhelmed and bewildered with uttermost perplexity when God clearly says to him, by some providence, "See thou tell no man!" What can it mean, that God should put to silence such gifts as his! But God knows his gifts better than the man does. There is many a man who supposes that his gift is to talk, who has really a splendid gift for holding his tongue, if only he would cultivate it.

There is often, doubtless, a Christian woman who frets at the barriers that nature and society have jointly put in the way of her wide, public usefulness, and turns back to the dull routine of housework and nursery-work, and takes up again the daily task that never seems any nearer to be finished, conscious of faculties that get no play in these occupations, and tempted to complain that God has given her no scope for the exercise of her best gifts. Gifts? What do you reckon among the best spiritual gifts? A gift for self-denying patience in steady work; a gift for discerning what is exactly right and

THE APOSTLE TO THE GADARENES. 161

detecting what is just a little wrong, and for going straight forward, without any words about it, to do the right and to refuse the not exactly right; a gift for keeping a sweet and serene temper in the midst of vexing and irritating trials—are there any diviner gifts than these? Covet earnestly the best gifts. The most excellent gift is charity.

On the other hand, there is many a man who shrinks from the task of public discourse—a man slow of speech, hesitating of utterance, of shrinking temperament, who says to himself: "My manifest calling is to serve God in some inconspicuous way, glorifying him by near and secret communion, but not hoping for any wide success or influence,"—many such an one, whom nevertheless God draws out from his seclusion as he did Moses, and gives him no time for his congenial meditation and retirement, but drives him into the very courses of public service from which he shrinks as being incapable. And how often it happens that this reluctant helper, so inwardly conscious of his incompetency, coming to his work with painstaking study and preparation, and with trembling dependence on the help of God, is found to be the very man for the place in which the facile and self-confident had failed!

2. It is a mere truism, but it is well to enunciate it in view of the illustration of the text—that when religious privilege and religious duty seem to conflict, the duty is to be preferred above the privilege.

It would seem as if the case of this nameless lunatic of Decapolis had been set before us here as an *a fortiori* case for all generations to the end of time. Who of us can ever say of himself that he is called to a more discouraging, a more hopeless duty? What one of us can ever be called to surrender that supreme religious privilege—the personal, visible companionship, the personal, audible teaching of Jesus the Lord? And if *he* might not choose, but must needs go away, untaught, untrained, to be alone from his Saviour, and be himself a teacher of others, can there ever be imagined a case between duty and privilege when you or I should be at liberty to hesitate? His longing to be with the Lord was like that of Peter when he heard the voice from out the excellent brightness, and beheld the vision of the glorified prophets in the holy mount. "Lord," he cried, "it is good to be here! Let us build us tabernacles and abide!" But he wist not what he said.

3. This is the final and manifest lesson of our story,—that duty, preferred and followed instead of privilege, becomes itself the supreme privilege.

You are right, in choosing a place of residence, to pay the gravest consideration to the question what will be for the best spiritual advantage of yourself and your family—what opportunities you and they will have for mental improvement, for the society of good men and women and children, for instruction in righteousness, and for the public worship of God in his Church. Would you have the right, for any light motive such as your betterment in business, to uproot your household from the midst of the beauty and glory of a Christian civilization and plant them in a community without schools, without Christian society, without Sabbaths, without churches, without the word of God? Would you not say "No! the interests of the soul are supreme. What will it profit them or me if we gain the whole world and lose our own souls"? And yet this is what the missionary does,—sacrificing the love of father and mother, of wife and children, and of native land, yea, and his own soul also, for the kingdom of Christ and his righteousness,— and receives his reward an hundred-fold in this present life— kindred and family, and houses and lands, an hundred-fold in spiritual blessings on his own soul, and in the world to come life everlasting. No! the interests of the soul are very great, but they are *not* supreme. And if they were supreme, they are not to be gained by running after them, but by letting them go. The supreme interests are those of the kingdom of God and his righteousness; and whoso, forgetting the interests of his own soul, shall follow after these, shall surely find that all

THE APOSTLE TO THE GADARENES. 163

things beside are added unto him. For he that will seek his own soul shall lose it; and he that will lose his soul for Christ's sake and the gospel's, the same shall find it.

See, now, as the illustration of this final lesson, to what honor came this nameless man at last. Having given up the infinite delight of the personal companionship of Jesus, behold him now promoted to this dignity, that he should be the first in the kingdom of heaven. The trained disciples, that had left all to follow the Lord, are passed over, and this highest honor, that he should be the first commissioned preacher of the gospel, is given to him who left the Lord himself, at his command, to do the Lord's work. And no man knoweth his name unto this day. But in the resurrection those unknown syllables shall be spoken again with "Well done, good and faithful servant," and shall shine above those of prophets and apostles, like the sun, and like the brightness of the firmament, forever and ever.

XV.

THE SIGN OF THE SWADDLING-CLOTHES.

A CHRISTMAS SERMON.

This shall be a sign unto you; Ye shall find the babe wrapped in swaddling-clothes.—LUKE ii. 12.

IT is safe to say that when the gospels were translated in our venerable version, it did not occur to any of the translators that this word *swaddling-clothes* would ever be an obsolete word, needing to be illustrated by a description of ancient or foreign customs. And yet so it is at this day. The usage which is alluded to in this word is to our American minds entirely strange. Few things among the old-world customs, I venture to say, strike some of us as more outlandish—more pitiable even—more entirely removed from our notions of good care and right training,—than the swaddling of little helpless babies, as it is practised, for instance, in Germany. I do not believe an American mother can generally pass one of those poor little *Wickelkinder*, strapped down on its back to a pillow by spiral after spiral of convoluted bandages, without longing to apply the scissors and let the little prisoner go free. And yet it is only a few generations since this way of treating new-born children prevailed, with variations and aggravations, in all nations, even the most civilized. We owe our own emancipation, in this land and century, from this and other artificial traditions, to no other single influence so much as to a remarkable book published in the middle of the last century by a citizen of Geneva—I mean, of course, the *Emile* of Jean Jacques Rousseau. It speaks thus of the universally prevalent treatment of an infant child as it had continued to his day: "Scarcely does the child begin to enjoy the liberty of moving and stretching its limbs, when it is placed anew in confinement. It is wound in swaddling-clothes, and laid down with its head fixed, its legs extended, its arms at its sides. It is surrounded with cloths and bandages of all sorts that prevent it from changing its position. It is a good thing if they do not even draw the bands so tight as to hinder respiration, and if they have the foresight to lay it on its side to avoid the danger of strangulation. . . . The inaction and constraint in which the child's limbs are confined must necessarily disturb the circulation, hinder the child from gaining strength, and affect its constitution. . . . Is it possible that such cruel constraint can fail to affect the character of the child, as well as its physical temperament? Its first conscious feeling is a feeling of pain and suffering. It finds nothing but hindrances to the motions which it craves. More wretched than a criminal in irons, it frets and cries. The first gifts it receives are fetters; the first treatment it experiences is torture."

Such was the practice of a hundred years ago in the highest families of the most civilized country in the world. In many lands, partly owing to this very protest, the practice is better now. But in the slow-going East the common practice of the nursery is no better, and it is probably no worse, than it was nineteen hundred years ago. But it is worse than anything we ever see or hear of in this part of the world. In fact, it comes nearer to the binding of an Indian papoose to a board, than to anything that we are accustomed to see in the families of Christendom. Once wound around with these swathing-bands, sometimes with an addition of fresh earth against the skin, and packed in their cradles like a little mummy in its coffin, the poor little babies are expected to stay there, all cries and complaints notwithstanding; they are not removed by their mothers even for such necessary occasions as to be fed. I have heard pitiful stories told by missionaries' wives and by missionary physicians, in the East, of the sufferings of little infants in consequence of the obstinate persistence of parents in a usage which we clearly see to be so unreasonable and unnatural.

It is obvious from the matter-of-course way in which the thing is mentioned, that when the virgin mother of the holy child, having brought forth her first-born son, swathed him in swaddling-bands, she was only following the ordinary tradition of the country. She did the best that she knew.

But now, you will ask, is it not strange that when the shepherds were given a sign by which they should know their newborn Saviour, their Lord and Christ, they should be told, not of something distinguishing him from all children beside, but of something common to all the infants that were born that night in all Judea? "Ye shall find him wrapped in swaddling-clothes." Why not say, according to the instincts of heathen mythology, Ye shall know him by the bees that gather to suck the honey of his lips, or the strangled serpents that lie about his cradle? Why not say, according to the suggestions of Christian legend and art, Ye shall know him by the aspect of supernatural majesty which it shall be the dream and the disappointment of all the world's artists to attempt to portray? Or, Ye shall know him by the halo of celestial light beaming from his brow, as in the *Holy Night* of Correggio, and filling the rude stall with an unearthly brightness? Or, Ye shall know him by some accessories worthy of so royal a birth, by gifts of gold and myrrh and frankincense that strew the humble shed? The very question brings its answer: You are to know him from all these natural dreams of a fond imagination, from the hopeful prognostications of pious Hebrew mothers, or the impatient fancies of fanatics, or the artful fictions of impostors taking advantage of the general expectation with which the very atmosphere of Palestine was saturated, to set forth some feigned Messiah—you are to know him from all these by the fact that he is just the opposite of all such imaginings—that he is to all appearance just a helpless human infant, the most helpless thing in the whole creation, bound and bandaged in swaddling-clothes. And if you would know how to distinguish him from other such, it is not by his grandeur but by his poverty. There is no room in the inn for such as he; and they have laid him in the manger, among the cattle.

To illustrate the use of such a sign as was given to the shepherds, let me suppose some traveler accustomed to the splendor and reserve of royal courts visiting the city of Washington, and asking on his way to the White House how he should find the President. We should tell him you may know him by this sign: He is a plain man, plainly dressed in a black suit, and you will find him in the centre of the thickest crowd, and everybody coming up to shake hands with him. First, he is not distinguished in the way you expect him to be, and secondly he is unmistakably distinguished in just the opposite way. But for some such "sign" as this our traveler might naturally mistake for the President some attaché of a South American embassy standing apart in a halo of dignity and a light blaze of gold lace. This "wrapped in swaddling-clothes and lying in a manger" was just the sign the shepherds needed. And we do well, if, looking for the Christ, we take heed to it ourselves. We are not yet safe from the error of them of old time, who thought to find the Lord clothed in soft raiment and dwelling in king's palaces.

"She wrapped him in swaddling-clothes." We accept the unconscious testimony of the evangelist against all those unbelieving theories concerning the person of our Lord and Christ which explain the mystery of his character and person on purely rational and natural grounds. "His mind was by nature of an exceptionally noble type" (so these theories run), "and being placed in circumstances of singular advantage, in a simple and natural state of society, the whole atmosphere of which was redolent with inspiring hopes of a coming Messiah and his salvation, in a family in which the traditions of royal descent were a constant living influence, and under a rare and perfect nurture under which all his faculties would have free play and exercise, it is no wonder that he should have developed into the consummate Man of men. Amid the artificial and sophisticated civilization of Rome or Athens, shut in by the narrow bigotries of Jerusalem, such a character would have been impossible. It needed the pastoral simplicity of that Galilean Arcadia, the peaceful seclusion of quiet little Nazareth, and above all, the wise, religious and normal influences of the natural home training of that remarkable family of Joseph and Mary, to produce the character of a Jesus." Thus the unbeliever ; and, at the other extreme, it is curious to see how the exaggerations of the medieval system lend themselves to the same view—ascribing divine perfections to the Virgin Mother, elevating Joseph to be " the third member of the earthly Trinity," and so surrounding the infancy and childhood of Jesus with supposititious miracles, as to make of the crowning miracle of his life and character almost no miracle at all. This is a striking instance, and one out of many, showing how the systems of unbelief and of exaggerated credulity play into each other's hands.

Now in vindication of the personal glory of Jesus, " the glory as of the only-begotten of the Father, full of grace and truth," I set over against all these unscriptural and anti-scriptural notions that represent him as cast from his birth into the lap of an exceptional, a natural and normal, even a miraculous and divine nurture,—I set, as an illustration of the actual, historic fact, this simple and, as one might say, unconscious testimony of Luke, " she wrapped him in swaddling-clothes ; " and I will show how the constraints of artificial training that were imposed upon the Holy Child in the hour of his birth, to make him like the rest of his generation and unlike himself, continued to surround him to his death ; so that he was not in any sense (as our modern dreamers dream so fondly) the product of his age, but its antithesis. He was what he was in spite of his age, not because of it. And having tasted continually, through his long life of grief, the bitterness of this protracted struggle against all the adverse currents of a corrupted world, and having triumphed against them all in dying, he invites us to drink of the same cup, and be baptized with the same baptism, as well as to sit down with him in the same kingdom.

And now observe to what extent this hampering of the body that was imposed upon "the heavenly Child" by a world which even in its tenderest kind intentions was utterly incapable of receiving its infant Lord, was a type of the limitations which beset him round from year to year.

1. First, there was the narrowness and ignorance of the most notoriously obscure—the most proverbially and almost illustriously insignificant—of all the petty out-of-the-way villages in Galilee. It was a little hamlet, wedged between the hills near Tabor, lying off to one side of all important thoroughfares. Probably modern Christendom can furnish no parallel to the inertness of life in such a village. A country hamlet in America, far removed from city and railroad, from shops and factories, seems to us to lead a somewhat irksome life of dull routine and narrow prejudice and domineering public opinion. But such a town in the atmosphere of America and of the Nineteenth Century, is largeness and liberty and variety itself, compared with a French or German country parish. And yet into the dullest of these consider to what an extent the breath of modern Christendom is breathed, with its daily mails and newspapers, its school and church, its educated minister, and its library. Imagine it with the most of these civilizing and animating influences withdrawn, and you have Nazareth. And do not think, carelessly, that in the prevailing listlessness, there would be naturally a greater liberty of thinking to one who should take it into his head to do anything of the sort. On the contrary, as we all know, there is no social tyranny so oppressive and domineering over individual liberty as that of the public opinion or prejudice of the

pettiest and most ignorant communities. What might be expected to come forth from Nazareth was well expressed in the question of Nathanael; and in the general feeling that the various prophecies that the promised Messiah was to be of the lowliest and unlikeliest antecedents, were all fulfilled in the fact that Jesus was "called a Nazarene." And yet in spite of these swaddling-bands, "the child grew, and waxed strong in spirit, filled with wisdom; and the grace of God was upon him."

2. There might seem to be prospect of emancipation from these hindering limitations, when at the age of twelve he passes the confines of the lonely village, and goes with the multitude that keep holy day up to the city of his father David. His place—so he told those who had sought him sorrowing—was there at his Father's house. And truly there were great men sitting there in the temple cloisters, whose wise words have come down to us in the dark, square, backward-written characters of many a Hebrew volume of traditions of the elders. What a longed-for opportunity it must have been to the Holy Child, full of wisdom and the grace of God, to escape from the circumscribed wisdom of the village elders, and listen at Jerusalem to those who sat in Moses' seat! But alas, the rigid narrowness, the fatal clinging to the letter, the fear to teach what was right and true and confessedly divine except it could be justified by some commentator upon a commentator! We are accustomed to speak of the books of casuistry taught in Roman Catholic seminaries as cramping and enfeebling to the mind; and so they are. But they are vigor and liberty itself compared with the traditions of these Hebrew elders. By his visits to the temple the growing boy learned, not what to imitate, but what to hate and shun, and by and by to denounce as the making void of his Father's law, in those days of solemn teaching when the multitude wondered at him because he "spake as one having authority, and not as the scribes."

3. I truly think that the Son of man found more congenial

fellowship, after all, when he came back to the village synagogue, than ever he found in his Father's house that had been turned into a den of thieves. At least he had escaped from under the shadow of that overbearing hierarchy which always oppressed him at Jerusalem. There might be prejudice at Nazareth, and narrowness, and the constraint which village public opinion always attempts to force upon the individual. But the synagogue, the type of the church, was a singularly free republic. The sole supreme authority was that written upon the scrolls of the law and enthroned behind the curtains of the little sanctuary. It was natural that the youth who was beloved throughout the neighborhood " growing in favor with man," should come (as it appears) to be the designated reader in the Nazareth synagogue. There, as afterward in the marble synagogue built by Gentile generosity for the congregation at Capernaum, he added his " word of exhortation " to the words of Moses and the prophets. But "his own received him not." At Capernaum they murmured at him. At Nazareth they sought his life.

4. If anywhere the Son of man could escape the hampering limitations which the society of that age and land imposed upon him, it would be in the select society of those whom he had "chosen out of the world" to receive the kingdom of heaven. According to the famous maxim of Cicero, "the orator is what his audience makes him." And it is a true maxim. If the orator creates the assembly, it is also true that the listening assembly makes the orator. Think of it, and lay it well to heart, my brethren, that you, by your thoughtful, intelligent attention, may add such force and inspiration to the preaching of the gospel as that other hearts shall be the more deeply reached and stirred.—Here, then, peradventure, may we not find some of the natural causes of the wonderful life and speech of Jesus Christ? Such listeners as Matthew, and John, and Peter—how much had they, not juniors but coevals or even seniors of the young Rabbi, to do with the develop-

ment of his great teachings? Now we cannot disguise the comparative greatness of these men. It is a striking argument in the evidences of Christianity to remark the sudden falling-off when we pass from the books of the canonical Scriptures to the writings of Polycarp and Hermas and even Clement. But the contrast between the first disciples and their successors is nothing compared to the contrast between them and their Master. The comfort and enlargement of mind which the Great Teacher could find, even in the selectest company of his disciples, was like that which some great dramatic poet may have when he delivers his verses to the actors and hears them mangled and murdered, all the tenderness and fineness of their meaning lost through coarse misappreciation; or such as the composer may have, when the harmonies that have sung themselves to him from the vocal page in the silence of his cabinet are turned to jangle and discord by the unskilled performers. He told them of the kingdom of heaven; and they began to scramble for the offices. He spoke of subduing the world by love; and they were ready to smite with the sword and imprecate fire from heaven. He told of the sufferings that must be, and they took him in hand to rebuke him.

And now behold him, so pent in by limiting and belittling influences from his rude cradle upward, as he grows in stature and in wisdom, and in favor with God and man. See, he looses himself alike from the swaddling-bands with which human affection, from the thongs with which human hate, have bound him. He takes off the grave-clothes in which he has been wrapped, and emerges from the sepulchre of a dead age and a dead church. And how majestic, and how solitary! Alone! Nay not alone, for the Father is with him.

The sign that was given to the shepherds is a sign also to us—that we find the Holy Child wrapped in swaddling-clothes Illustrious men have sometimes had an honest pride in inscribing upon their escutcheon, beneath a noble crest, the symbol of the humble mechanic rank in which they had their origin. So the Church of Christ, beneath the diadem of supreme royalty, quarters upon its shield, beside the cross and the thongs, the manger and the swaddling-bands, and invites the world to read the blazon. That family group which the painters of every later age have been essaying to depict,—the carpenter with his simple, uninquisitive faith obedient to heavenly visions, the pure Virgin with her unskilled maiden tenderness pondering strange memories in her heart, both leaning over the Wonderful, but understanding not the saying which he speaks to them,—these speak over again to us the language of that prophet who first called his child *Immanuel*, " Behold we and the Child whom the Lord hath given us are for signs and for wonders from the Lord of hosts."

XVI.

THE CHILDREN IN THE TEMPLE.

A PALM-SUNDAY SERMON—TO CHILDREN.

And the multitudes that went before him, and that followed, cried, saying, "Hosanna to the Son of David: Blessed is he that cometh in the name of the Lord: Hosanna in the highest."—MATT. xxi. 9.

As I looked out into the evening sky, a week ago, and saw the slender little new moon following the sun down into the west, I thought to myself, There it is, once more,—the passover moon. When this moon is full, will be the time when, all the world over, the Jews will be making ready to eat the passover, and the time of the passover is the time when Christ our Lord was crucified. When the passover-moon was new, our dear Lord was getting ready to go up to Jerusalem where he was to suffer. And next Sunday (so I said to myself) will be the anniversary of that first day of the week, eighteen hundred and fifty years ago, when Jesus Christ arrived at Jerusalem, and made his entrance into the city with the multitudes and the palm-branches, and the children crying Hosanna in the temple. Of all the Sundays in the year, it is the children's Sunday. We must bring the children into the temple, that they may sing their Hosanna to the Son of David, who cometh in the name of the Lord.

That was the strangest procession in the history of the world. It was a great multitude that fell into line behind Jesus and his disciples all the way from Jericho, up the steep, narrow, rocky road, shut in by great cliffs on each side, that leads to Jerusalem. And of all that great crowd, we do not certainly know but two persons—two blind beggars whom the Lord had just healed near the gate of Jericho, and who at once had come into the procession and "followed Jesus in the way." But knowing who these were, we may naturally enough guess who some of the rest were. It would be strange if in that great company on their way to Jerusalem for the feast, there were not many of the five thousand, and of the four thousand, who had been fed by the Lord when they were hungry and fainting in desert places in Galilee, not many months before. In such a crowd from beyond Jordan and from both shores of the little lake, there would surely be some of the palsied and lame who had been brought to him through all these years, and had been made to "leap like a hart" at the sound of his gracious voice. Among those that flocked about him to see "the King in his beauty" must have been some of those whose eyes he had unsealed from midnight blindness; and among the voices that broke out in Hosannas till the wilderness and the solitary place were glad with joy and singing, there would not fail to be some which the touch of his healing finger had loosed from dumbness during those three years of doing good which were now drawing to a close. I can almost see that great, glad multitude that had come down the green Jordan valley, making everything gay with their pilgrim psalms and their bright holiday garments, as they make the sharp turn at Jericho, to climb through the steep ravine toward Jerusalem. I should look among them to see if I could recognize the form and face, once so fierce and dreadful, but now radiant with serene peace and love, of one who had once been an outcast, dwelling in tombs, possessed of unclean spirits. Somewhere, close beside the Lord, I should expect to find a widow from the little town of Nain, leaning on the arm of that only son whom the Lord had given back to her from his bier. Do you think that the good centurion and the servant whom he loved, would be far away? And would not the crowd make way to give a near place by the

Master to Jairus, the ruler of the synagogue, and his little girl? We are not distinctly told that any of these were there; but we know that the crowd was full of those who had memories like these, for they were shouting and singing praise to God for the wonderful—"the wonderful things which they had seen."

Toward the end of the hard day's walk, just as they come to the last steep climb, the road passes two little villages, one of which, Bethphage, has quite disappeared, so that we cannot find any trace of it; but Bethany, where Martha and Mary and Lazarus lived, is still there on the mountain side. Here they find a young ass, and place Jesus on it, and lead him along with shouts, as if it were a king's triumphal march to his capital. There were plenty to sneer, no doubt, and say, "Not much like a king—poor, tired-looking, dusty, travel-worn man, plodding along on this homely little beast!" But oh, what king or conqueror ever had such a retinue, or brought such captives in his train?

And now the procession comes to that wonderful point—how well I remember it!—where the road from Jericho turns the shoulder of the Mount of Olives, and all at once the ancient city, gloriously enthroned upon her triple hill and crowned with her diadem of walls, emerges upon the view. It is a fair sight to-day, but far more glorious then, when the Temple of God, roofed with gold, threw back the sunlight from its pinnacles! And as they halt here for awhile, the crowds from the city begin to pour forth and up the mount to meet them and escort them in. This made two great choruses—"the multitude going before and the multitude following after"— and hark! now, as they move on, strewing the road with garments and palm-branches,—hark! they are going to sing. The two multitudes toss back and forth the responses of the psalm to each other, "Hosanna—Save now—Blessed be he that cometh in the name of the Lord." It was a part of the great passover psalm, the one hundred and eighteenth, that they

THE CHILDREN IN THE TEMPLE. 177

were singing. I have read from it to you this morning. Read it again, at home, and see how fit it was—how full of prophecy. Our Lord loved it. It was daily on his lips through all this week of anguish. It was the last song of the little company at the Holy Supper, before they went out again into this Mount of Olives, in that night in which he was betrayed. Think what it must have been to them all, as they shouted it amid the waving palm-branches, and made the dark valley of the Kedron, and the recesses of Gethsemane, and the steep of Moriah to echo with its Hosannas! So they came up, at last, to the temple-gate—the "gate of the Lord into which the righteous should enter,"—and the King of glory entered in.

And now it was that the children came in, in crowds; and they caught up the same chorus that the rest were singing, and took it with a great shout, "Hosanna to the Son of David." I suppose that children in Jerusalem were much like children in Philadelphia, in this, that they were glad when a friend came back amongst them. And Jesus *was* their friend. No child ever seemed afraid of him. He never drove away a child that wanted to speak with him. His disciples wanted once to drive them away, and he said, "No! forbid them not! suffer them to come! of such is the kingdom of heaven." And now the great men about the temple complained to him of the children's coming in and singing Hosanna; and he answered, "Let them sing! What does the Psalm say?—'Out of the mouth of babes and sucklings thou hast perfected praise.'" I wonder whether he did not think, at this moment, of that time, twenty years before, when he had been brought for the first time, a little boy of twelve, to this house of God his Father. At any rate, he who had always preached to grown-up and educated men that their way into the kingdom of heaven was to become like little children, was not the one to rebuke the children who were only claiming that he was their king too, and trying to sing their Hosanna with the rest. But he did sharply rebuke those that were jealous of the children and wanted to stop their singing; and he made it to be understood, from that day to this, that wherever he had a church, there was room in it for every little child to sing his praise and pray to him with all the rest. This is so like Christ, and so unlike the world in general, to declare that being ignorant, and weak, and of very little consequence, is no reason to hinder God's tender love, or to stand in the way of Christ's salvation. I have heard people, often enough, protesting against the folly of trying to give the joy and hope and comfort of the gospel to very feeble-minded folk, to very light and superficial minds, to very degraded and ignorant races,—of trying, in fact, to seek and save that which is lost. Some people never can get over thinking that Christ's chief delight ought to be in very superior people, educated and refined,—in the best nations and races. It is by laying this gospel well to heart that you will get the better of this foolish and wicked pride, and be content to confess your sin and need, and to sing with the rest of us out of this Hosanna Psalm, that THE LORD is your Strength and your Song, and that he also is become your Salvation. This was the song with which the old and young came trooping together into the temple, on that Palm Sunday, swinging their palm-branches, and shouting, "Hosanna! Save, Lord, we beseech thee."

Now let us all, old and young alike, beware of the foolish mistake of supposing that there is any virtue or merit in just being young. There is nothing in being ten or twelve years old which is in itself more acceptable to our Lord, than being fifty or sixty years old. Certainly he never thought of blaming us for growing up, and growing old and feeble. And he always taught that even very aged people could be like little children, and ought to be. Nothing in all the gospels is more truly childlike than what is told us of one of the splendid Roman army-officers, who trusted Christ so like a little child, and of whom it was said " I have not found so great faith, no, not in Israel." That little child, Samuel, when he called out in the dark, "Speak, Lord, for thy servant heareth," was not more childlike than venerable old Abraham when he answered, "Lord, here am I." Young Timothy, taught in the holy Scriptures at the knee of his mother and grandmother, was childlike just as "Paul the aged" was, when he wrote to Timothy, "I am ready to be offered." The childlike virtues are loveliest when we find them in the strong, the wise, the learned. The dear old man, who numbers his days and learns how frail he is, and gently leans upon the arm of his Father in heaven, and fears no evil, as he totters down into the dark valley, is just as dear and childlike a child as the little boy that simply honors and obeys and trusts his Father on earth.

And as a grown man may be like a little child, just so a little child may have grown sadly like an old man—having all the traits of mind from which the old man needs to be converted. A pitiful thing it is to see! My friend, Mr. Charles Brace, who has given his noble life to rescuing lost, outcast children in New York, tells of the *old* look that they wear—the lines of doubt, distrust, suspicion, drawn prematurely about the lips and eyes—the set, pinched expression of self-reliance, at an age when they ought not to be relf-reliant, but happily, trustfully reliant on the love and wise guidance of others—the air of self-importance and of knowing-it-all, as if nobody could teach them any thing, which makes them seem so unlovely to most people's eyes. We have sweetly childlike old people, and we may find unchildlike children, anywhere—suspicious children, that can't trust; wilful children that can't be taught; and self-conceited, self-important children whom people generally laugh at and sneer at, but whom they that have the mind of Christ tenderly pity, knowing through what tribulation and mortification they must pass, if they are ever to come into Christ's kingdom *like* little children. It is a question for every one of us,—how can we be as little children—in simple faith, in straightforward humility, in willingness to be helped and taught and forgiven and saved? How can we keep and cherish these traits of character? how can we recover them if we have lost them? how can we gain them if we never had them—these traits that are the glory of childhood and the greater glory of a Christian manhood and womanhood?

There are two more questions that will come up in some minds in connection with this story of the Palm Sunday; and when I have tried to answer these, my sermon will be done.

1. What became of this great multitude of shouting and singing followers of Christ during the awful week that followed? Ah! it is a sad question to ask. What did become of them? We do not seem to see much of them afterward, in any of these four gospels. There may have been some of them among the disciples that "followed afar off." Perhaps there were some of them scattered among the throng in the high-priest's palace; perhaps some were among the crowd before Pilate's house; but we don't hear of their crying Hosanna, then; I wonder if perhaps there were any who had already learned to shout, "Crucify him." I love to think that there may have been some who stood with the "daughters of Jerusalem" beside the way, and wept when they saw the Lord go by bearing his cross toward Golgotha. But we miss them just when we would like to hear more of them—these two great multitudes. And if you think this quite unaccountable, just ask yourself where would you be this week, if some such awful tragedy of persecution were to be enacted over again. Here we are singing Hosanna on Sunday, with the multitude. If persecution were to arise because of the word, and the multitude should begin to fall away and scatter, is it quite sure that we should still be following the Master close at hand?

2. How was it possible that one so beloved and honored by the people on the first day of the week, should be cried on to a cruel death by the clamor of the people, before the end of the week?

And for the answer to this question, also, we have only to look carefully at the plain story, as it is plainly told, and then

THE CHILDREN IN THE TEMPLE. 181

look into our own hearts. This awful deed of the crucifying of the dear and blessed Lord and Christ was wrought by common human motives, working in common human hearts; by common human sins, like yours and mine. Each day of this sad week bears witness against our hearts. This *Sunday* reproaches us with the instability of our friendships, the shallowness of our conviction, the transiency of our devotion. The *Monday* will tell us, in the story of the cleansing of the temple, how the selfishness of common everyday interests was enlisted against the Lord. The *Tuesday*, with its sharp debates in the temple cloister, will tell how the acrimony of theological hatred was added to the confederacy; on the *Wednesday*, while Jesus seems for a little while withdrawn from view, we see his own disciple Judas plotting with the priests—basely deserting a falling cause, as men will and do, and yet disguising his guilt to his own conscience; on the *Thursday* we see emerging into view, in the council of Caiaphas, that motive of the glory of God and the good of his cause, without which it would seem that the greatest crimes against humanity are never perpetrated; and when, at last, the weary dawn of the *Friday* breaks above the Mount of Olives, it needs only the very common, very human policy of Pilate, subordinating all duty to his allegiance to Cæsar and his purpose to be Cæsar's friend, and the very common, very human unreasoning rush of the crowd in the direction of the loudest shouters and the apparent majority, to achieve the crucifixion of the Lord of glory. There is nothing in it all, but plain common sins like yours and mine. O hateful sins, that have wrought this deed! Vile greed of gain; hateful sectarian emulation; base shrinking from the falling cause; unworthy faithlessness to God, that would do evil for God's sake; mean ambition; vulgar rushing with the multitude to do evil;—I know you all. I heard you whispering in the plot. I saw you following to the garden. I saw you smite with the bloody scourge, and buffet with the hand, and plait the thorny crown. I heard your blasphemies, your shouts of Crucify, your sentence, "Let him be crucified." I heard your driving of those cruel nails; and through the darkness the railing voices which I heard scoffing at the Sufferer were yours. O sins that slew my Lord, henceforth begone! O mind that was in Christ, be thou henceforth in me!

XVII.

THE PETITION OF CERTAIN GREEKS.
AN EASTER SERMON.

Now there were certain Greeks among those that went up to worship at the feast: these therefore came to Philip, which was of Bethsaida of Galilee, and asked him saying, Sir, we would see Jesus. Philip cometh and telleth Andrew: Andrew cometh, and Philip, and they tell Jesus. And Jesus answereth them saying, The hour is come, that the Son of Man should be glorified. [With the following verses.]—JOHN xii. 20-33.

THIS being, in some respects a difficult Scripture to intelligent readers (it presents no difficulty at all to the unintelligent) is presumptively a specially profitable Scripture to as many as shall come to understand it. For it is God's method in the difficulties of sacred Scripture, first to provoke and stimulate inquiry, and then splendidly to reward it.

The questions that arise on the first reading of this story are several: first, what is the importance of the incident, that it should be mentioned at all? secondly, why there should have been so much hesitation and consultation among the disciples over so simple a matter as this request of "certain Greeks?" thirdly, why it should be that after the request had been related with so much particularity, nothing is distinctly said of what came of it—whether it was granted or not? finally, what was there in this seemingly trifling incident, just mentioned by one evangelist and then dropped, not so much as mentioned by the other three, that should so have agitated the soul of the Son of man that he should almost be ready to say, "Father, save me from this hour"? What is the connection between the message of Philip and Andrew to their Master that certain Greek visitors to Jerusalem at the Passover wished to see him, and the answer that he made—"the hour is come; the Son of man is to be glorified—but only through death. This grain of wheat, if it be preserved, will be but sterile: it must fall into the ground and die, and then shall it bring forth much fruit"? If we would know these things, we must study deeply into the spirit of the four gospels, if by any means we may attain to the fellowship of Christ's sufferings.

The message of the Greeks came to the ear of our Lord just at that juncture in his ministry when he began to feel with its heaviest weight the meaning of those words of the prophet Isaiah, which he had been wont to read aloud in the synagogues of Nazareth and Capernaum—the words "despised and rejected of men." There had been days—the earlier days of his Galilean ministry—when all who heard him seemed ready to bow in homage before the words which he spake with such authority. In the presence of his mighty works of healing, the voice of selfish bigotry itself seemed to be stricken dumb, and the contradiction of sinners to be abashed and put to shame. Here at Jerusalem, amid the pride of learning of the scribes, and the pride of "place and nation" of the priests and rulers, it was different; but even here such crowds followed to gaze upon the man who had raised up Lazarus from the dead, that it was said among his enemies, "Behold, the whole world is gone after him." And yet, for all this, it is evident, even to an unprophetic eye, that he is rejected of his own nation. He has come to his own, and his own receive him not. For long months the bigoted Pharisee and the skeptical Sadducee, who never have agreed on anything before, have been working with one accord to entangle him in his talk, and embroil him either with one party or with the other. Scribes and priests and rulers have been dogging him from one retreat to another as spies upon his words and deeds. They have plotted murder in private. They have tried to provoke the

THE PETITION OF CERTAIN GREEKS. 185

mob to bloody violence in the temple court. Already they are beginning to draw the heathen governor into their plans, and to tamper with one of the twelve disciples with proposals of treachery. His near friends will not believe it when he tells them; but there is no illusion in his own mind. He knows the set, fanatic purpose of his enemies to take his life. And, notwithstanding many evidences of popular affection, he knows the circumstances that are combining to abet that purpose. How soon the bloody end of that lovely and blameless life shall come is evidently a question only of a few days. From amidst the incessant cavilings, disputes, intrigues, treasons, conspiracies with which all this part of the story is filled, two incidents, which come close together in the Gospel of John, stand out in delightful contrast with the rest. The first is that jubilant processional entrance into the city and temple with the palm-branches and hosannas of the multitude; and the other is this petition of "certain Greeks."

Looking carefully into the language of the story we find some slight but clear and unmistakable indications of what sort of people these Greeks were. The tense of the Greek verb used is significant: they were "among those who were *in the habit of coming* to the feast"—not chance-comers, passers-by on a journey, but habitual attendants at the Passover feast. And, secondly, they were not mere tourists, or sight-seers, such as doubtless did gather to witness that wonderful pageant, so unlike anything the world beside could show—a whole nation congregated to solemnize the memory of a divine deliverance; *these* Greeks were among those who were wont to come up to the feast, not to gaze but "to worship." These minute but distinct indications mark this group of inquirers after Jesus as representative men. They belonged to a class destined to fulfill a great and important part in the subsequent history of the kingdom of Christ—the class described again and again in the Acts of the Apostles under such titles as "devout Greeks," "devout persons," "they that feared God." The phrases are familiar to all attentive readers of the book of Acts, and you recognize how great was the part which this sort of people fulfilled in the spread of the Gospel to the ends of the earth. They were not converts to the Jews' religion, you understand. They never had received the sacrament of naturalization and adoption into the family of Abraham, nor acknowledged the obligation on them of the ordinances of the Mosaic law. Outwardly they were Gentiles still; but Gentiles who had seen the folly and falsehood of the heathen idolatries, and were seeking for something better. Such unrest and dissatisfaction with the "outworn creeds" of Paganism were felt throughout the Roman world. Some tried to rest in a general disbelief of all religion. Some tried to borrow a religion from Egypt or the East, and under the pressure of this demand the importing of foreign religions grew into a trade. [This was the ready explanation that occurred to some of the Athenian idlers as they listened to Paul and his "new doctrine" from the benches of the Areopagus—that "he seems to be one of those introducers of foreign divinities."] But in the midst of men's waverings and gropings, these "devout Greeks" had found what they were looking for in the Jews' synagogue. For already the Jews were wandering everywhere, and wherever a few families of them sojourned, there was the synagogue. Every seventh day they met to read in Moses and the prophets of the hope of Israel, and with them, not only the converts who had entered into the Hebrew citizenship, but neighbors and fellow-worshipers who knew no citizenship but that of Rome—men who, seeking thoughtfully from one school of philosophy to another the answer to the questions, What is happiness? What is virtue? What is the highest good?—had found, at last, in Moses and David, teachers greater than Plato or Aristotle. The synagogue meetings used to be full of these outsiders. The Jews had a name for them, calling them, not converts, for they were not such—calling them "proselytes of the gate," as if hinting that they did not get beyond the

THE PETITION OF CERTAIN GREEKS. 187

threshold.* Such an one was the devout centurion Cornelius at Cesarea; another such was the good centurion at Capernaum, who built the marble synagogue because he loved the Jewish people. They were very apt to be centurions or soldiers. Such were the "honorable women which were Greeks," whom Paul more than once found among his eager listeners in the synagogue. They were very apt to be women, revolted by the wickedness of heathen religions. Such were the multitudes at Antioch in Pisidia, who listened gladly to the Gospel, when the Jews blasphemed and contradicted, until Paul and Barnabas waxed bold and said to the Jews, "Seeing ye put from you the word of God, and judge yourselves unworthy of eternal life, lo, we turn to the Gentiles." Wherever the apostles went, it was the "devout Greeks" that were the open door by which the Gospel entered upon its triumphs in the Roman world. Neither was the preparation of the heathen mind for the Gospel limited to these half-proselytes. Through the heathen literature of this period, the scholar is startled every now and then to come upon thoughts that seem strangely Christian as we read—thoughts of a holier God, of a higher morality, of a larger humanity—they are the thoughts of men who are straining their eyes to find the light, and who already begin to get some glimpse of that true Light which lighteth every man that cometh into the world.

And alongside of this preparedness to receive the Gospel, which is discovered in the heathen mind of that age, is that marvelous providential preparation to dispense it, which is the admiration of all intelligent history. How often we say to each other, over the morning paper, "We live in a wonderful age!" The men of Paul's time and of Jesus' time lived in an age just

* Dr. Edersheim (*Jesus the Messiah*, vol ii., p. 390, note) gives a reason which is hardly conclusive, for reckoning the Greeks who sought to see Jesus, as "proselytes of righteousness" This view might be admitted without substantially weakening the argument of this discourse.

so wonderful. Then, as now, the world had been brought into one place. The multitude of wrangling principalities, whose perpetual warfare had kept the earth in turmoil, had blocked the paths of commerce, and had disturbed the retreats of philosophy and the sanctuaries of religion, have been suppressed and supplanted by a universal empire, which may plunder and oppress, but will suffer none beside to do it; the track of whose conquests is the pioneering of great highways of peaceful trade; and whose title of *Roman citizen* is a panoply and safeguard to its wearer to the ends of the earth. And with the universal empire has grown up the universal language of literature and thought and commerce—the Greek. On this incomparable language it seemed as if the providence of God had conferred a sort of Pentecostal gift, that by means of it men of the most widely different lands and religions might hear and know his wonderful works.

It is evident—more evident to us than it was to the men of that generation—that the world was ripe for some great change. The nations, an-hungered, were seated by fifties, and there was a hush as of expectation that One should break and bring to them the bread of life.

Bearing these great facts in mind, we turn back to the story of the request of certain Greeks for audience of the great Teacher, and we find that in its method it seems marked with a sense of the grave importance of it. They would not venture to come with it directly to the Lord. They took careful counsel. They sought the only one of the disciples whose Greek name, Philip, seems to mark him as the right man for their message. And it is not without deliberation and consultation with his fellow-townsman, Andrew, that he ventures, coming with Andrew, to communicate to his Master that petition of certain Greeks, which, being announced to the Lord, seems to agitate him with so deep a revulsion of feeling.

The Greeks were calling for him. And why not go? Why should the Master hesitate? It seems to have been a thought not wholly foreign to the mind of the Lord or the mind of his enemies. In this same Gospel of John there is a striking passage which receives light from this in the twelfth chapter, and reflects it back again. Said he to them that would lay hold on him: "Ye shall seek me and shall not find me, and where I am ye cannot come." The Jews, therefore, said among themselves, "Whither will this man go that we shall not find him? will he go unto the dispersion among the Greeks, and *teach the Greeks?* What is this word that he hath said?" [John vii. 34–36, R. V.]

And now what nobler possibility had ever presented itself to one who felt that he had brought a great light into the world? Thus far his light had seemed to be hidden under a bushel. That little patch of historic soil at the junction of three continents, itself so secluded from them all by desert, and mountain, and ocean—that narrow beat from Galilee to Jewry and from Jewry back to Galilee again—had been the sole scene of all his life and teaching. It does not appear that he ever once set foot upon the shore of the Great Sea; although the broad vistas of it must ever and anon have opened up before him, as from hill-top to hill-top he trod the weary distance to and from Jerusalem. Only once, exhausted with the burden that he bore, of our infirmities and sicknesses, he ventured over the rocky boundary of heathen Tyre; but then it was only to rest, not to labor. "He was not sent," he said, "but to the lost sheep of the house of Israel." But now the prospect that seems to open itself before him is as when from out the secluded little Galilean vale of Nazareth one climbs the sightly eminence of Tabor, and before him spreads not only the land of Israel, the distant cliffs of Judah, the teeming valley of Jordan, and the goodly mountains of Lebanon, but also "the great and wide Sea"—the highway of the nations, the avenue of the world's commerce, the central scene of universal history and empire. This petition of the Greeks to Christ—how like it was to that voice which came a few years later to Paul as he slept beside the ruins of old Troy—a far distant voice, heard faintly across the surging of the Hellespont, as of one clad in the garb of Macedonia, saying, in the language of another continent, "Come over into Macedonia and help us!" Oh heavenly vision, to which he was not disobedient! but following it, told the story of his Gospel until "his lines had gone out into all the earth and his words to the ends of the world." What if it had been, not Paul, but Jesus, who, being despised and rejected of his own, had said to the seed of Jacob, "Seeing ye put from you the word of God and judge yourselves unworthy of eternal life, lo, *I* turn to the Gentiles!" Suppose it had been Jesus, not Paul, who, following these seekers of his light back to their Gentile homes, had taught the longing nations of life and immortality! Suppose it had been he, who, speaking as never man spake, had stood in the busy streets of Corinth, had climbed the marble steep of the Areopagus, and taught the Stoic and the Epicurean with such authority as he had used upon the Galilean Mount!—who had proclaimed amid the proud towers of Rome "to swift destruction doomed," the coming of the kingdom that is not of this world—the kingdom that cannot be moved!—who had sped him like some auspicious star, through paths of light and "trailing clouds of glory," until the world had beheld and owned his glory—"the glory as of the only-begotten of the Father, full of grace and truth!" We long to lay upon the brow of the despised and rejected Master whom we serve this chaplet of success and triumph; and as we read the victorious career of Peter and of Paul, we grudge that the servant should be above his Lord.

And now we turn back from the contemplation of this splendid possibility, and look to see what is that alternative which stands awaiting him at Jerusalem—the priestly plot, the heathen judgment-seat, the lictor's thong and scourge, the cruel gibbet and the open sepulchre beside it, and we cry like Peter, with his great love and little faith, "Be it far from thee, Lord; this shall not be unto thee."

But where, then, would have been the Gospel? This successful and triumphant Messiah, that turns a defiant front on failure, that will not accept defeat but tears his victory out of the very jaws of hostile fate, that demands success for his great mission from the Father, and, with retorted scorn upon those who have despised his message, turns to new lands and races, resolved that the world shall hear him whether it will or no— what sort of gospel could such an one as this have bequeathed to the world? One more of those gospels with which the world was plentifully supplied already—a gospel of heroism and triumph, stimulating heroic natures to strenuous endeavor, and to every sacrifice—but one. The world is full of gospels for heroes. You can read them by dozens in "Plutarch's Lives." History goes on adding to them in every generation —the story of the Luthers, the Fredericks, the Napoleons. But whither could we have turned to find a gospel for the great multitude of us who have found out, by some sad experiences of ourselves, that we are not heroes at all, but very human men and women?—a gospel for the unsuccessful and the disappointed, for the tempted and the sinful; for those who have got past the heroic point of saying of deadly sickness, "I will not give up to it," and have owned, at last, that they are sick and in need of healing; for those who have got so far beyond the fine elation of self-reliance and "self-help," that in default of some help from outside, they are settling down into something like despair—where could we have found a gospel for such as these, who make up so large a part of human kind?— a gospel to stand by us in failure and tribulation, and be our support and comfort in sorrow and heart-break—our victory in death?

No, no! It cannot be. This golden grain of wheat must fall into the ground and die, else it cannot bring forth fruit. The agony of soul must be endured. The supreme surrender must be made. With life just entered on, with great beginnings made, with the world opening to him, with the hope of near achievements within reach, this young man Jesus must prepare himself to die. "For this cause came he to this hour." It is the law of the kingdom of heaven to which he bows himself, thus leading many sons to glory. If ye will bear fruit, ye, too, must make the like surrender—must die to your personal plans, hopes, ambitions; die to your selfish loves and hates; die—Oh last struggle of the best and worthiest souls!—die to your longings and purposes of useful service in God's kingdom, so far as these are your purposes and not God's—that so God may glorify his name in you—yea, and glorify it again.

How hard it was for the disciples to see the purpose of this waste! How hard it is for some to-day! So great a teacher and example as he was! These two or three years of public life; these few pages of recorded sayings; how they have blessed the sinful world! How rich the world would have been if that fair and lovely young life could have been lengthened out, illuminating all the vicissitudes of human joy and sorrow with its blessed light, till it had filled the round of three-score years and ten!—if the recorded sayings of those holy lips could have been increased to volumes; if the hand which wrote no syllable but those unknown words upon the ground, soon to be effaced by trampling feet, could itself have given us gospels and epistles out of the fullness of his own heart! Oh the calamity to the world, that shall cut off this divine life from among men! We may well believe such searchings of heart to have mingled with the whispers that ran through the little circle when Philip telleth Andrew, and Andrew and Philip come and tell Jesus that the Greeks desire to see him.

It was the judgment of human hearts. But how different the estimate which men put upon the value of Christ's life and work, and the estimate which he put on them himself! He turned away from Greece with all her schools; from civilization with all its forces; from the West, then, as now, having the world's future in itself—turned away from these stretching out their hands to receive him; and gave himself instead into the hands of treacherous Judas and jealous Caiaphas, and vacillating, truckling Pilate, saying to the Greeks that would speak with him, "No, not yet; it is not teaching that can save the world; but I, *if I be lifted up*, will draw all men unto me."

It is not thus that the world estimates the fruitfulness of a life. It glorifies success. It loves to witness a career of strenuous resolution, a will bent on success, lashing all untoward circumstances, like fractious steeds, into obedience to its purpose; and when the purpose is worthy and beneficent, they say, "There is a fruitful life; that life accomplished something!" "Success is a duty," they say; "nothing succeeds like success." And that highest virtue of the Gospel, triumphing over the last and noblest of temptations—the virtue that is willing for God's sake and righteousness' sake to fail and die—the virtue that can stand by and see a good and holy cause go down, and can go down with it, rather than lift one unrighteous finger to save it—this is what the world calls failure and folly and waste; and herein, sometimes, the Church seems no wiser than the world.

So men spake with one another on that Sunday which was the first of all Lord's-days, when the great feast was over, and, like the melting of the snows on Hermon, the streams of home-returning pilgrims poured down the slopes of Zion and Moriah. "We trusted that it had been he which should have redeemed Israel. Think what he might have accomplished with a little prudence, a little tact, a little concession to prejudice, a little reservation of unwelcome truths, a little conciliation of people in high places! He might have led the whole nation—people and priesthood. He might have won the very Gentiles to him. But he wouldn't. He wouldn't concede. He wouldn't compromise. He wouldn't so much as humor the time and the situation—and you see the result."

And only a few weeks later, so good men spoke to each other when Stephen died. How they had loved Stephen—so full of faith he was, so full of the Holy Ghost! What hopes of great things for the Church had centred upon Stephen! What an irreparable loss was his untimely death! Thus good men "bare Stephen to his burial, and made great lamentation over him."

And no long time afterward, when the ranks that had been thinned by persecution began to be filled up, they led forward to the baptismal water a young man, a convert of the aged apostle John, on whom, for the great hope they had of him, they named a new name, Polycarp, which is by interpretation *much fruit*. In his happy and useful old age, the fierceness of the heathen persecution bore him unresisting to the amphitheatre and to the stake. And when the flames divided on either side, and refused to consume the martyr's life, the executioner came with a spear and quenched the embers with the old Christian's heart-blood. Thus, said they, will we cut down this fruitful tree, that it bear no more fruit.

The history of the advancement of Christ's kingdom is a long record of sore disappointments. You may go to the old burying-ground of Northampton, Massachusetts, and look upon the early grave of David Brainerd, side by side with that of the fair Jerusha Edwards, whom he loved but did not live to wed. What hopes, what expectations for Christ's cause went down into the grave with the wasted form of that young missionary, of whose work nothing now remained but the dear memory, and a few score of swarthy Indian converts! But that majestic old Puritan saint, Jonathan Edwards, who had hoped to call him his son, gathered up the memorials of his life in a little book. And the little book took wings and flew beyond the sea, and alighted on the table of a Cambridge student—Henry Martyn. Poor Martyn! Why would he throw himself away, with all his scholarship, his genius, his opportunities! Such a wasted life it seemed! What had he accomplished when he turned homeward from "India's coral strand," broken in health, and dragged himself northward as far as that dreary khan at Tocat by the Black Sea, where he crouched

THE PETITION OF CERTAIN GREEKS. 195

under the piled-up saddles, to cool his burning fever against the earth, and there died alone, among unbelievers, no Christian hand to tend his agony, no Christian voice to speak in his ear the promises of the Master whom, as it seemed to men, he had so vainly served. To what purpose was this waste?

But out of that early grave of Brainerd, and that lonely grave of Martyn far away by the plashing of the Euxine Sea, has sprung the noble army of modern missionaries.

And the blood of such as Polycarp, sinking into the sands of many a fierce arena, was the seed of the Church that has sprung up in many a land to wave like Lebanon, and bear its healing fruits.

And from that most sad spot, hard by the city gates, from which men bore away the mangled form of Stephen to his burial, there went pricked in the heart the young man who had kept the executioners' clothes, who by and by should take up Stephen's message as from his bleeding lips, and bear it afar among the Gentiles.

And from that sealed and guarded tomb by Golgotha came forth the Lord of glory, King of kings and Lord of lords, declared to be the Son of God with power by the resurrection from the dead.

XVIII.

CREATION.

In the beginning, God created the heaven and the earth —Gen. i. 1.

In the matter of the origin of the universe, Christendom, which was for many ages of one accord and one mind, is now vexed with a grave debate between two opposing and incompatible views. How shall we entitle them? If we describe them as the Scriptural view and the scientific view, we beg the question, or we give up the question, as the case may be. We imply that men's habitual and traditionary impressions from the Scripture *are* the Scripture; and we imply that the favorite speculations and hypotheses and strong arguments of scientific people *are* science. Without using any terms that may thus tend to prejudgment of the case, let us first roughly sketch them side by side—the *traditionary view*, which is certainly derived mainly from the Bible, whether by correct interpretation or by incorrect; and the *speculative view*, in which is certainly contained a large element of science, that is to say, of settled and demonstrated truth.

The comparison of these two views is forced on us by the talk of every thoughtful circle, and the news of every journal. It is not only in the scientific lecture-room that the question emerges; it is suggested in the highest flights of poetry, and the most genuine inspirations of art. One cannot rehearse the majestic cantos of the Paradise Lost, or listen to that "tone-poem" in which the most pictorial of composers has set forth the scenes of the world's beginning as the minds of men for many centuries past have been accustomed to conceive them, without having the question forced upon the mind.

CREATION. 197

The comparison between these two conceptions of the creation, the old and the new, will come up, must come up, ought to come up, before your minds, even though it should bring with it vague misgivings as to the result, and indefinite dread as if the very foundations of all faith were giving way. I propose to sketch them rapidly, one after the other, in rough outlines, and set them side by side, that we may deliberately think about them in their bearings on our Christian faith. You are not afraid to do this, I hope. Why should you be?

First, then, there is the *traditionary* conception of the creation of the world. It is identified not only with much of the preaching and theology of the Church, but it enters into the poetry, the music, the painting, of the Christian ages. Stated roughly, it represents to the mind mere vacuity and unoccupied space as subsisting from eternity, until, at the beginning of time, the shapeless masses of brute matter were evoked out of nothing by the uttered voice of God. Unknown ages passed by, unmeasured, unrecorded, until the business of bringing a world of order out of this shapeless mass began with a divine interference, and the word Let there be light. And there was light; and there the work of creation halted for the night that was to usher in the second day—how long a night, whether of hours or of millenniums, no man can know.

By successive acts of creation, the order of which, if not arbitrary, is sometimes very perplexing, were produced the expanse of the sky, and the disposition of the earth's surface into sea and land. Then were wrought those miracles of divine skill and adaptation as well as power, in the vegetable world, calling forth from the earth the grass, the herb, the tree. And not till then, and after the night that preceded the fourth period of creation, was the infinite marvel of the starry system inaugurated, with its vast order of poises and counterpoises, its suns and planets and satellites, and the heavens declared the glory of God. Again creation rested, and night came down on the unfinished work, and when the morning of the fifth day dawned, there was a new forth-putting of divine power, and at once the infinite variety of fishes and of birds sprung into perfect life. Once more creation ceased, and again it recommenced, now for the last time. With a word, the earth was made to bring forth the creatures of the dry land,—the beasts and the cattle and creeping things. And to crown the whole, out of the dust of the earth, but in the image of God, was man created, male and female, and given dominion over all. Thus the heavens and the earth were finished, and the host of them; and for the evidence of the divine work, we point to the divinely wise, mighty and perfect workmanship, and exclaim in adoration, " Great and manifold are thy works, O God; in wisdom hast thou made them all!"

And now consider, secondly, what we call the *speculative* conception of the origin of the world.—Not that it is all of speculation. As the traditionary view of the beginning of things is made up partly of Scripture statement, and partly of our habitual inferences and interpretations of Scripture, so this speculative view is made up partly of scientific facts, and partly of the hypotheses and guesses and fancies of science. It introduces us, as far back as its remotest conjecture is able to reach, to a vast, illimitable cloud of variously mingled gases, white with a fervent heat at which the solid elements of which mountains and main continents are builded up would not only melt but fly off in subtle vapor. This nebulous mass of fiery vapors, the raw material of a universe, is what scientific speculation shows us at the beginning, or as near that awful brink of material existence as it dares to venture. Whence it came, how it came, the boldest speculation does not pretend to know, but only dares to guess that it may have been from eternity. But there it is, matter enough for all suns and constellations and planetary systems, and motion enough—turning of atom upon atom and whirling of cloud upon cloud—motion enough to be wrought over into all the forces of the universe. In that dance of atoms is contained all the heat, light, electricity, gravitation, yes, and all the living forces of vegetation or animal life, or even nerve and will-power, that shall ever be to the end, if it is possible that there should be an end, and that either matter or motion, could ever really begin to be or cease to be. By and by, as the momentum of this fiery whirl grows fast and furious, there is shot off from the mass a lesser cloud that goes careering away through space and yet is held in relation to the mass from which it breaks, by the power of gravitation that steadies it in an orbit of its own. And as we have seen a rocket, sent aloft, burst into stars of many-colored fire that go dancing forward in the same parabola, just so the cooling and condensing mass breaks into planets that go sailing onward still, and circling round their central sun; and from each planet starts its rings or moons. Thus came into existence this ball of our earth. The cooling, the shrinking, the contortion and rupturing of its crust made mountains and hills—made ravines and valleys and ocean basins, which the condensing moisture filled with streams and seas. The surface was shaped and finished and provided with soil by grinding glaciers and wearing winds and by the rush of many waters. And by and by there came of itself into being (if only scientific speculation could guess how) out of the mud and ooze, some germs of life. And the germs that were strongest and best and fittest pushed aside the weaker, and ever, with the tendency of life to vary, the best varieties remained and multiplied, and so life grew higher and stronger. New members, and new senses, and new faculties became developed. Worthless types of life faded out, and left their traces imprinted on the rocks, and nobler forms kept coming in. Fixed circumstances engendered habits, and hereditary habit became instinct, and instinct took on the form of a brute intelligence, and by and by, somewhere and somehow, existence slipped over the immense transition, and intelligence flashed up into reason and conscience, and man became a living soul. And all this in the steady, unbroken, unassisted working of a succession of natural causes, from the original whirling cloud of incandescent gases, down to the finished, or at least the well advanced and populated earth and heavens of to-day.

Such are these two pictures of the origin of the world—two so mutually antithetic, seemingly so mutually contradictory and destructive. And when we have made all allowance for the parts of this speculative view that are *mere* speculation, thus far, but yet contemplate the splendid and daily augmenting mass of evidence that makes in favor of it, we are bound, here in the church and in the pulpit, to ask what shall we do about it? What shall we learn from it?

Learn this, then, first:—

I. This theory of the origin of the world does not in the slightest degree weaken the argument of *Natural* Theology. But rather it expands and adorns and illustrates it to a grandeur and splendor never before conceived. How vast, how sublime, how overwhelming and bewildering in its magnificence, the conception that we now get of the wisdom and power of God! Of old we were wont to learn these in detail from the exquisite mechanism of the eye, the hand, the heart; from the infinite contrivances of mutual adaptation in the lower forms of life; or from the mathematics and mechanism of the heavens; and to say of each several object and combination, "Here behold the wisdom, power and love of God! My Father made them all!" And now that this wonderful and harmonious result is referred to a chain of natural causes, and that science, the prophet of nature, the interpreter to us of God's natural works, seems solemnly to beckon us backward toward that fiery laboratory where dumb but giant forces are busy fusing, mingling, stirring, and pounding into shape the materials of this orderly universe, and whispers to us her surmises that the whole course of nature has proceeded thence without interruption in the sequence of effect from cause, we see, as never before we saw, the amazing glory of the Creator. The forest oak is a majestic object, as it sits rooted upon its rocks, looking forth toward all the winds, and watching the seasons come and go.

The apparatus of an intricate life is playing in a million of veins and arteries, adding each year its ring of robust strength to the concentric circles on which you may mark off the centuries, girding about it anew its coats of shaggy bark, and painting its leaves with the tender green of spring and the ruddy hue of autumn. It is the grand production of His word who bade the earth bring forth her grass, her herb, her tree. But you bring to me, half hidden in its rustic cup, an acorn, and tell me that in the white kernel within that brown shell are imprisoned all the possibilities of the future oak—not some chance tree, it may chance of beech or elm or of some other tree, but the oak itself with all its lordly traits, its giant boll, its stretch and grasp of root, its tough fibre, its shaggy bark, its deep-cut leaves of shining green—that all these, to the last detail, are provided for in that little nodule of starch, and I say, this is a greater wonder still! This is excellent in working, for it cometh from His word who bade the earth bring forth the fruit-tree yielding fruit whose seed is in itself after its kind. The glories of this finished world are vast, are wonderful. If every adaptation of all the combinations that have been the delight of natural theologians had been shaped, moulded, fashioned by the pressure of a divine finger, how full of God's power and love the world would be! But if science will but stand beside us, holding us by the hand, while we bend gazing into that abyss of primeval vapors in which are seething and boiling the elements of the projected universe, and will dare assure us that there already are prepared the order and harmony of its countless millions of perfect adaptations—that out of that chaos, simply by the operation of the forces that are busy at their wild play therein, shall come marching forth at the appointed hour, like a debouching army, the steadfast order of the constellations and the punctual movement of the planetary systems,—that without word of command, or touch of external power, the foundations and walls of geologic structure shall fall into place, and that in gradual succession the forms of life shall come forth to take their several stations, moved and stirred with brute instinct and affection, until man at last appears, with exalted reason, with conscience of right and wrong, with polity and invention, with love and with immortal hope, then we turn to science that has showed us this wonder, and demand—Who measured out the ingredients of this enchanted chaos? Who stirred it round and round into its wonder-working whirl of motion? Who spoke the spell that made it pregnant with a universe of matter and with a world of intellect, and love, and hope? And science cannot tell. She only gazes and is dumb. But what science cannot guess, faith *knows*— "that the worlds were framed by the word of God, so that the things that are seen were not made of things which do appear." These marvelous thoughts of the method of creation before which timid theology stands trembling and shuddering, do really sing such a psalm of praise to the far-reaching wisdom and wonder-working power of God, "as never was by mortal finger strook" from "psaltery or instrument of ten strings." No hymn of praise is more enkindling to devout rapture than the Nebular Hypothesis; and to a religious mind, there is no more religious book than The Origin of Species. These do not forbid the praise of God—they do not hush the choral song of the universe to its creator. Notwithstanding all the discoveries, all the conjectures, of science—notwithstanding? nay, all the more because of them—the birds still sing in the branches, the sea roars, the trees clap their hands as of old, and "the patient stars" go

"singing, as they shine,
The hand that made us is divine."

I repeat it, then, the modern theories as to the processes by which the world has come to be, do not in the slightest degree weaken, they rather heighten, deepen and strengthen, the argument of Natural Theology. And now let us not fear to add,—

II. That they do not conflict with the *religious* teaching of the Scriptures. And when I speak of the teaching of the Scriptures, I do not mean our tradition as to what the Scriptures teach, or our lazy, habitual interpretation of them. The language of the Scriptures is not to blame for men's gross reading of it. What better expression for the outgoing of creative power than that word, "*And God said*"? Is the Scripture to blame, that we have indolently and grossly dreamed of one shouting out into chaos and the abyss, in Hebrew syllables? What fitter poetic phrase with which to mark the close of each succeeding chapter in "the marvelous work," than that great refrain—" and there was evening, and there was morning—Day the First; and there was evening, and there was morning—Day the Second"? Is the Scripture to blame, that when it points us back into the past eternity, or ever there were signs or seasons or days or years, we have had no more apprehension of the nature of the subject than to try to time creation by an eight-day clock?

But putting aside tradition and prepossession, let us ask again, What is the *religious* teaching of the Scripture concerning the creation of the world?—I do not mean in the way of the details of a scientific cosmogony—these we have no reason to expect in a divine book given by most human men. And if we look for them here where we have no right to expect them, we are liable to be misled, as so many have been misled, into a false cosmogony, founded on the crude conceptions, vague, unscientific, of the primitive ages before science had begun. But what do the Scriptures, thoughtfully read, teach us of God's way of working in the creation?

1. Contrary to our natural conception of the Almighty and All-wise, to whose work is no need of any lapse of time, whose thought, will, word, is itself creative,—the Scriptures teach us that the work of creation was a *protracted* work, reaching from epoch to epoch through such vicissitudes as may be expressed, for the scale of eternity, and as human language may utter the things of God, in terms like *day* and *night*, *activity* and *rest*.

2. Contrary to what our conceptions of God's way might be, but conformably to what our latest science discovers to have been, the Scriptures teach us that this protracted work was also a *gradual* work, moving forward by orderly and consecutive stages, from matter up to man.

3. Plainly the Scriptures teach (though men have so often missed the meaning of them) that God, in his *protracted* work, in his *methodic* work, of creation, did not scorn to use material and natural causes, but rather wrought by means of them, making his own work to be his own instrument and agent, bidding the waters bring forth and the earth bring forth, and it was so.

But these things are incidental. The one main lesson which the Scriptures, with majestic dignity and authority, set themselves to teach, is that concerning which science, in its nature, is incompetent either to affirm or to deny—that the power and wisdom that pervade those processes which we explore by observation, computation and conjecture, are the power and wisdom of a God of righteousness and love—that the Former of our bodies is the Father of our spirits;—and to this declaration of the holy word, the heart and soul and mind of man respond, "Amen; our Father which art in heaven!"

From such contemplations as these, we turn back to our Milton and our Haydn, and smile while we admire; so poor and inadequate we find their grandest conceptions, their most imposing utterances. For to us it has been given to behold, both in the Word and in the Work, new grandeurs, such as had never entered into the heart of man. We seem to be admitted as spectators of the very processes of creation. Seated in the astronomer's pendent chair, beneath the dome of the observatory, to gaze upon the floating nebulæ; standing before the slow-grinding glaciers at Grindelwald or Chamounix to observe, still busy at their work, the very forces that shaped and equipped the continent on which we dwell; nay, even in such a common thing as in the garden, the market and the cattle-show, witnessing the new creations wrought from year to year by human culture;—it is as if we had come into the laboratory of the Creator, where his obedient servitors are still toiling at their tasks, and had read there the inscription, in the words of the Son of man, "My Father worketh hitherto, and I work."

So amplified does the knowledge of God become in the advancing light of science! So transfigured, as with an unearthly lustre, is science in the light of faith! But to him that hath no light *but* science, how is the light itself become as darkness! How wretched an idolater is he whose only god is a cloud of superheated gas! For this is his god—this nebulous divinity—this goblin of smoke. It made the eye; but it cannot see. It made the ear; but it cannot hear. It made the reason; but it cannot understand. It filled the ordered worlds with forms of beauty, with symmetries of number, and fashioned the invisible air to be the vehicle of music; but in it is no thought of harmony or beauty. Inert, apathetic, dead, it has no sympathies, no affections; yet out of its dull and senseless bosom it brings forth the tender instincts of the birds and beasts, the mutual loves of kindred, the sweet pieties of home, the noble pride of native land. There is no conscience therein, no hate of wrong, no love of righteousness; yet hath it created man, not in its own image, but in such an image as it never knew, with instinct of duty, and remorse for sin, and forthreachings after an immortality to which he cannot attain, and blind gropings after a Father whom he shall never find, and famishing desires which there is no eye to pity, and aspirations breaking into prayers which there is no ear to hear. It has no heart, but only a resistless, relentless hand of inexorable fate, of iron, mechanic destiny, holding you here in life, then plunging you to death. Behold your god! For is it not your god? Is it not this that hath made you, and not you yourself! Go, worship it! go, pray to it! sing to it happy psalms of thanks! Take on your knee your little child, when first he comes to you with questions about God, and teach him the lesson of this grim despair! Seek out the tempted ones, held back from depths of wrong by thoughts of divine judgment and divine salvation, and whisper in their ears your new and dark evangel! Hasten upon the track of the missionary who brings into gloomy regions of the shadow of death the light of a new hope full of immortality, and quench that light, and bring the darkness back again! And then come back to happy death-beds, where soft voices speak to each other tender, trustful words of victory over death, of the endless life with Christ, of the sure promises of God, and where hearts rise together in believing prayer—come with your atheist religion to these sorrowful rejoicing ones, and tell them there is no soul, no sin, no Saviour, and no God but incandescent hydrogen, and great is gas!

O men and brethren, shall this dead god be your god? Or shall yours rather be the living and true God, the God and Father of our Lord Jesus Christ, and our Father, and our God? Choose ye whom ye will serve.

XIX.

A COROLLARY OF EVOLUTION.

I gave my heart to seek and search out by wisdom concerning all things that are done under heaven: this sore travail hath God given to the sons of men to be exercised therewith.—ECCLESIASTES i. 13.

It needs no great attainment in the intelligent use of the Scriptures to recognize that whatever of divine wisdom is communicated to us through this book of "The Preacher" is conveyed by means of the experiences and speculations of a most undivine man. Whether the book be regarded as the actual writing of Solomon, or (as is more likely) of some much later poet speaking in the character of Solomon, it delineates before us a vain endeavor to solve the problem of the universe by wisdom, and the *blasé* despair with which the writer gives up the inquiry at last, acknowledging that it is too much for him, and that further study does no good, and settles down in the conviction (which is the real lesson of the book) that he must leave all to the wisdom and justice of God. This "conclusion of the whole matter" is that which well rewards us for following him through his Epicurean experiments and conjectures, and his pessimist despair. But on his way to this conclusion he lets fall many a nugget of worldly wisdom, many a shrewd, sometimes cynical, observation on men or society; in his old-world aphorisms we see the reflection of many a modern experience. In undertaking to get a theory that shall include all phenomena, he differs not at all from our very latest philosophers, and there is solid and sober truth in him when he looks on the universe, with its unsolved problems, as God's invitation to our inquiries —the task divinely set to us for the schooling of our reason.

It is the justification of philosophy, even in its most futile labors. These scores of centuries of toilsome speculation, in which each school has achieved so little except to refute the rest, have at least not put scorn on the divine invitation to human inquiry. They have done their task at the great problem; even though the "sore travail" of accounting for the facts of the universe still remains, and is likely to give exercise to our posterity as it has to our forefathers. Let us hope that they may not be less wise than the Hebrew "Preacher," who, when he had come to the end of his studies without reaching the solution of his questions, found "the conclusion of the whole matter" in "fearing God and keeping his commandments."

That theory of the universe which, at the present day, in the English-speaking countries, is most in vogue, is known as Evolutionism. It is only as a theory of the universe that I propose to regard it this evening. As a doctrine of natural history, of more or less extended application, it has wide approval on the part of many scientific men who either have no interest in it, anyway, as an explanation of the system of the universe, or as such very decidedly repudiate it. But it is only in this latter relation—as a theory of the universe—that the doctrine of evolution greatly concerns the theologian. The question of the origin of vegetable and animal species by development and survival is one of fascinating interest, but has (as I conceive) none but incidental bearing on any important religious question. The theory of evolution as an explanation of the universe is another matter. It is, in terms, a denial of the creation of the world, in any sense, and a negation of God, or, as many of its expounders would prefer to say, an ignoring of God.

But I beg you all to observe that, distinctly hostile as this system is to the teaching of the Scriptures, and even to the very essence of all religion, it is no part of our present argument to controvert it directly; but only to state it, mainly following the most conspicuous of its English apostles, Mr. Spencer: and then to point out an inevitable corollary from it, which seems to me to have been curiously overlooked both by its advocates and by its antagonists.

Evolutionism, then, is that theory of the universe which finds all the facts of the universe, past, present, and future, to be fully accounted for by the existence of matter, uncreatable, indestructible, capable of indefinite variation in form, but incapable of varying in amount; and the existence of motion, also invariable in amount, but capable of being changed, not in direction only, but also into other modes of motion, such as heat, light, electricity, vegetable and animal life, thought, emotion and volition. Given matter and motion (and these, it is claimed, *are* given, both being essentially uncreated), by successive stages the universe will come to be as it is, with its planetary and sidereal systems, with its geologic structure, with its plant life, and its animal life, each working up from the lowest to the highest orders, with man and his faculties, with society, from its rudimentary barbarism up to the highly organized and complicated forms of civilization: that the whole order of things as known to us would thus—we will not say *be made,* for that would imply some power from without impressed upon the chaos; we will not say *grow,* for that would imply some principle of life within it—but that out of mere atomic matter and motion would automatically *come of itself* the whole order of the heavens and the earth, including all life and humanity in history and society.

In favor of this view are to be alleged a great mass of unquestionable scientific facts. 1. All those astronomical facts which tend to confirm the Nebular Hypothesis—a hypothesis which itself gains strength by being adopted into this larger system or theory. 2. The modern demonstrations of the conservation and correlation of forces, which prove that heat, light, sound, chemical reaction, electricity, magnetism, are all different forms of the same force, that each may be transmuted into motion, and motion into each, and each into every other. 3. The proofs of a close mutual connection between physical motion, in these mutually interchangeable forms, and vegetable and animal growth, and muscular power, and even mental action. 4. The facts, already many and impressive, and steadily accumulating, though always falling short of conclusive proof, which draw us more and more toward the belief of the origin of new species by development from former species. These undisputed facts, among others, combine with the charm which we all find in connecting diverse truths together in a simple and unique system, to give to the system of evolutionism its unquestionable currency and vogue at the present day.

On the other hand, this system has some grave difficulties to contend with: 1. To begin with, there is the difficulty of the starting-point. How matter can be eternal without being infinite—how it can be self-existent without being existent everywhere, is a metaphysical difficulty which soon becomes a mathematical one. For the first conditions of evolution require that the mass of unformed matter should have both surface and centre, and immensity has neither. Again, the system of evolution must make a beginning in time. It needs vast cycles of time in which to have wrought the universe, but not too much time; if you give it eternity, you kill it. And how can it make a beginning in time? How is it to start without being started?—the old question of the *primum mobile*. Then, 2, is the question about the beginning of life, which, at the first, is doubtless very feeble, very rudimentary, hardly perceptible, but which, after all, does have to begin before it can exist. The notion that matter, if only you grind it fine enough, make it moist enough, stir it long enough, keep it warm enough and not too warm, will somehow or other begin to live of its own accord without the introduction of any germ of life from without, is a notion which it is not easy to prove or to believe, and which it requires a certain measure of audacity to enunciate. It is easy to resolve the results of life into heat and motion,

A COROLLARY OF EVOLUTION. 211

but not to transmute heat and motion into life, except by the agency of life itself. 3. There is the grave difficulty about the beginning of mental action—thought, emotion, volition. Just where we are to find the point at which mental action begins, it may not be easy to show. No doubt we see signs of what looks like it very low in the animal scale. But it is none the less certain that it begins *somewhere* in the system of nature; and how thought, emotion, volition, the attributes of mind, should first come into the universe, of themselves, when there had been no mind in the universe before, is another of those grave difficulties which beset the theory of evolution considered as a way of accounting for the universe.

And it must, in all fairness, be borne in mind, in considering these and other difficulties, that this theory of the universe is a chain which is no stronger than its weakest link. Let it be conceded, that at the beginning of motion, of life, of mind, or at any other point, it requires to be supplemented by a feather's weight of aid from outside, and it is no longer an adequate theory of the universe. It has gone to pieces, and become nothing more than a very interesting and valuable series of observations in physics and physiology.

I have stated these among the difficulties that beset the theory of evolution over against the masses of scientific fact that are alleged in favor of it, as being essential to a just statement of the subject. Let me once more remind you that I am not now controverting the theory of evolution, but only setting it forth with a view to some of the inferences to be drawn from it. For the purposes of the argument, we waive all these difficulties. For the time being, we accept the theory of evolution. We suppose the volume of matter, vast but not infinite, and the quantum of motion eternally constant in amount, beginning its plastic work before all calculated ages. We will try to suppose (as Mr. Spencer demands;—see "First Principles," Sec. 82) that motion is transformed into life, and into mental action, just as into heat and light and electricity

—that "motion, heat, light, chemical affinity, etc., are alike transformable into each other, and into sensation, emotion, thought—these, in their turn, being directly or indirectly retransformable into the original shapes." "How this metamorphosis takes place—how a force existing as motion, heat, or light can become a mode of consciousness; how it is possible for aerial vibrations to generate the sensation we call sound, or for the forces liberated by chemical change in the brain to give rise to emotion—these are mysteries which it is impossible to fathom. But they are not profounder mysteries than the transformations of the physical forces into each other." (Sec. 82, *ad fin.*)

The statements of this representative philosopher leave nothing to be desired in point of distinctness and perspicuity. Those actions which we are accustomed to speak of as mental —thought, emotion, volition—are, according to him, simply modes of physical motion like heat, light, and electricity. They are "each transformable into the other," and then "retransformable into the original shapes." "Each manifestation of force can be interpreted *only* as the effect of some antecedent force; no matter whether it be an inorganic action, an animal movement, a thought, or a feeling." (Sec. 84.)

This, then, is the final achievement of evolution, when at last moving matter, which, without any agency of life from without itself, has of itself begun to live—does at last, without any agency of thought or reason from outside itself, begin of itself to think, to reason, to love, to hope. The known universe is now complete. It has made itself, out of brute matter and mechanic motion. And man, the latest product of this marvelous self-made automatic machinery, who but just now has attained to the knowledge of it and of himself, may well give himself pause and look about him. It seems a lonely universe compared with that we used to know. The firmament is silent now. The songs of the morning stars are hushed. The dumb heavens no more declare the glory of God. Around us the ten thousand proofs of wise design and fatherly tenderness which we used to think we saw are blotted out, and instead we see nothing but the automatic grind of inexorable Force, in which is no thought nor purpose, and if there can be said to be any principle of action it is this: Crush the feeble. As we gaze upon the fashion of this new world, we are as those who have come back to some old temple in which they had been wont to worship, and find it transformed to common uses. The words of faith and consecration that had been carved high above the portal have been covered up with gilded sign-boards. Within, the house of prayer has been made a place of merchandise. No holy law nor promises of God are heard therein, and from the tombs of saints that slept the words of pious hope are rudely obliterated. The laver of holy baptism is desecrated to a common bath, and the board whence men had been wont to eat of the bread that came down from heaven, to a table of thankless feasting. Instead of the harmony of organs and the voice of choral hymns are heard the clank of soulless machinery and the clamor of selfish traffic. O desecrated world, from which ye have taken away the Lord! We look within us, and find there reason that lays hold upon the Infinite, and "thoughts that wander through eternity," and a "hope that is full of immortality," and love, and duty, and mercy, and forgiving tenderness, which we had dreamed might be the lineaments of a certain divine likeness, the impress of a divine Maker. We find, withal, a craving instinct of worship, drawing us as if into relation and communion with a heavenly Father, whom not having seen we love; and we had thought of this as if it might be itself "the evidence of things not seen," the still voice by which he would draw us and welcome us to himself. But we are undeceived at last, and disabused of these fair illusions. All these thoughts, reasonings, hopes, affections, cravings are simply modes of physical motion, like light, heat and electricity; they have only used up so much of the invariably constant amount of the molecular and molar motion of the universe, prior to being translated back into light, heat and electricity again. Doubtless it is well to know the truth, even if this is the truth. Let us not be walking in a vain show. But somehow the world seems lonely now. Of old the good man was never lonely. He would say, as David, "O Lord, thou compassest my path and my lying down, and art acquainted with all my ways.... When I awake I am still with thee;" or, as the Son of David: "Alone! yet not alone, for the Father is with me." But now there is no Father, and we are orphans. Ah, the noblest utterance that this new materialism has yet made is the wail that broke from the heart of him who among all its brilliant minds was the most brilliant, versatile and symmetrical, the most logical and consistent in the blankness of his unbelief, the young, the lamented Professor Clifford, when he cried out, in the solitude and bereavement of his soul, "The great Companion is dead!"

I said a few minutes ago that, under the system of Evolutionism, when at last it has reached the point at which all the forms of mental action are accounted for as simply and solely other forms of physical motion, its account of the known and actual universe is complete. It has said its last word. But not so concerning the possible future universe. Evolutionism has not half done itself justice in speaking of the possibilities which it involves. It has "lacked a sacred bard," and either told

"in mournful numbers
Life is but an empty dream,"

or, in the language of its latest expounder on the psychological side, Dr. Maudsley, bewails itself in pessimistic vaticinations of the inevitable future diminution of solar heat and light, and consequent decline of development and degeneration of all things, "until at last a frozen earth, incapable of cultivation, is left without energy to produce a living particle of any sort, and so death itself is dead;"* or, in the words of its chief apostle,

* In "Essay on Body and Will."

Mr. Spencer, declares it to be "beyond doubt" that we are "manifestly progressing toward omnipresent death," forced to "contemplate, as the outcome of things, a universe of extinct suns, round which circle planets devoid of life."* But evolution should be ashamed of such coward foreboding in its disciples. There are fairer prospects before the universe than it has ever known, if only the work of development that has gone so far shall go farther in the same line. Out of the one unvarying fund of motion in the universe, unvarying in amount, but infinitely convertible and reconvertible in form, how little, thus far, has been transformed into the highest form—the form of thought, emotion, and volition! What splendid progress still remains to be accomplished, until the various correlated forces of the world, the motion, gravitation, light, heat, electricity, chemic action, and vegetable and animal life, shall all have been transmuted into their equivalents in mathematical and metaphysical reasoning, in imagination of beauty and sublimity, in far-seeing contrivance of means to ends, in meditation of righteousness and holiness, in tender mercy, in long-suffering, in forgiveness, in love; for by the very "first principles" of evolution all these mental acts are measurable by their equivalents in foot-pounds; and just as it is conceivable and probable that the total forces of the universe once existed in the sole form of molecular motion, so it is not only conceivable, but wholly possible, that all these forces may by and by be transmuted into the sole form of mental action. Nay, more; since matter itself is known to us only as a mode of force, being manifested simply by equivalents of resistance or of gravitation, it results that matter also is capable of being commuted into the various correlated modes of motion of which mental action is one; and thus that the whole universe may come to exist as a spiritual being, as thought, emotion, volition; wisdom, love, might.

---

* First Principles, § 136, cf. § 141.

This is the splendid consummation of the system of evolution: That, given the senseless and shapeless nebula, with its aimless whirl of atoms, out of which have been evolved already the order of the heavens, the structure of the earth, the chemic and mechanic forces, the ranks of vegetable and animal life, and, finally, the forms of spiritual activity—it is capable of taking on altogether this spiritual form, no atom's weight of force being lost, but all being securely transmuted into spiritual forms, into thought, emotion, volition; wisdom, love, and might; which are again reconvertible into their former shapes of physical, vegetable, and animal existence—into matter and force.

And now I ask your consideration of one more inference from this system, which is the one I had in view when I announced the subject of this sermon, "A Corollary of Evolution." It is this: According to the principles of evolution the original form, in which the universe existed from eternity, *may have been* the spiritual form—thought, emotion, volition; wisdom, love, might; omniscience, omnipotence, and infinite benevolence—a form perfectly convertible into gravitation, motion, light and heat. And against the supposition that the original form of the universe was that of spiritual existence, there is, under the system of evolution, no reasonable presumption or probability, and no just objection, except that it is orthodox.

Some hasty and inconsiderate philosopher may object off-hand that it is contrary to the known course of evolution that the higher forms of motion, like thought and feeling, should precede the lower, such as heat, light and vegetation; that, in fact, the lower forms always precede the higher in course of development. But the answer is obvious: that this objector has forgotten to what scale his "known course of evolution" has been mapped; that what he knows of the course of evolution does not really represent a curve long enough to furnish the elements for computing the course of nature. He dreams that his paltry millions or billions or trillions of years make rather a long time from which to estimate the rest; whereas they are only a tick of the clock. He speaks of *the* course of evolution, as if there might not have been a score of successive and diverse courses of evolution, from the nebula back to the nebula again, since time began. He speaks of time, and we are speaking of that which was before time, from eternity—concerning which his science and his speculation are alike confessedly and hopelessly at fault; he has relegated it all to The Unknowable. He has to deal with two elements, and only two, that make up the universe—matter and force; both of them variable, convertible, and reconvertible in form, both of them indestructible and uncreatable in essence. As they cannot cease to be, so can they not begin to be. *Unless* they are from eternity, the system of evolution, as an explanation of the universe, is impossible; and *if* they are from eternity, the system of evolution is likewise confessedly impossible. The only hypothesis which can save this elaborate system, the fruit of such toil of thinking, the object of such magnificent contributions out of the treasury of science, from utter self-destruction, is that hypothesis the possibility of which is a corollary of the system itself: that from the beginning, or ever the earth and the worlds were made, the forces of the universe lay hidden in that mental form to which they are correlated—in eternal and infinite wisdom, love, and power, and subject to the summons of the Almighty will. There, in limitless foreknowledge, was marshaled the order of the steadfast stars; there the massy architecture of the earth was planned; there tender mercy took counsel with unfathomed wisdom over creatures that were yet to be, and cared for the fall of sparrows and the cry of the fledgling ravens; there the contemplation of wise design "did behold our substance, yet being unperfect, and in its book all our members were written, which in continuance were fashioned, when as yet there was none of them." It is evolution that teaches us that this *may* have been, and if it may have been, then it *must* have been. The necessary premise of the system, its inevitable consequence, is this, which already "by faith we know":—"In the beginning God created the heavens and the earth." It is "the conclusion of the whole matter," the same now as in the day when "Ecclesiastes, or the preacher," "gave his heart to seek and search out by wisdom concerning all things that are done under heaven." For now, as then and ever, science is religious, even though the scientific man may be materialist and atheist.

O timid fellow-Christian and theologian! does not this argument rebuke our unworthy fears of what materialism can do? So often the defenders of religious and spiritual truth have seemed to be seriously concerned that men were framing theories and systems of simple materialism, in which was place for neither God nor soul of man, but which derived all spiritual and mental facts from merely physical causes; thus building a bridge, from the material side, over that great gulf between matter and spirit which thought and knowledge have always found impassable. Be not afraid! God is not mocked. There can be no bridge from the material over to the spiritual that is not, in every sense, just as much a bridge from the spiritual over to the material. Whatever line of reasoning deduces mind from matter makes it equally plain that matter may be the creation of mind. There is no breach that materialism can make in the defenses of religion which may not become a sally-port for our sorties and reprisals.

XX.

THE NATURAL THEOLOGY OF THE SPLEEN.

PREACHED TO A CONGREGATION OF STUDENTS IN MEDICINE.

All things were created by him, and for him.—COLOSSIANS, i. 16.

IN the argument which I am about to submit to your attention, I pass over the most impressive thing about this text—the fact that it is found, as others like it are found, in epistles from the same pen, in the midst of an impassioned lyric ascription of glory to the Lord Jesus Christ. With such doxologies, as we may call them, the letters of Paul abound. His swift logic seems to take fire from its own velocity, and flame up in songs of praise, in which the inalienable glories of the one living and true God are wonderfully ascribed to "God's dear Son." Lyric odes, I have called them, outbursts of poetic and worshipful emotion; and not the less such for being set in their orderly place in his great arguments to men's understanding and reason. *They* must needs fail wholly to understand them, who fail to see that the divine inspiration which breathes in them is also a poetic inspiration. Grammar and dictionary are not the only apparatus required for the interpretation of the Pauline epistles, even when used by a devout spirit. There is many a learned and pious exegete who has less successfully caught the meaning of these hymns of St. Paul, and less intelligibly expressed it, than that great interpreter of Scripture, Felix Mendelssohn.

I leave here, at the threshold, this amazing ascription of the glories of the Creator to him who is himself declared to be the First-born of the creation, and turn to the two syllables, *By* and *For*, in which are indicated the two aspects of the Creation, the Origin and Means of it, and the Object and End of it, from these to unfold the twofold argument that leads from the Creation to the Creator. The former of these syllables, *By* him, points us backward to God as the original cause of all causes; the latter of them, *For* him, points us forward to God as the final purpose of all purposes and end of all designs.

The former argument, from facts to their causes and through these to the First Cause, is the common and familiar argument of Natural Theology. The multitudinous and cumulative illustration of it has been the delight of religious literature, especially in England, for the last three or four generations. And how splendid are the monuments of it in all libraries! The statement of it in Paley's "Natural Theology" is the finest masterpiece of lucid statement on such a theme in any language. The "Astronomical Discourses" of Thomas Chalmers show what power has great reasoning on a great theme to kindle the imagination and stir the feelings. And the successive volumes of the Bridgewater Treatises, though they show the old tide-marks of science which have long since been passed by the advancing flood, will never cease to command the respect which great and worthy minds of each generation love to pay to the great thoughts of generations past. Doubtless many of the forms under which this argument from fact to cause has been set forth have been successfully criticised and controverted; but the substance of it stands, and will stand till the heavens have ceased to declare the glory of God,—till day no longer speaks to day, and night to night.

This argument let me first rapidly review, before proceeding to another and correlated argument, which is to be the principal theme of this evening's discourse.

The old, accustomed argument of natural theology rests on an axiom—that every fact which has a beginning must have a cause—and leads us back from any given fact (that is not an eternal and self-existent fact) to the cause of it, and thence to

THE NATURAL THEOLOGY OF THE SPLEEN. 221

the cause of that cause, and so on until we come to the First Cause, the cause that had no beginning, that is essentially self-existent, eternal. Short of this, the mind may pause, but it cannot rest. It is in suspense and unsatisfied until it has reached the end of that chain. It is not another axiom, but the same under another statement, that the cause of every fact—whether simple cause or indefinitely complex—must be an *adequate* cause. There must be nothing in the fact for which the cause is not sufficient; so that knowing the character of the fact, we may infer the nature of the cause. It is pretty safe to presume that the progress of science is not likely to disturb the authority of this axiom. In fact, it is this principle of causation that is the foundation of all scientific discovery, and, like all good foundations, it is only made the firmer by the growing massiveness of the superstructure.

Well; taking this principle of causation, Natural Theology has been accustomed to study the facts of the universe, and to find in them such indications as prove in the cause or causes of them the attributes of intelligence, of benevolence, of righteousness. Especially has it delighted in the study of the parts and the unity of the human frame, as being the confessed master-piece of nature's fine work, and affording the best illustrations of these divine attributes. One famous "Bridgewater treatise," "*Bell on the Hand,*" is devoted to the study of the mechanism of that member, its marvelous aptitude for its various functions in the service of man, as contrasted with the hands of the apes, which are exactly fitted for the apes' wants, but utterly unserviceable for men's. The favorite illustration of Paley, perhaps, is the mechanism of the eye, with its arrangement of lenses of different densities and qualities, and its mechanical appliances for the adjustment of the focal distance, which are in such curiously exact analogy with the contrivance of the achromatic refracting telescope. Another illustration is the construction of the heart, a double pump, with its exquisite valvular apparatus, exactly fitted for the function which it fulfills. To such examples as these, Natural Theology has been accustomed to point in triumph and say, "This evidence of design is proof of a designer."

But now there comes an answer to this summary argument, that the form of it is a begging of the question. "Design, you say, is proof of a designer. No doubt. But this is nothing more than playing back and forth between equivalent words. Of course, design proves a designer. The very question is, *is* the correspondency between structure and function *design;* or is it simple correspondency, attained by processes from which design was absent? We are prepared to show you traces of the actual processes by which the hand, the eye, the heart have come to be what they are through long processes of yielding to the plastic influences of their surroundings, from the earliest and lowest stages of life in the jelly-globule."

Now, my friends, neither you nor I are in a position where we can afford to sneer at such statements of scientific men as these. We are not, indeed, to be shut up by them, or cut off from the right to use our judgment about them; but that man does not stand to-day in any pulpit whose gifts of intellect or attainments in knowledge give him the right to *sneer* at the grave arguments and the splendid accumulations of facts which the earnest and devoted students of nature adduce in favor of their theory of development. For myself, I listen to these men with wonder and admiration,—I might almost say, with reverence. I beg them to show me, floating on the tide, or dredged from the mud and ooze underneath the deep sea, that shining gelatinous particle, with its rudiments of sensation and of motion, in which the possibilities of fish, bird, beast and man are hid as the oak is hid in the acorn,—and I gaze on it with profoundest awe. O more wonderful than hand, or eye, or heart of man, bright bud of existence, precursor of history, progenitor of heroes, founder of all founders of art, polity, philosophy, first pattern of maidenly and manly beauty, prototype of mind, affection, conscience, forefather of humanity,—hail, wondrous jelly-speck! I survey anew the world of human life, intelligence and society, and then turn again to look upon the flat and flabby mass in which is shut up the "promise and potency" of all these, and exclaim, with new depth of conviction and feeling, What must be the height and depth and length and breadth of that divine creative wisdom which could implant in this viscid lump of agglutinated cells the possibility, the prophecy, of the human hand, eye, heart, intellect and soul!

And if, again answering, you say, "Nay! not so fast with your inference of creative power and wisdom! but let me show you that even this rudimentary form can be traced along the line of causation to the chaotic whirl and stir and grind which did triturate the particles exceeding small, and tumble them about, and moisten them, and cool them, and warm them, and ferment them, and play on them with light and electricity and every mode of motion and chemic change, so that the cosmos was all contained in the chaos, and came forth of itself,"—I look again on man, "with native worth and honor clad, with beauty, courage, strength adorned," and turning back adore the divine plan, forethought, wisdom and omnipotence which created such a chaos, having such a destiny. For when the time shall come, if ever it does come, that science shall have said her last word and missed no step in the orderly arrangement of the facts of the universe, according to the order of cause and effect, and has accounted for every fact of the tremendous series, it then remains for her to account for *the series.* And this is beyond her scope. She finds herself, in this inquiry, in an atmosphere that can sustain neither her respiration nor her flight, and she falls gasping, fluttering, bedraggled to the ground. The best that science, the magnificent natural science of this latest of the centuries, has to offer in answer to this question, is the poor old pagan device of the Dance of Atoms— that if only this dance were kept up long enough the atoms might fall into the existing form, and then—who knows? —perhaps something—as consciousness, affection, intelligence, will—something might have come out of them that was never in them. Impossible! But granting this impossible thing, conceding that it might have been so, *we know* that it *wasn't so*. We look upon the face of nature, and it answers back our reason. We read The Origin of Species, and confess that that great book *might* have been produced by unconscious ravings of a lunatic or an imbecile, dropping without design into the form of coherence and consecutiveness; but we know that it *was* produced by a tenacious, orderly, perspicacious reason. Is there more evidence of reason in *expounding* the order of the universe than there is in the order of the universe itself? Does less wisdom, forsooth, go to the making of the system of nature, than to making a book about it?

In all this, I have done little more than rehearse, under another form, the old familiar argument from *fact* to *cause*. From the existence of the organ, we infer a cause. From the fitness of the organ to its discovered function, we infer the intelligence of the cause. From the beneficence of the function to which it is fitted, we infer the benevolence of the cause. This is the natural theology of the hand, the eye, the heart.

But in our exploration of the organs of the body, we come by and by upon one, the function, use, purpose of which has long been in doubt, and cannot yet be said to be fully and determinately settled, and that is *the spleen*. It has been studied for two thousand years. It has been examined with the scalpel and microscope and retort; in health and in disease; in man and in the brutes. And yet there it lies in its place among the viscera, and defies us to answer the question, What is the use of the spleen? It is the opprobrium of physiology. From the days of Hippocrates, in the fifth century B.C., there has been no lack of ingenious suggestions as to what it might be for, and conclusive arguments to show that it could not be for anything else. Hippocrates and Aristotle say "it is to draw off the watery parts of the food from the stomach." Another of the ancients says "it is to prepare the chyle for the liver." And another says "it is to draw the melancholic humor from the blood." Coming to more modern times, one says "it is to prepare blood from the chyle." And another finds its use to be "to ferment and separate the melancholic juice." Still another has a theory that it is "to secrete an aqueous humor to be supplied to the nerves," and finds two writers to agree with him. And by and by comes the great Malpighi, who completely overthrows all preceding theories, and does not succeed in putting anything satisfactory in the place of them. But still they don't give it up. Mayow thinks that it is a sort of vial for effervescent mixtures; and Drelincourt that it is to dilute thick blood; and Dionis that it is to refine gross blood; and Leeuwenhock that it is to propel stagnant blood; and one original Englishman has a theory that it is to elaborate the synovial fluid for lubricating the joints.

At length, in 1722, Stukely suggests that it is a reservoir for maintaining the balance of the circulation, and this seems to be accepted in our day as containing some part of the truth. But a half-century later Hewson held that the use of the spleen was to elaborate the red corpuscles of the blood; and this, too, might have enjoyed a general currency in our own day, except, unluckily, for the interference of three eminent German and French savants within a few years, who prove to their own satisfaction that the use of the spleen is to *destroy* the red corpuscles of the blood. Sir Everard Home divided his distinguished life between three different and highly original theories of the use of the spleen, which he successively demonstrated, and repudiated. And Oesterlen and Simon hold that it is meant to provide a small sinking-fund of nutriment; and Arthaud holds that it is an electrical battery.*

---

*For the ample history of scientific conjecture on this subject, see Gray's monograph On the Spleen.

Now, into the midst of all these mutually incompatible conjectures as to what is the purpose of the spleen—conjectures (the whole of which time would fail me to mention) extending over a period of twenty-three hundred years and still adding to their number—may I be allowed to interject a question?— What is your reason, gentlemen, through all these centuries, for supposing that the spleen *has* any purpose that it is adapted to? What makes you think that it is adapted to anything? Have you any reasonable objection to *this* theory—that the spleen has no purpose nor use? There is certainly as much experimental evidence for this theory as for any other. It is one hundred and fifty years since it was proved that the organ could be excised without apparent loss to the system. Two writers of thirty years ago give the result of repeated experiments of the kind, in very decided language. They "show conclusively," says Gray, "that its abstraction did not in the least interfere with the functions of life." In many cases, the subjects even improved by the operation. And Crisp, who writes in support of a somewhat different theory of the use of the spleen, and to expose the "glaring and fundamental errors" of Gray, declares that after the extirpation of the organ "the animals were more active and could run faster," and that there was "no abnormal change in their condition." And yet they go right forward to discuss the never-ending question, What is the purpose of the spleen? and nobody ever stops to ask the prior question, Is there any reason for supposing that the spleen has a purpose? Is this scientific—to spend twenty-three hundred years in inquiring what is the purpose of it before settling the question whether it has a purpose? Why not rest content with the assumption that it has none at all, and so save yourselves all this inquiry and debate?

It is easy to imagine the unanimous reply of men of science, "Oh, but you can't do that, you know. You can't help asking what is the use of such an organ. It must have a use, you know, or else it wouldn't be there. Why, there never would have been any science of physiology if we had not assumed that every organ had its function and object, and had not recognized it as a first principle of scientific research that the inquiry as to the function and object of every organ was to be followed up until that function and object were discovered— no matter how many centuries it might take,—and not to be given up like a bad conundrum. No; the suggestion that this viscus is simply useless is one to be rejected at once, as contrary to the fundamental principles of science."

Well, then, since I have been so unfortunate in my first essay at a theory, let me make another effort. I offer the hypothesis that the use and purpose of the spleen is simply for packing—to fill up waste room in the great cavity. And I have no sooner got the words out of my mouth than I am told that my hypothesis is unscientific, entitled to no consideration at all,—in fact, unsupposable. Packing, forsooth! Why, if we could suppose Nature, in her fine work, to be reduced to such awkward shifts, a mere wad of adipose tissue would serve her turn. The suggestion does not suffice to account for so elaborate an organ, with its intricate vascular and nervous arrangements. The purpose suggested is not an *adequate* purpose for such a structure.

This is getting to be very discouraging. But be patient with me once more. Practically, the spleen is best known to us as the *nidus* of certain diseases, some of them distressing and dangerous. The fact has been well known to all physiologists through all the period of active, restless inquiry as to the purpose of the spleen; and yet, with all their countless theories, there has not been a man of them to make the obvious supposition that this is the purpose of it—to promote distress and pain. Why has this been excluded, all the time, from among possible hypotheses? and why would it be cast out now, if I should have the temerity to offer it, as being untenable and unscientific? What is the scientific presumption against it, which makes it unworthy of consideration? For manifestly, whether tacit or expressed, science *has* such a presumption. And manifestly it is this, that in seeking for the purpose of an organ, a malignant purpose, or any other than a benevolent purpose, is unsupposable.

In short, we find, from this least understood viscus, that those things which we have been wont to prove in long and cumulative detail from the *results* of science, by the discovered proofs of design, of wise design, of benevolent design, in the facts of the universe, inferring the wisdom, power, benevolence of the cause—these things we find to be all *presumed* by science from the outset of her work, as among the necessary postulates upon which she works. Consciously or unconsciously, science has held in the one hand the axiom that everything which has a beginning must have a cause, and an adequate cause; and, in the other hand, with hardly less firm a grasp, has held it as an axiom that everything which has an end must have a purpose, an adequate purpose, a good purpose. Scientific men have sometimes been faithless, or thought themselves so; but, consciously or unconsciously, science itself is a believer. The truths of pure religion are her inspiration and her guide. Her postulates, her methods, her unsolved problems, the progress of her uncompleted work, all declare it. Paley, and the Bridgewater Treatises, with their vast array of demonstrated facts, may step aside. In claiming the universe for its King and Maker, we need call no witness from the great realm of human knowledge. We summon testimony from the vaster realm of the unknown. Through all the explored regions of the universe we follow reverently the lead of science, and above us, and beneath us, and on either hand, we hear the voices of the whole creation testify of God. And when we have followed our guide to the end of her trodden paths, and stand beside her on the awful brink of the unknown, and hear her solemn and inquiring voice cry out into the dark, a voice rolls up from that abyss, and answers, GOD.

In no respect do the processes and methods of science more

distinctly reveal the principles of true religion as being its own principles, than in the constant, pertinacious, inexorable demand for unity—unity of origin, unity of law, and (as we are beginning now to see) unity of purpose. The latest born of the sciences, the science of language, does not so much see the common origin of human speech, as it prophesies it as a thing to be discovered, declaring that there can be no such thing as a science of language, unless on the presumption that all languages are of one. Chemistry is not content with having simplified the universe down to its few dozen of elements, but must keep on in the quest for the one ultimate atom; as astronomy is exploring for the universal centre, having long ago proclaimed the unity and universality of law. It is not so much true that physics has at last discovered that all forces are one force, as that it has always felt this to be true, and now at last is finding out how to prove it. Even the craving and groping for proofs of an unbroken line of causation from eternity hitherto and henceforth to eternity again, are utterances of a like instinctive conviction. Our inquiries into nature are predicated on the unity of nature. The first axiom of the logic of scientific inquiry is virtually this: *The Lord thy God is one God.* And this, whichever way we reason, whether from the fact to its cause, and so through prior causes to the First Cause, or from the fact to its purposes, and so through remoter purposes to the Final Purpose,—this is virtually the last conclusion: *The Lord thy God is one God.* Here on our moment of time we stand and witness the entrance of some new fact into being. Small or great—the crystallizing of a snow-flake or the catastrophe of an empire—every fact is a link between two chains that reach out into two eternities, past and future. At the point where these meet, our minds can not stand still. They are impelled in each direction. We ask the cause of the fact and the cause of the cause. We ask the purpose of it, and the purpose of the purpose. Atheism, driven thus toward the infinite in one direction, comes back to be impelled alike toward the infinite in the other;

and on either shore of the known and finite world it stands aghast, confounded and shuddering, gazing blankly into the dark. But holy Wisdom finds, at either bound, no darkness at all, but light. It does not slink back confounded from the endless quest. Erect it stands upon the verge of time and matter, and plumes its wings of faith for flight into the unseen. For unto it the darkness beyond is illuminated, and the void immensity is filled, and eternity is inhabited, by Him "of whom, and through whom, yea, and *to* whom, are all things; to whom be glory forever."

The soul that comes back from such a vision of God finds the visible creation to be a different place from what it was before. The dead universe has become alive with God. The air is full of God. The earth is full of him. So is the great and wide sea wherein are things innumerable, both small and great. And, above all, the soul is full of him, and dwells in God, and God in it.

For as we tread along this track of reasoning from purpose to remoter purpose, which leads at last to God as the great End and Final Purpose of all, we find, at first, that all things seem to point more or less directly toward the soul of man as the immediate object of creation. The world seems made for man. Nature is his servant, and ministers to him, even when maltreated and abused—nay! all the more faithfully when toiling through her retributions of pain and travail, than when exulting in her original and joyous destiny. All things are for man. The sun and moon and the seven stars come forth, as in the dream of the dreamer, and make obeisance to him. The flowers and the grain are for him, but not more than the thorns and the thistles are for him. The glad and wholesome atmosphere is for him, but not more truly than the miasm and the breath of pestilence. The heart is for the soul's sake, and the veins that throb with the happy consciousness of living, and the nerves that are busy with carrying messages of pleasant sensation to the seat of life; but oh, how often have these been more wonderful and more true servants to the soul, when the heart has heaved heavily and slowly, or the fevered blood has burned through all its channels, and the shattered nerves reported nothing to the brain but one long complaint of weariness and pain;—how often have they wrought out thus for the soul, through sorrow and trouble, what they never could have wrought through health! So health is yours, and sickness is yours. Life is yours, and more wonderfully death is yours. Yea, all things are for the soul of man. But for what purpose is the soul? Verily, the soul is Christ's and Christ is God's.

O souls of men, created by him and for him, consider well the Source from which you are sprung, the image in which you are created, the Father from whose home you have been wandering. Think how all things are made to minister to you, working for your good, that you should serve and glorify the eternal God. Consider this, the chief and final purpose of your existence—" to glorify God, and enjoy him forever"— and that if this be missed, whatever success beside you may achieve, your life is a disastrous failure. In all your consciousness of ignorance, weakness, wickedness, commit yourself to the everlasting arms of strength, to the infinite heart of forgiveness,—trust, and be not afraid; and exult to find the Beginning of all causes, the End of all designs, the Solution of all mysteries, the Fountain of all knowledge, the Goal of all inquiry, the Satisfaction of all aspirations, in Him by whom, and for whom, were all things created. Let your anxious questionings of nature begin, and your triumphant solutions end, with the humble confession which is at the same time a hymn of thankful praise:—

> "From thee, great God, we spring, to thee we tend,—
> Path, Motive, Guide, Original, and End."

XXI.

THE SCRIPTURAL DOCTRINE CONCERNING SCRIPTURE.

Ye search the Scriptures, because ye think that in them ye have eternal life; and these are they which bear witness of me; and ye will not come to me that ye may have life.—JOHN v. 39, 40.

THE volume which we call *the Bible* is the subject of our continual study as a congregation of Christian believers. Twice every Lord's Day you assemble to hear the discussion and exposition of its texts. Again during the week many of us spend an evening together in the methodical study of it. On Sunday afternoons, our children, simultaneously with millions of other children, sit down to the careful scrutiny of an appointed lesson from it. And in every home it is a domestic guide and a personal counselor. As a book, to teach, guide, strengthen and inspire us, we know it well, and mean to know it better.

I am not sure that we know the Bible as well, and consider it as duly, *as a fact to be accounted for*. Considered thus, it is a phenomenon unique in history. I will not venture to frame words of my own with which to describe the Bible as it stands among the facts of human life and history to-day, lest you might think I had fallen into the pulpit fault of over-stating my case; still less will I take the statement of some advocate pledged by his theological position to extol and defend the Bible. I will rather ask you to listen to the statement of a most unfriendly witness, the delight of whose life was to affront and offend the sensibilities of those who regarded the Bible with any measure of religious reverence and to treat its claims of authority with contemptuous and insolent disparagement. Let me read you his language:

"This collection of books has taken such a hold on the world as no other. The literature of Greece, which goes up like incense from that land of temples and heroic deeds, has not half the influence of this book from a nation alike despised in ancient and modern times. It is read of a Sabbath in all the ten thousand pulpits of our land In all the temples of Christendom is its voice lifted up, week by week. The sun never sets on its gleaming page. It goes equally to the cottage of the plain man and the palace of the king. It is woven into the literature of the scholar, and colors the talk of the street. The bark of the merchant cannot sail the sea without it; no ship of war goes to the conflict but the Bible is there. It enters men's closets; mingles in all the grief and cheerfulness of life. The affianced maiden prays God in Scripture for strength in her new duties; men are married by Scripture. The Bible attends them in their sickness, when the fever of the world is on them. The aching head finds a softer pillow when the Bible lies underneath. The mariner, escaping from shipwreck, clutches this first of his treasures, and keeps it sacred to God. It goes with the peddler, in his crowded pack; cheers him at even-tide, when he sits down, dusty and fatigued; brightens the freshness of his morning face. It blesses us when we are born; gives names to half Christendom; rejoices with us; has sympathy for our mourning; tempers our grief to finer issues. It is the better part of our sermons. It lifts man above himself; our best of uttered prayers are in its storied speech, wherewith our fathers and the patriarchs prayed. The timid man, about awaking from this dream of life, looks through the glass of Scripture and his eye grows bright; he does not fear to stand alone, to tread the way unknown and distant, to take the death-angel by the hand and bid farewell to wife and babes and home. Men rest on this their dearest hopes. It tells them of God and of his blessed Son; of earthly duties and of heavenly rest. Foolish men find it the source of Plato's wisdom and the science of Newton and the art of Raphael. Men who believe nothing else that is spiritual believe the Bible all through; without this they would not confess, say they, even that there was a God.

"Now for such effects there must be an adequate cause. That nothing comes of nothing is true all the world over. It is no light thing to hold with an electric chain a thousand hearts, though but an hour, beating and bounding with such fiery speed. What is it then to hold the Christian world, and that for centuries? Are men fed with chaff and husks? The authors we reckon great, whose word is in the newspapers and the market-place, whose articulate breath now sways the nation's mind, will soon pass away, giving place to other great men of a season, who in their turn shall follow them to eminence and then oblivion. Some thousand famous writers come up in this century, to be forgotten in the next. But the silver cord of the Bible is not loosed nor its golden bowl broken, as time chronicles his tens of centuries passed by. Has the human race gone mad? Time sits as a refiner of metal; the dross is piled in forgotten heaps, but the pure gold is reserved for use, passes into the ages, and is current a thousand years hence as well as to-day. It is only real merit that can long pass for such. Tinsel will rust in the storms of life. False weights are soon detected here. It is only a heart that can speak deep and true to a heart; a mind to a mind; a soul to a soul; wisdom to the wise, and religion to the pious. There must then be in the Bible, mind, heart and soul, wisdom and religion. Were it otherwise, how could millions find it their lawgiver, friend and prophet? Some of the greatest of human institutions seem built on the Bible. Such things will not stand on heaps of chaff, but mountains of rock." *

This is the language of Theodore Parker; and with characteristic aptitude at missing the best point in his subject while hitting all around it with well chosen words, he omits the one most notable and exceptional thing in the career of the Bible through history—that it is identified with those well authenticated cases of vital and revolutionary change in personal character, by which some individuals (not to say multitudes of them) from being selfish, impure or otherwise radically bad, have been transformed into noble types of human excellence. You must add this transforming virtue which seems, if not to reside in the volume, at least to be associated with it, if you would fully know the measure of the phenomenon which is to be accounted for.

It is not very essential to the line of inquiry which we pursue this evening, whether we look for the explanation of this

* A Discourse of Matters pertaining to Religion, by Theodore Parker. Boston, 1847. Pp. 301–304.

impressive and solitary fact in human literature inside of the marvelous volume, or outside of it. When Mr. Parker goes on in one scornful page after another to disparage the contents of the book whose effects on society and humanity he is compelled to bear witness to, he is only making his problem the more portentously difficult. By just as far as he succeeds in proving that the book itself is nothing but a common book, not essentially distinguished from other books of human literature, by just so far he enforces the inference that there is a *power behind the book* that is competent to these prodigious results, for which human forces in every age, literatures, philosophies, priestcrafts, governments, have toiled in vain. The results of the book are confessed; and he who confesses the results confesses the power adequate to produce the results. It is from the results that we estimate the power. And the power that is adequate to such results, so mighty beyond the achievement of human forces, so beneficent, so spiritual, so holy, is a power for which we have no word but this—*divine*. Construe it as you please (it is indifferent to my present argument), whether as a power within the book, or a power behind the book, or a power attending on the book, there is a power there somehow, which by all its characters is certified to be of God; and which impresses on the book, in some measure, more or less, the stamp of a divine warrant and approval. So much as this, then, I shall presume to be admitted (and it is not presuming very far)— that in an exceptional sense of the words, in which they are not true of other books, there is something divine in or about that book which we call the Bible.

Now there is a ready inference which suggests itself at once to many minds as soon as this presumption is accepted as a premiss. Do not accept it hastily, but scrutinize it well; and I think it will strike you as at least a very natural inference, and a very plausible one. It is this: that that volume which has been impressed with a divine sanction and indorsement, whether by mighty works attending it, or by divine wisdom and virtue infused into it, will be divinely perfect in all its parts and details. How natural this inference is, may be more readily seen from a human analogy. If a scientific man of the highest eminence for attainments in knowledge and judgment and original discovery, should choose to confer great authority before the whole public upon the book of some other author, by aiding in the preparation of it, by enriching it with his own best thoughts and discoveries, and by sanctioning it with strong practical expressions of approval, so that the book came into wide currency and effective influence, I hardly see how the great man would fail to be deemed responsible before the public for the character of the book in all respects. If the book thus floated into effective and influential circulation by his masterly suggestions and contributions is found to abound in vicious and blundering scientific processes, his scientific reputation will suffer. If the book includes, incidentally to its scientific pages, some mischievous political or theological notions, it will be felt that they are given weight and currency by his great name, even though his name does not stand alone on the title-page. And even rhetorical and grammatical blunders in the book will shed discredit upon him, if he is known to have had full knowledge of the whole course of the preparation of it, even down to the proof-reading. The only limitation to his responsibility for the book which he has lifted into influence and success, and over which, at every stage in its progress, he has had full control, is in his own disclaimers and disavowals.

It is not a strange thing, therefore, but a very natural thing, that in the case of a book which, through a certain divine influence and sanction, has attained to an authority quite without parallel in human literature, men should infer that since the divine knowledge and control over its whole preparation has been complete and absolute, therefore the divine authorization must extend to its uttermost details. And when this easy inference has been favored by a supposed necessity of theologians, and they have argued that if a possibility of human error and weakness was to be admitted anywhere in the divine book, then all the foundations were gone and there was no more ground of confidence about anything,—it is no wonder that for these many generations the stout assertion, on the part of theologians who assumed the highest rank as orthodox and evangelical, of this claim as to what the Bible *ought to be* and *must be*, has discouraged or precluded any patient, diligent inquiry as to what the Bible actually *is*. The poorest pages of our systems of theology, the most worthless shelves in our theological libraries, have confessedly been those occupied with treatises on this subject. It has been pre-eminently the unsettled point of theology. The claim too often made on the one hand, that the Bible must be nothing but divine, or else not divine at all, has too often been conceded on the other hand, and has divided thoughtful men into two hostile camps, one party claiming that in the Bible were no traces of human weakness, the other that in it was no evidence of superhuman wisdom, leaving between the two a neutral multitude, having no very well defined views of their own, doing their best to avoid being hit by the shots of either party. A very miserable plight had theology got itself into, on this subject, when, not out of the facts of the Scriptures, but out of its notions of what the Scriptures ought to be, and out of the exigencies of its own controversies, it had contrived an unscriptural and untenable theory of Scripture, and then given the world its choice between that and infidelity.

And yet if we turn back to that argument and analogy which seemed to point us so clearly toward the conclusion of a divine authorization of every word of Scripture, we find a limitation in it which modifies the whole aspect of the case, and suggests to us a method of study in which we may hope to reach the true doctrine of Holy Scripture; and this—*the right method of studying the question*,—is the subject of this evening's discourse. The *right application of this method* is too extensive a subject, and involves too great a multitude of particulars, to be more than touched upon incidentally, from point to point, by way of illustration.

We have seen, in that analogy of human duty and responsibility which we have drawn, that the only limitation to one's responsibility for a book which he has lifted into influence and success, and over which he has had full control, lies in his own disavowals and disclaimers. If, on the title-page, he says that his contribution to the book is limited to the furnishing of certain information, and that he is not to be understood as guarantying the scientific soundness of the rest of the book; if he announces in a preface that he has no sympathy with such political or theological notions as the writer has mixed up with his scientific arguments, or that he has refrained, for good reasons, from any attempt to improve his young friend's literary style, or retouch his grammar, or even correct his proof-sheets; —then there remains no longer any just ground either of discrediting a great and honorable name by imputing to it unworthy defects and errors; or, on the other hand, of giving mischievous currency to false notions, by clothing them with the authority of the great name.

And now taking once more into our hands this confessedly incomparable and in some sense divine book, let us examine to see whether it contains any disclaimers and disavowals of divine agency and responsibility for any part of it, or whether, according to an opinion that has had much currency, and has often been defended as essential to Christianity, it has the guaranty of divine perfection in all details. We do not need to look for such disclaimers in a preface or a title-page. It may well be that, if we are only willing to see them and be taught by them, we shall find them looking us in the face at the opening of the book. The signs of a divine perfection, in some respects at least, are not difficult for us to recognize; and if openly on the face of the page we find distinctly set the indubitable mark of human fault, it is the clearest announcement that the book could give us of the limitation of the divine warranty.

SCRIPTURAL DOCTRINE CONCERNING SCRIPTURE. 239

1. The first question is: Has there been a divinely infallible and perfect preservation of the original text of the Scriptures? And very short and prompt is the answer to this question from every page of the critical Greek Testament with its one hundred and fifty thousand various readings.

The unquestionable, palpable fact was long flatly denied in the name of orthodoxy. Men said, "Of what use is it to have an infallible Word of God, unless we have an infallibly exact copy of it?" They set up a solemn warning: "If you make the least concession that there may be mistakes in our copies of the Scriptures, you give up the whole case to the enemies of religion." So they refused to learn from the Scriptures what the Scriptures, by the facts of the case, plainly teach us about themselves. We know better—no credit to us; we have been taught better in spite of ourselves; the myriads of facts have been forced upon us until we cannot help knowing that we possess the Scriptures in more or less imperfect copies of the original writings. If this is not the sort of Bible we wish we had,—if it is not such as we think we need,—it is nevertheless such as God has thought good to give us, with his own warning written plainly across the face of it, that we are not to count on the infallible accuracy of the copies.

It is very easy to say that the variations do not affect any important matter of instruction*—easy to say it, but not to maintain it. That the only categorical statement of the doctrine of the Trinity in all the Bible is known to be a spurious text—that the history of the woman taken in adultery has a questionable right in the gospel of John—that the story of the

---

* "It is the *unanimous* testimony of Christian scholars, that while these variations embarrass the interpretation of many details, they neither involve the loss nor *abate the evidence* of a single essential fact or doctrine of Christianity!" Prof. *A. A. Hodge*, "Outlines," 75.

"Extravagant words are weak words" was a maxim of Daniel Webster which has no more important application than its application to theological exposition.

resurrection of Jesus at the end of the gospel of Mark is of doubtful genuineness,—these are *not* facts unimportant to Christian truth. And be they great, or be they small, when the question is on the absolute divine infallibility of the text, one little error will disprove it as much as ten thousand great ones.*

Without pausing over the minor question whether or not we have, on the face of the Scriptures, any like disclaimer of divine infallibility in points of taste, rhetoric and grammar, I inquire,—

2. Whether the Scriptures themselves do or do not distinctly disavow any perfect and divine freedom from error in facts of nature and science. And I find the material for an answer in such a text as Mark iv. 31, which declares that the mustard-

---

* It was a fundamental point of the orthodoxy of the post-reformation age—the age of the Westminster Confession—to maintain the infallibility of the received text: that "God not only took care to have his word committed to writing, but has also watched and cherished it ever since it was written up to the present time, so that it could not be corrupted." Thus the *Formula Consensus Helvetica*, 1675, which proceeds to denounce the questioning of the Hebrew vowel-points as "imperiling the foundation of our faith." In like manner the Westminster Confession declares that the Greek and Hebrew texts, having been by God's "singular care and providence kept pure in all ages, are therefore authentical"

It is curious to observe that in our degenerate day it has become an essential point with the sworn defenders of the Westminster Confession not only to deny this "fundamental" proposition, but also to deny that the Church ever held it! (*A. A. Hodge*, "Outlines," 75.) It is found to be an essential condition for defending the infallibility of the Scriptures against the allegations of discrepancy, boldly to disclaim the infallibility of the Scriptures as the Church now possesses them, and to assert it only of "the original autographs" which no one has seen for seventeen hundred years, and no one expects to see again. The ingenuous neophyte in training for the gospel ministry is instructed, when pressed by those abundant facts with which the Scriptures would teach us concerning themselves, to run for a double corner of the checker-board, and move to and fro between (1) the obscurity of Scripture and doubtfulness of all in-seed "is less than all the seeds that be in the earth;" or in Leviticus xi. 5, 6, and Deuteronomy xiv. 7, which declare that the hare and the coney chew the cud. I mention these as two of the most distinct and obvious—I might say intentionally obvious—instances. It looks as if it had not been the divine purpose that we should be left in any doubt as to whether the Bible was miraculously exact on such points, by permitting two such inexact statements, on points so easily determined, to look us in the face from the Old Testament and the New. For the hare and the coney are not ruminants, but rodents; and the mustard-seed is larger than the seed of the poppy, or the rue. Now when the Scriptures have so distinctly notified us that they are not to be held responsible for exact scientific

---

terpretations; and (2) the sheer impossibility of ever proving anything to have been in "the original autograph." Holding these two points, he may safely bid defiance to all "rationalist critics," and to all efforts of the Bible to teach him about itself. (*Ibid.* 76.)

Concerning this theologizing I have to remark:

1. Whatever else it may be, it palpably is not the doctrine of the Westminster Confession; and, on the part of those vowed to maintain this document in all its details, can best be defended on the equity-principle of *cy-près*—that when the Confession becomes hopelessly untenable, then it is right to hold the thing that seems to come nearest to it.

2. The "original autograph" doctrine is futile and useless. The question of practical importance to the Church is this:—what sort of Scriptures are these which we actually possess; not whether the Church once had infallible documents which it has now lost.

3. The doctrine as stated in the text-book in question is lax, unsafe, and unsettling to the foundations. The advice that when you are hard pushed with a discrepancy you can always conjecture a corruption from the "original autograph," is a repudiation of the conservative principle of sound criticism that the difficult reading is the probable reading. It invites the wildest license It is in the worst sense of the word "rationalistic criticism" If we may resort to this imaginary "autograph" to evade a troublesome discrepancy, why not to escape an unwelcome doctrine?

statement, is it worth our while seriously to fret ourselves because the first chapter of Genesis puts the birds before the reptiles instead of after? And does it really pay for us to cover any more shelves of our libraries with dull books to reconcile Genesis to Geology?

3. Do the Scriptures give us any intimation as to whether or not their writers were divinely guided into an infallible exactness of historical statement? There is one very remarkable characteristic of the structure of the Bible from beginning to end, which is peculiarly adapted to give us light on this point. Its historical narratives are written in duplicate, or in triplicate,—in the most important parts, in quadruplicate,—so that by reading different narratives of the same event side by side, we may judge of the degree of exactness or of variation which they bear in comparison with each other. We have two separate stories of the creation, partly overlapping, and not precisely agreeing. We have two different stories of the deluge, manifestly by different writers, and wrought together by the author and compiler of the book of Genesis in a way so inartificial as if it were meant that every reader's attention should be invited to whatever there is of repetition or coincidence or discrepancy.

This characteristic, which appears on the very first pages of the Bible, goes through the whole of it. The narrative of the book of Exodus is duplicated in parts in the books of Leviticus and Numbers, and then recapitulated in Deuteronomy, and briefly reviewed in certain of the Psalms, and finally rehearsed, with some notable variations, in the speech of Stephen in the Acts of the Apostles. When the two narratives purport to give a transcript of the same document, and that a document of supreme importance—the very writing of God in the Ten Commandments,—we are thereby invited to observe whether the transcription is exact or inexact, and whether the discrepancy affects matters of any importance. [See Exodus xx. 2–17; and Deuteronomy v. 6–21.]

We go forward in the volume, and come to the books of Samuel and Kings, parallel to which we find the two books of Chronicles, and these again duplicated in part by some chapters of Isaiah. We find the same document professedly given in 2 Samuel xxii., and in Psalm xviii.; and may observe how far the two copies tally.

Without delaying on such details, which are multitudinous, we turn to the New Testament, and, as in the Old Testament, we find a distinct warning on the first page, as to whether or not the historical statements of the book are to be regarded as set forth with a supernatural infallibility of exactitude. Matthew i. 17, reads:

"So all the generations from Abraham to David are fourteen generations; and from David to the carrying away into Babylon are fourteen generations; and from the carrying away into Babylon to Christ are fourteen generations."

Count them on that very page, and see how it comes out; and then refer to the genealogies of the Old Testament, and see whether you find the evidence of a divine miracle of exactness in the way in which they are transcribed, or the evidence of very human work indeed. Has the first page of the New Testament any lesson for us on the subject of the alleged verbal and mathematical infallibility of the Scriptures?

The whole series of the four gospels invites us to observe discrepancies. "He went up into the mountain," says Matthew, and preached the Sermon on the Mount. "He came down to a level place," says Luke. "He healed a blind man as he was coming to Jericho," says Luke; "he healed two blind men as he was leaving Jericho,"—and with the same language and circumstances,—says Matthew. There are three varying reports of the words at Christ's baptism and four varying transcripts of the title on the cross; and four varying reports of the solemn words of the Lord at the institution of the Holy Supper. Is there any way which could have been taken so effectually to renounce and repudiate, in behalf of the Scriptures, those pretentions to a supernatural exactness of historical statement which they never set up for themselves, which by their very structure, from beginning to end, they so openly disavow and disclaim, but which the ignorant zeal of theologians in the last two centuries (for this is a very modern heresy with which we are contending—this infallibility dogma of Protestantism) has been forcing upon the Scriptures in spite of themselves.

"But is there not some way of harmonizing or getting around these discrepancies between parallel Scriptures, consistently with the infallible accuracy of each one?" Oh yes, indeed and alas, there are many and many such ways! It is one of the most sorrowful chapters in the sorrowful history of the abuse of the Scriptures, the chapter which records the doublings and twistings and turnings of interpreters, in passages like these, when they apply all their resources of learning and ingenuity in the effort to make believe that something is not there, which visibly and palpably *is* there. It is a strange sign of a teachable spirit, when men come to regard the very facts and phenomena of the book which they affect to be taught by, as something to be dodged, evaded and got round. It is a strange sort of reverence for the Bible, when, in the interest of an artificial dogma of their own contriving, men set aside the teachings of the Bible itself.*

Now in these arguments I have done little more than give some illustrative instances of the *method of study* that must be pursued if we would come at the Bible doctrine concerning the

---

* Dr. Charles Hodge [Theology, I., 170] says: "Not less unreasonable is it to deny the inspiration" [he uses the word as equivalent to *supernatural infallibility*] "of such a book as the Bible, because one sacred writer says that on a given occasion, twenty-four thousand, and another says that twenty-three thousand men were slain. Surely a Christian may be allowed to *tread such objections under his feet*."

Undoubtedly, in a land of religious liberty, this class of Christians "may be allowed," under claim of special reverence for the Bible, to

SCRIPTURAL DOCTRINE CONCERNING SCRIPTURE. 245

Bible. We have asked, 1, whether there is any evidence on the face of the Scriptures of a miraculous care for the exact preservation of the original text of its component documents; and we have found full and conclusive evidence of the contrary. We have asked, 2, whether the facts on the face of the Scriptures countenance the claim of a miraculous infallibility in matters of natural science; and we have found that instead of countenancing it, by very distinct implication they disclaim it. We have asked, 3, whether the Scriptures give us any intimation that their writers were guided into an infallible exactness of historical statement; and we have found that the Scriptures seem to be so constructed in systems of parallel narrations as to afford answers to this question from page to page, and that these answers are as conclusive in the negative as it is possible for such answers to be.

In like manner we may seek in the Bible itself for an answer to the question, 4, whether this book, so manifestly approved, sanctioned and blessed of God, in which are such manifest signs of a divine influence, has been supernaturally secured in all details from error in its *predictions*. It contains in its own pages the books of the history alongside of the books of the prophets, and it invites us thus to compare spiritual things with spiritual, and say whether or not the history exactly tallies in its particulars with the particulars of the prophecy that went before it. What are they there for, side by side, unless it is that we may learn this?

We may go on and ask, 5, whether the course of the Scrip-

"trample under foot" the evidence to which the Bible so frankly invites the attention of all readers, bearing on the question of its miraculous accuracy on historical and statistical matters. They have no better use for some of the most conspicuous and characteristic facts and phenomena of the Scriptures, than to be blinked, or concealed, or "trodden under foot of men." A truer reverence for the Bible, and a stronger and calmer faith in the God of the Bible will give courage candidly to examine these teachings of the Bible, and docility to learn from them.

tures has been miraculously guarded in such a way as that even in the darkest and most barbarous ages, no error of *moral* judgment, no expression of approbation of any wrong act or spirit has anywhere entered them through the imperfection of their human writers. It is right for us to ask the question, and it must be answered out of the facts of the Scriptures themselves; not out of our preconceptions and predeterminations of what the Scriptures ought to be. It is not a difficult line of study— to compare the song of Deborah with the first epistle of John— the book of Joshua with the Sermon on the Mount—the sixty-ninth Psalm with the prayer of the Crucified—and say whether or not the moral judgments and sentiments of these different passages are alike representative of the one unchanging, eternal, absolute standard of right and wrong; or whether we are able to discover some differences between them, and to recognize, in the long series of books that lead at last to the gospels in which the glory of God shines out upon us in the face of Jesus Christ the profoundly instructive and most hopeful and helpful record of the way in which the Father of this wandering, sinful human race has led his wayward children, through all the ages of primeval darkness, up to where the true light now shineth.

These are only examples of the questions which need to be asked of the Scriptures, if we would know from the Scriptures themselves what it is that they claim to be and do. And these are only illustrations of the frank and unreserved way in which the Scriptures are ready to answer, if only dogmatizers would get out of the way with their pettifogging "harmonizings" and "reconcilings," and let the honest old book speak for itself. More than these I have not time to give; for this subject, which I have thus touched on for an hour, could not be adequately treated in a volume.

I know with what serious and anxious dread the questions will be put, "If we concede one jot of all these claims of criticism, where are we going to stop? If we have not a Bible that is infallible in every word, how shall we know what we can rely on as infallible? If we admit that there is human imperfection anywhere, what good will our Bible do us?" Dear, timid brethren, these questions have been put again and again, at point after point, by the defenders of extravagant and untenable statements — unscriptural statements concerning Scripture—as they have reluctantly evacuated them and fallen back; and the Church of Christ still lives, yea! and is like to live, in spite of the gates of hell, in spite of the timorousness of its own defenders. It is very little that we need concern ourselves, in this inquiry, about what sort of Bible you think you ought to have, or feel as if you could not do without. Our concern is to know the Bible as it has pleased God that it should come to us, and to make the best we can of that. If you think it a small and useless thing that you have in your hands a volume attested as no other human history has been attested, for its substantial truth, bearing in its gospels marks of a simple honesty and integrity that are themselves the token of a divine inspiration, full of disclosures of God that approve themselves to the touchstone of the conscience and the reason, containing incentives of holiness that show transforming power over the heart of man, and change the face of society and the course of history;—if you put away as an unworthy thing the words that bring you into acquaintance with the very Son of God made man, and scorn them because they come in human humbleness, withdrawing themselves from factitious honors which men thrust upon them, wearing no halo of supernatural exactness in things indifferent to their great purpose,—then I pray to be delivered from a share in your ingratitude. I reach out my hand to take to myself this treasure of his gospel, yea! though it be brought to me in earthen vessels, and seek that it may be to me his wisdom to salvation.

Is it a light thing that you have a gospel that is able to bring you to Jesus Christ? Take heed lest you provoke upon your own souls the rebuke contained in the text with which we began—a text the true meaning of which, long hidden from English readers, is now made clear in the Revised Version. Take heed lest you renew that olden folly of the unbelieving Jews, who searched the Scriptures because they thought that in *them* was eternal life—but would not come to Christ of whom they testified.

XXII.

RESURRECTION IN CHRIST.

The witness is this: that God gave unto us eternal life, and this life is in his Son. He that hath the Son hath the life; he that hath not the Son of God hath not the life.—1 JOHN v. 11.

THIS day, with all its brightness and joy, reminds us, by the shadow that it casts, that we have come, within these last few years, to a new period of religious thought. The world has moved forward (if we ought not rather to say *backward*) to a time when many serious, thoughtful, *religiously* thoughtful souls are gravely doubting whether there is any future life for man. So far as I know the history of religious opinion, this is something new in Christendom. Of course, there have been irreligious and anti-religious people before now, in every age; there have been gross materialists and sensualists who have loved to say "let us eat and drink, for to-morrow we die;" there have been professional scoffers and defamers of the gospel, who have spit out their contempt on the doctrine of a future life, as being part of a system they detested. Less than a hundred years ago, in a characteristic fury of reaction from the abuses of the church, the French people carried their sudden and brief hatred of everything Christian so far as to paint up over their graveyards "Death is an Eternal Sleep." But they soon painted the words out again. There have been instances enough of this gross, sensualist unbelief of any life to come, especially in the last century. But they have been exceptional cases, and commonly not very respectable cases. They have been cases to be pointed at as something abnormal and pitiable. There have not been enough of them to modify the general proposition that the serious thinking of all the Christian nations, since there began to be Christian nations, has been pervaded and impregnated with the thorough conviction that man is to live again after death. The literature of Christendom, even its infidel literature—its Rousseau, its Voltaire, its Byron—has presumed the fact of the life to come, or has even distinguished itself by insisting on its own doctrine of the natural immortality of man, as being part of its system of natural religion. All along there have been plenty of arguments and debates about the future life, as to what sort of life it should be,—how, where, with whom, in what body, whether in any body at all and not rather as purely spiritual existences, we should live after death. But on the great question—"If a man die, shall he live again?"—there has been a prevailing harmony of views. The affirmative has been commonly taken for granted by sober, earnest writers of all schools, through all these Christian centuries. Says Dean Milman: "Since the promulgation of Christianity, the immortality of the soul and its inseparable consequence, future retribution, have not only been assumed by the legislator as the basis of all political institutions; but the general mind has been brought into such complete union with the spirit of the laws so founded, that the individual repugnance to the principle has been constantly overborne by the general predominant sentiment." This Christian doctrine of the life to come, the same solid and sober historian declares to be "the parent of all which is purifying, ennobling, unselfish in Christian civilization."*

But now, as I have already said, as we come near the beginning of the twentieth century after Christ, we have struck upon a new period in the history of religious thought, in which, not by flippant and violent blasphemers, nor by sensualists contriving doctrines to suit their vices, but by studious, thoughtful truth-seeking men and women, of honorable, pure and upright

---

* History of Christianity, I., 354.

lives, the subject of the life to come has become a subject, sometimes of painful doubt and hopeless ignorance, sometimes of settled disbelief. Perhaps I could not quote a more apt example (though I might give you many and distinguished names) than that of one of the greatest women of our century, Harriet Martineau. No one can deny that she was a woman of some high qualities, intellectual and moral; and that in some great works of authorship—notably in her history of the Thirty Years' Peace of Europe—she nobly served her own and later generations. In her autobiography, we find her, a thoughtful, earnest, philanthropic woman, meditating on the shortening span of life and the approach of death, without an expectation, and, as she declares, without a desire, of any life beyond the grave. She has tasted life with delight, but has had enough of it, and has no wish to repeat the draft. She has had the satisfaction of accomplishing some good for the world in her time; but she has done enough, and thinks now that the world has no further need of Harriet Martineau. She has chosen to draw her own portrait in this attitude—an old woman sitting on the further brink of life and looking out into the dark without hope and without God. She is not an exception, she is a representative—one of a multitude of noble intellects of our time that have sunk down into the same darkness. Has such a thing been known before in Christendom? Said I not well that we have come to a new period of religious thought?

And if you ask, does not all this betoken a dreadful outbreak of human depravity, or of diabolical deceit, that so many of the best minds of our time should bring themselves to this position, from which, as we are wont to say, human nature instinctively recoils, abhorring the thought of extinction:—if you ask, is it not a fact of awful and alarming portent, as if we were drawing near to a general "eclipse of faith,"—I answer, it does not so seem to me. It does not appear that these minds have come to their gloomy and forlorn position by any so very irrational a course. It seems rather as if they had been betrayed into it, by having been taught the doctrine of a future life on fallacious arguments, and then, looking sharply into these arguments, having found them to be insufficient. These people have been so trained in the school of scientific investigation, that they will not take a proposition on insufficient evidence. For these many and many ages, and especially in recent ages, Christian theologians have been accustomed to speak of this doctrine of human immortality as a doctrine of natural religion, which the gospel merely comes in to confirm. And when these keen, severe critics come to look into the arguments alleged to prove that it is the nature of man to be immortal, they find that the arguments will not hold water. They go back to Plato, and read that touching dialogue that tells of Socrates dying by poison while he sits among his disciples discoursing of the immortality of the soul;—and they say, "Oh yes, it is all very beautiful, but it does not prove anything." And they are quite right. It *doesn't* prove anything. And if it does not prove anything when you read it in heathen Plato or Cicero, neither does it when you read identically the same argument in Christian Augustine, or Bishop Butler, or Joseph Cook—this argument from the uncompounded nature of the soul, or from the analogy of the chrysalis and the butterfly, or from the vague impressions of a previous existence, or from the longings or the prevalent beliefs of men. The argument does not prove anything; and these men see that it does not; and they are logical disbelievers of the truth to-day, because, for these many centuries, it has been the fashion for men to believe the truth illogically.

And further, their disbelief is confirmed by the study of the unity of nature, which is the noble lesson of modern science. Theologians have always loved to make much of the pre-eminence of the human race, as being completely separated from the brutes; having reflection, reason, conscience, a soul, while "the brutes that perish" have no soul at all—only an instinct. Now the course of modern science leads along pretty steadily in the direction of believing that "the brutes that perish" do have the same kind of faculties with men—that the difference between them is not a difference of kind, but only a difference of degree. Whole books of science, and most valuable and interesting books, have been written on the evidences of reason and conscience in "the brutes that perish;" and if the brutes perish, how do we know but that men perish too? So these minds reason. They try their weight on those arguments of natural theology—those old heathen arguments for the immortality of the soul, that it has been the fashion through sixteen centuries for Christian theologians and preachers to rely on— they try their weight on them, and they give way under their feet. Outside of the church, the world is beginning to lose its belief of any future life.

And how is it within the church? What kind of consequences have followed from this long inveterate habit of talking as if man was immortal of himself, by his own nature, as the heathen used to teach, instead of having no immortality but what God gives him through Jesus Christ? For it has gotten into our theologies, and our preaching, and our habits of speech—this notion of the soul of man as essentially incapable of death. It is taught as belonging to natural theology, a fact of nature which men can know by their reason, and which is only confirmed by the Gospel. And is it altogether strange that after the church had been trained for some centuries to believe that all men are sure of immortality any way, it should occur to some, by and by, to doubt whether there was any such great importance to the world in the resurrection of Jesus Christ? and if the resurrection of Christ was not essentially needed, how very unlikely that there was any resurrection of Christ! So reasoned David Strauss, and lost his own faith in the risen Lord, and shipwrecked the faith of thousands of others with his own. Immortality is safe enough, he said. The soul in its own nature cannot die. What need have we then of this old story of the risen Saviour? And so he threw it overboard. But mark you the result upon his own soul. When he had lost from under him the solid fact of the resurrection of Jesus Christ, he found all the rest of his religious hopes and convictions crumbling piece by piece away. And at last that proud, vain notion that man is an heir of immortality in his own right, and not only as being a joint-heir of Jesus Christ—this went too. And that illustrious Christian scholar, that great but perverse student of the life of Jesus, passed the gloomy evening of his days "without hope, without God in the world," without a Saviour, so far as he knew, or a soul to be saved. And this is the position of many and many a thoughtful and not irreverent mind in these days. I really believe that they have not sought this position. Certainly they are not of those who want to disbelieve in order that they may give rein to their lusts. They dread the possible moral consequences of their disbelief, and are anxious to fortify men's minds against them. They let it go unwillingly, this old philosophical doctrine of man's natural immortality, and simply because they can find no proof of it.

And now from these hopeless pages of sincere, faithful, honest science, out of which the old cherished notion of man's natural immortality has faded, in the advancing light, as mist and cloud are dissipated before the fierce shining of a summer morning, we turn to the Scriptures of the New Testament for some evidence that man by nature has immortal life in himself. And we do not find it. It is not there. Oh what wonderful things *are* there, concerning resurrection, and immortality, and eternal life! From gospel through to apocalypse the pages are aglow with a divine and holy hope. There are distinct asseverations in the name of God, there are sure and immutable promises, there are visions of immortal bliss and glory—the innumerable company of angels, the perfected spirits of just men, and God the Judge, and Christ the Mediator—and there are songs of everlasting joy, and love and holiness that cannot perish. But it is always as God's gift, never as man's inalienable possession, that this endless, deathless life to come is spoken of. Men's theologies may talk of the souls of men as "not dying because they are of an immortal subsistence;"* but the divine Scriptures declare plainly that it is not man who hath immortality—man, whose breath is in his nostrils; that it is He, the blessed and only Potentate, King of kings and Lord of lords, who *only* hath immortality. That which man hath is just this little span of mortal life, and then death. This brief life he holds by a precarious tenure; but death is all his own, his heritage, his birthright from his fathers, the wages of his personal sin and of the world's sin. But eternal life is somewhat that must come to him from without himself;—it is the gift, the free gift, of God.

Here, in this dim world, now these many centuries, the authors of many a philosophy, the founders of many a religion, the explorers in many a field of science, have been hoping, longing, strenuously arguing, to show that man is not the frail, damaged, perishing creature that he seems to be. And the latest result of the calmest, clearest, coolest reasoning seems to be this, that all this hoping and longing and strenuous endeavor are in vain, and that in the increasing light the proofs of man's natural immortality are fading out, and the grave is growing gloomier, and life more vain and less worth the living.

Into such a world as this has entered one made like to the sons of men, but declaring himself to be the Son of God, and boldly saying, "I am the Resurrection and the Life." O mortal men, "I give immortal life." To this race of men, doomed to death but shrinking from the grave's mouth, recoiling with an awful instinct of abhorrence from the dark and void abyss, he declares, "He that believeth on me shall not perish, but shall have everlasting life. I will raise him up at the last day." The word of Christ is full of this. It echoes back the despair of human reason. It extinguishes the dim flicker of the old philosophic hope. And it brings in a better hope—a "hope full

---

* Westminster Confession, XXXII., § 1.

of immortality"—a "hope that maketh not ashamed, because the love of God is shed abroad in our hearts by the Holy Ghost that is given us."

The salvation of Jesus Christ is a greater thing than men have thought. Reading the Gospel with a vail upon our hearts, we have deemed that Christ was come into the world to reveal to us the immortality of which we were already ignorantly in possession. We read again, with cleared vision, and discover that it was not to show us what we had before, but to bring us the eternal life which we had never had, and never should have had without him.

This new period of religious thought of which I spoke at the beginning, and which seemed so full of evil portent, is not of evil portent only. This philosophic despair is sent to call men away from confidence in a vain philosophy which has no true hope of immortality, and send them to their only sure hope—Jesus Christ, the Son of God. The light of this fair resurrection-morning* shines the brighter on the open and empty tomb of the Lord of life, for the darkness that is settling down all around us on men's mere speculative hopes. Through all the homes of unbelief the darkness is growing denser,—a darkness that may be felt; but there is light in the dwellings of the righteous. And soon, let us hope and pray, the very gloom of their darkness shall drive them to Him who is the Light, and again it shall be fulfilled which was spoken by Isaiah the prophet, "The people which sat in darkness have seen a great light; and to them which sat in the region and shadow of death, light is sprung up."

The tidings from the broken tomb are tidings of great joy. The light that beams thence enlightens every man. Even the shadowy places of the earth are the less dark by reason of this great light, this promise in Christ that God will raise the dead. The shadows are the less dark; but they are the more

---

*This sermon was preached on Easter morning.

RESURRECTION IN CHRIST.

manifest. We should not know that there were shadows but for the shining light. But now the true light is come, and the shadow that it casts is dark indeed. For this very promise of life, eternal life, through Jesus Christ, itself declares that out of Christ lies the domain of death.

The infinite and blessed gift is offered to as many as will receive it. It is offered to you, O men. Will you not believe in him and have life everlasting? Or will you rather put from you the word of promise, and judge yourselves unworthy of eternal life?

XXIII.

RESURRECTION OF THE UNJUST.

If I make my bed in hell, behold, thou art there.—PSALM cxxxix. 8.

ONE of the best services which we are about to gain from the Revised Version of the Old Testament * is through the use of some less misleading word to indicate the state, or the abode, of the dead. This large and vague thought, as it lay in the minds of the ancient believers, was represented by a single word which comprehended all that they knew or thought concerning the condition both of the wicked and of the righteous dead. Our translators evidently felt themselves at a loss for an equivalent word, and so they varied between two words neither of which expresses the idea. About half the time they translate this word "the grave"—simply the place of interment of the dead body—and the other half the time they translate it "hell," which in modern English means the final abode of the wicked in eternal punishment. It is of immense importance to the proper understanding of the English Old Testament, that we clearly apprehend that the word translated "hell" *never* refers to the state of punishment or suffering, nor to the state of the wicked dead, but simply to the state of all the dead, irrespectively of their suffering or happiness, their good or ill desert. In the New Testament there is a difference. There we have two words, one of which means, like the Old Testament word, simply the state of the dead, irrespective of their good or ill desert. It is translated, in the common ver-

* This sermon was preached just before the publication of the Old Testament Revision.

sion, sometimes "hell," sometimes "the grave," but in the Revised Version it is rendered "hades," which is simply the Greek word in English letters. But there is another word in the New Testament, which is not in the Old Testament, at all, —a word which, by its origin and by its application, carries with it the most solemn and awful significance of utter perdition and fiery destruction; which is applied only to the doomed abode of the wicked; and which is constantly translated by the word "hell;" and is used as in contrast with the words "paradise," or "heaven." If we would read intelligently, we cannot too distinctly apprehend that in the Old Testament there are no names used to indicate separate abodes for the righteous and the wicked after death. We find there that most characteristic thing of all the Scriptures—the clear division of all mankind into perfectly distinct classes, the righteous and the wicked, and no intermediate class between them. We find also the declaration of God's intense, awful, immutable hatred of wickedness, and his love of the righteous. And withal we find glimpses, from time to time, of a life to come; very dim and vague they seem to be at first, growing more frequent, more clear and confident, in the later prophets and psalmists; but by no means vivid, full and distinct, down to the very end of the Old Testament, for it is only "in the *gospel*" that "light and immortality are" fully "brought to light." We have no word for heaven as the abode of blessed souls, in the Old Testament, and no word for hell as the prison-house of the wicked.

In all this I have told you nothing that is new to critical students of the Bible, and nothing that is in doubt or dispute, but simply what is perfectly known and admitted among all scholars.

A very striking illustration of it is to be found by comparing this Psalm cxxxix. with Psalm xvi. In Psalm xvi., the righteous man, in language which finds its complete fulfillment in Christ, the wholly righteous, expresses his trust in God not only through all the changes of life, but in death and after death—that even in that dim unknown, that realm of silence and darkness into which, according to the vague conceptions of these ancient believers, the departing soul goes out—even there the God whom he has always trusted will be able to find him, and keep him, and bring him forth. It is by far the clearest hope of the life to come that is to be found recorded in the Old Testament, at least until you come to its very latest writings—this trust of the righteous soul that God will not lose him in that darkness of the world of the dead. He has no confidence in any immortality of his own, but in the Eternal and Almighty and Faithful God. "Thou wilt not leave my soul in hell—the abode of all the dead—neither wilt thou suffer thy Holy One to see corruption."

And here, in Psalm cxxxix., we have the like thought presented from the opposite point of view. It is a profoundly solemn utterance of the fear and awe of sinful man, as he feels himself to be under the hand of the Almighty, under the eye of the Omniscient, and before the face of the Omnipresent. Oppressed with the tremendous sense of such knowledge and such power, he shrinks away as if to seek some hiding-place. Shall he "take the wings of the morning"—the eastern breeze which, rising from the Syrian desert, sweeps down over the crests of Lebanon and Carmel, and ruffles the waters of the Great Sea that stretch illimitably westward—shall he spread his sail, and fly upon this blast beyond the confines of the land, beyond the track of all exploring keels, and find a dwelling in the utmost tracts of unknown seas? But God's eye would see him there. Shall he climb into the starry heights? But God's presence would confront him there. Or, breaking away from all visible scenes, cutting loose from life itself, should the sinner hope that death would hide him at last from God in the gloom of that unknown into which the departing life fades out from all human cognition? Even in that abode of the departed he could not escape from God. God's hand could reach him there, and pluck him back from the abyss whose darkness cannot hide from God. It is the same thought which is at once the hope of the righteous and the fear of the sinner; the thought of God's omnipresence, and omnipotence, and eternity. The righteous man exults in God, "for thou wilt not leave my soul in hell;" the sinner trembles before God's face: "If I make my bed in hell, behold, thou art there."

And this, throughout the Scriptures of the Old Testament, is the only fear, as it is the only hope, for the life to come. Not a word anywhere of that which appears so often in modern and mediæval theology and preaching, not a word about the soul as being of "an indestructible essence," or of "an immortal subsistence," but everywhere a deep consciousness of man's precarious tenure on life which it needs omnipotence to sustain; and here and there the hint that he who has hold on the eternal God has laid hold on eternal life, and a warning, like this in the text, that even if one should seek to hide himself from God in the dark shadows of the grave, God can reach after him and bring him forth.

It would be difficult to mention a subject that better illustrates two of the striking characteristics of the Bible than this subject of the future life of man: these two characteristics are, 1, the progressive method of revelation; and 2, that which Dr. Chalmers has described, in a memorable phrase, as "the alternative character of the Gospel"—that all the light of it casts a shadow—that just as fast as its promises come to light, age after age, they are attended by its warnings; that the disclosure of its privileges, as it grows brighter from age to age, keeps no more than equal pace with the disclosure of its responsibilities. See how this appears in the matter of the hope of a future life. In the early chapters and books of the Old Testament, no announcement of it, hardly anything from which an ordinary reader would draw the inference or conjecture of it; later on, in the Psalms, the pretty distinct gleam of a hope of the future life, through God's resurrection-power, and with it, in exactly proportional distinctness, the shadow from it—the *fear* of a future life. And when at last, in the very late book of Daniel, we do come to the distinct announcement of at least a partial resurrection, there is something besides a promise in it; there is a solemn threatening with the promise. "Many of them that sleep in the dust of the earth shall awake, some to everlasting life,—and some to everlasting shame and contempt."

Thus, through all the Old Testament, this growing light has been casting a more and more definite and awful shadow, and at last the New Testament opens, and it is broad daylight. There comes one into the world who says, "I am the Resurrection and the Life." There are those, his followers, who speak, as never men have spoken before, with such absolute, definite, positive confidence, with distinct assurance, with faith and hope so clear, so unhesitating that they do not fall short of knowledge, of the life to come of which these dim foregleams appear in Moses and David and Asaph and Isaiah and Daniel. But here, too, you will observe that it is not high noon all at once, even when the Sun of Righteousness has risen. Put the books of the New Testament in the order of their date, and you see how the light grows unto perfect day. This light of the immortal life is most clear and vivid in the latest of the gospels, and the latest of the epistles. It is the Gospel of John, by far the latest of the four, which is pre-eminently the gospel of light and immortal life. It is the Epistle of John and the later Epistles of Paul that tell us most of what we want to know. And as before, the light casts a shadow. There never were such solemn and dreadful words of warning spoken by any ancient prophet or psalmist, as are spoken by the gentlest, kindliest, most pitying and tender lips that ever opened to teach men concerning things invisible. It is he, and he alone, this meekest and lowliest One, that takes the quenchless fire, the undying worm of those abhorred offal-heaps of uncleanness in the valley of Gehenna, for a type of punishment in the world to come—he, who that very hour has been pouring out his sweet beatitudes on the meek, the peace-maker, the poor in spirit. And when we rise to the height of his promises of what he will do in bringing back the dead, he, by his word, and power, and by the life which he hath in himself, does it not seem that the fair and beatific hope might be left to rest as a comfort and encouragement to us in this despairing world, without being dashed with the dark strokes that show us the converse of the promise? But no! if we begin, we must read on. If we delight to listen when we hear him say these wonderful things, how that "as the Father raiseth the dead and quickeneth them, even so the Son quickeneth whom he will. . . The hour cometh when the dead shall hear the voice of the Son of God, and they that hear shall live. For as the Father hath life in himself, even so gave he to the Son also to have life in himself. Marvel not; the hour cometh in which all that are in the tombs shall hear his voice and shall come forth; they that have done good unto the resurrection of life"—if we love to listen to these great hopes thus far, we may not turn away at this point, and stop the ears and refuse to hear the rest. Those closing words will follow us and stay with us. The more we try to forget them the more they will stick in the memory, and prick the conscience and cut the heart,—the words: "and they that have done ill unto the resurrection of the judgment." So when we stand in the court of Felix, and hear the defense of the apostle Paul, as he declares the Christian hope, there comes the same solemn cadence to his promise of the resurrection:— "the resurrection of the just—and of the unjust." No; it does not seem that ever in this world we can have this great light without its shadow.

And now I want you to observe one more impressive fact concerning the divine revelation of the life beyond the grave: —that it is given in a purposed, almost disdainful disregard of the thoughts and beliefs, and knowledge (if we may call it knowledge) concerning the life to come, which was possessed or claimed by any the wisest of men, as held by them in their own right or through their own wisdom. In fact when God would take a people and instruct them concerning the life to come, it would seem that the first stage of the process consisted in disabusing them of all reliance on the hopes that the heathen cherished. Moses leads forth his fellow-countrymen on that heroic pilgrimage through the desert, and lays for them, under a divine direction, the foundations of a new polity, a new civilization, a new philosophy, a new religion. And in all his work how largely he uses the resources supplied through his providential equipment with "all the learning of the Egyptians!" The arts of war and peace, the frame of government, even the rites of religious worship, subsisting in Egypt, all these he freely used. But that which pervaded the religion, the government, the philosophy, the social usage of the Egyptians, like a vital atmosphere, the doctrine of future life and future judgment, he used not at all. The Egyptian ritual of the dead is saturated with it; not a mummy-case in all the catacombs but testifies of it; and yet the books of that Moses who was learned in all this lore have nothing of it. He would seem, according to our customary way of estimating, to be starting this people of Israel on a lower plane of religious knowledge than that of the heathen from among whom he had led them forth. He rejects the whole of this fully developed eschatology, and gives instead of it only this: that the Lord is God of Abraham and Isaac and Jacob,—a thought out of which by and by, after many ages, the clarified mind might be taught to deduce the great inference. Why this method in the divine teaching?

Among the apostles to whom was committed the training of the infant church were two, at least, to whom the speculations of past and contemporary philosophy concerning the immortality of the soul were intimately familiar. Paul had not studied in the schools of Tarsus without knowing the arguments of Cicero and Plato; and John was well-informed in the teachings of

Philo and the Alexandrians—all of these so clear and positive about the immortality of the soul. How is it that going forth to teach the world the gospel of life, they make no use at all of these arguments, all ready to their hand, which the later theology of the church relies on as so indispensably useful? They pass them by with contemptuous silence. Not a word of all this scholastic jargon about "indestructible essences" and "immortal subsistences." *Why* not?

Paul might have spoken to his audience of philosophers at the Areopagus of the inextinguishable immortality of the soul, and he would have found the way all prepared for him; there might have been disputation, with a great party on his side of the question; but there could have been no derision. But he declined this argument, and spoke rather of *God's* raising one from the dead; and they mocked. They to whom the Gospel and Epistle of John were sent were surely not indisposed to be taught in language borrowed from the Alexandrian teachers. But this apostle, like his fellow, refuses all aid from such wisdom, and points to the Lord Jesus Christ as the only hope of life beyond the grave.

And how bright this hope! how clear this confidence! Such faith as theirs is itself an evidence. In the wonderful pathos and dignity of the dying hours of Socrates, we have, by the common agreement of the ages, the highest attainment of which unaided human reason and virtue are capable. With cheerful calmness the sage "consents to death," saying to the disciples who weep beside him: "We go our ways, you to live, I to die; and *I know not* whether is better." Speaking, like Socrates, out of the gloom of a condemned cell, the apostle declares, not, I know not, but "*I know* whom I have believed," and has never doubted that "to be with Christ is far better."

The Platonic philosophers longed for a faith in their own nature, that in them was somewhat of immortal essence which might elude the stroke of the executioner, and continue by its own indefeasible vitality. The Christian disciples had no such faith in themselves. For their hope of eternal life, they "looked out and not in." They believed in God; they believed also in Christ. They knew whom they believed, and that he would not lose them "in the land of forgetfulness." Therefore their heart is glad and their glory rejoiceth.

And according to the measure of the joyful confidence of these was the dread of those to whom their message came, but who, stubborn in heart, would not obey the gospel. They found quite another sort of argument to deal with, from those Platonic speculations the too fine edge of which was so easily turned by the rougher weapons of their Epicurean and Stoic wit. It had been so easy to say, in the verse of one of their own poets, "If the guest is bored by the entertainment, let him step out." It was growing so easy, and so frightfully common, as now it grows to be wherever materialism eclipses the light in Christian lands, for men thus to "step out" by suicide into the outer darkness. But now they are warned that there, without, is wailing and gnashing of teeth. Now they know that if there is not within us some elusive particle of "immortal subsistence," there is above us the eternal and almighty God, whose everlasting arm is underneath those who trust in him, to bear them up when heart and flesh shall fail them, and can reach into the abode of death to drag forth the culprit who would hide himself there from the jurisdiction of the Most High.

And what the warning of the gospel was to them of old time, it is also to us:—that there is but one safe hiding-place in all the universe from the just anger of the almighty God, and that is under the shadow of his wings.

XXIV.

GOD'S EQUITABLE JUSTICE.

That servant which knew his lord's will, and made not ready nor did according to his will, shall be beaten with many stripes; but he that knew not, and did things worthy of stripes, shall be beaten with few stripes.—
LUKE xii. 47, 48.

THIS is one of the places in which the gospel seems to protest in advance against the overstatements of those by whom, in after ages, it was to be preached.

For through all the Christian centuries, the gospel has suffered not only from understatement, but from overstatement. There have been those who, holding the Christian doctrine doubtfully, hesitatingly, partially, have enunciated it feebly. And there have been others, receiving it unreservedly, with complete faith and profound feeling, holding it not for themselves only, but as a trust for other men, have been impelled into the other fault, of bettering their gospel by intensifying it. Now to intensify the gospel is to caricature it. It is as if one should take some perfect statue, the admiration of the world, and attempt to make its beauties a little more beautiful and its perfections a little more than perfect. There is beauty in the curve of that full lip—let us add something to the fullness, and emphasize the curve. What life and animation in the distending of the thin nostril!—retouch it, then, with the chisel, and we will have *more* life and animation. How exquisite the arching of that eyebrow!—good! we will bend the arch a little more, and it shall be more exquisite still. What a Jove-like sublimity in the towering of that forehead—that dome of thought!—go to, now! let us intensify this excellence and elevate this sublimity to a yet higher degree! And so saying, we take that fatal but easy step which leads downward from the sublime. Our improved Hyperion is a monster. The travesty is not the less damaging for having been made with excellent intentions. Almost every great and original poet is thus burlesqued by the extravagances of his admiring imitators; just as the gospel has sometimes been caricatured by honest and intensely earnest preachers. It is hard, sometimes, to be caricatured by one's enemies; but to be caricatured by one's friends, out of the very zeal and warmth of their friendship, is a good deal harder, and more damaging.

"Overdoing is the devil's way of undoing," said Richard Baxter two centuries ago: and he illustrated his remark by historical instances,—how that when Christianity began, the devil struggled against it with all the powers of darkness, until he found that it was of no use, and then the devil turned Christian and began to *overdo* Christianity. By and by came the Reformation, which made havoc with his kingdom until at last he bethought him to turn reformer, and to undo that work by overdoing it. And at last, in Baxter's own time, arose the Puritan revival, and went on from conquering to conquer, until it had established itself in success, and then the devil changed sides and turned Puritan, and began to overdo Puritanism, and so undo it. And Puritans as we are, I do not see but that we must confess that we have not entirely got the devil out of the Puritan churches from that time to this. But, finally, it is the obvious policy of the adversary to corrupt the church of God by heresies: and yet when heresies are crushed, and truth is triumphant, how common for Satan to take the orthodox side;—and when he does, who is so orthodox as he is? Nothing will satisfy him but the very intensest statements, the most exorbitant enunciations: and so his overdoing of orthodoxy is his way of undoing it.

I have known churches in which all the bad, selfish, malignant passions have been combined for the vindication and intensification of orthodoxy; and in which the whole behavior of those so exercised has given proof of a Satanic work. Alas, for those, who, instead of receiving meekly the ingrafted word of God, become possessed thus of an orthodox devil! It is a kind that goeth not out but with prayer.

Nearly every department of Christian doctrine has suffered more or less, at one time or another, from this Satanic policy of undoing by overdoing. The errors of Roman theology may mainly be described as overstated truths. It required only a little intensification of the teachings of the New Testament, often, doubtless, a very well-intended intensification on the part of those whose zeal for Christian truth outran their discretion, to produce from the sober doctrine of the Gospel the notions of transubstantiation, of the sacrifice of the Mass, and of the confessional, and the fabric of sacerdotalism in general.

But those parts of Christian teaching which have most suffered from this sort of influence are those which lie near the threshold of every system of theology—the doctrines concerning Sin and Punishment. It is the form in which these doctrines are held, in any system, which logically seems to determine the character and grade of that system in comparison with the evangelical standard. In proportion as any system apprehends the exceeding sinfulness of sin, and the awfulness of divine punishment, it apprehends also the greatness of salvation, the infinite dignity of the Saviour, the radicalness of regeneration. Just in proportion as the apprehension of the guilt and punishment of sin grows weak, the sense of man's need and of God's salvation is weakened; Christ's work seems less, and so his person seems of less account; and conversion seems less like a change from death to life, and more a matter of degree, a difference of more or less. How natural, then, that the zeal for intensifying and improving Scriptural statements should seize, most of all, on these two points.

Now the true Scriptural doctrine of sin, solemn and inexorable as it is, is, nevertheless, a most reasonable doctrine. It is nothing but the doctrine of common sense and common conscience illustrated by God's law and Christ's example—the doctrine that all have sinned, that there can be no right purpose but a purpose to do wholly right, that in lack of such purpose men lie before God in wickedness. Zeal without knowledge lays hold of this plain, sober truth, and puts it into an intensified form, labels it with an extravagant and misleading name, as "Total and Universal Depravity," and gives it out as if it meant that every man is as bad as he can be; and that everybody is as bad as everybody else—or worse.* When language gets to be as orthodox as this, it ceases to be orthodox at all. It becomes a burlesque of orthodoxy. It is unscriptural and anti-scriptural, as well as irrational, in denying the New Testament doctrine of gradation in human guilt.

Just so with regard to the Christian doctrine of future punishment. The words in which Jesus delivered it are few, solemn, awful. "Outer darkness," "unquenchable fire," "the undying worm," "weeping and gnashing of teeth,"—these are the features of the picture, and behind them, in dim, far-receding perspective, the sombre background sketched in such words as "eternal," "forever and ever." Such few, awful words spoken, oh, with what tenderness of pity! with what sternness of inexorable truth! sufficed the Son of God when he would warn the guilty multitude to flee from coming wrath. Zeal without knowledge, being, therefore, all the more zealous, betters the instruction, and intensifies and aggravates, instead of simply and humbly and tremblingly repeating it with such tenderness as they do well to use, over whose own heads the sentence of the law has hung. I say nothing of the taste

---

* See, for example, Payson's Works, I., 159: "I preached, last Sabbath, on man's depravity, and attempted to show that by nature, man is, in stupidity and insensibility, a block; in sensuality and sottishness, a beast, and in pride, malice, cruelty, and treachery, a devil. This set the whole town in an uproar." And yet some people wonder why there should have been a Unitarian reaction!

of those who delight to practice their raw imaginations in such work as overtasked the lurid genius of Dante—in describing the implements of infernal torture, and demonstrating the morbid physiology of everlasting anguish. But I protest, by the authority of Christ himself, against those who, claiming to declare his doctrine of punishment, distort it by their extravagance out of all likeness to itself. If there are those who have joined to an unscriptural doctrine of *indiscriminate* depravity, the denunciation of *indiscriminate* punishment of all unbelievers, I condemn them not. They have one that condemneth them, even Jesus Christ himself; who himself declares, in this text, the doctrine of gradations in human guilt, and gradations in divine punishment. It is on these points, among others, that Satan, using the overzeal of men, has undone the teaching of the church by overdoing it. He could not, to so considerable an extent, have alienated the reason of men from the truth of Christ in these matters, unless he had first perverted the truth under unreasonable terms. But the Gospel is its own vindicator, against its friends as well as against its foes, and one reading of such a text as this should be enough to bring back the perplexed minds both of believers and of unbelievers to that primary axiom of all theology—the axiom that stayed the failing faith of Abraham—the Judge of all the earth will do right.*

Taking now a single species of sin for an example, I wish to study this doctrine in its personal application. I take the sin of *unbelief*, one which is pointed to in the Scriptures as

---

* The useless and groundless speculations of some recent theologians on the possibility of a "probation after death" seems to have this genesis: that having adopted an eschatology that is repugnant to their sense of justice, they are driven to go exploring in the unknown for a theodicy. What they seem to be groping for is a new probation not for the culprit, but for the Judge; as if they were apprehensive that, according to their scheme, He would not do the exactly right and infinitely kind and merciful thing the first time.

radical and elementary among sins, and I appeal to our own consciences (a standard by which God himself asks that his justice may be judged) for an estimate of the gradations in the guilt of it.

I. To begin with, concerning a great class of cases, the conscience declares that in them the specific and explicit fact of unbelief in Christ is simply without guilt—the cases of those to whom he has never been made known; as it is written, "faith cometh by hearing;" "how can they believe in him of whom they have not heard?" It is one of the first lessons of divine justice which God has written on our hearts, that men are not held guilty for not performing impossibilities. Christ did not come into the world to condemn the world, but to save the world. The world is condemned already, without Christ. The wrath of God is on it, for its sins,—an awful burden, which from those who trust in Christ the Saviour, is lifted off and rolled into his sepulchre; but on those who believe not, even though they have heard not, "the wrath of God abideth," —not cometh upon them, for it is on them already, and there it stays. God is not unjust, but abundantly merciful in his justice, and with few stripes, proportioned to the measure of their guilt by a Judge omniscient and so mighty that the temptation to undue severity cannot come near to him, he visits those who in partial darkness, have nevertheless sinned against the little light they had.

II. In the second place, there are those who, having heard the gospel of Christ, are not satisfied, with intellectual conviction, that it is a message from God, and that Christ is a sufficient Saviour to all who put their trust in him. In this class is included the widest range of gradations in guilt. This class includes those to whom the gospel has come in utter ignorance, or in worse, in deep, inveterate, hereditary prejudice against the gospel—has come with its frank, open invitation, "Come and see"—"come let us reason together;"—it includes those whom the Spirit of God pronounced "noble," because they

GOD'S EQUITABLE JUSTICE. 273

were *not* satisfied on slight evidence, but "searched the Scriptures daily whether these things were true:" and it may also include those who, when the Light of the world draws nigh, hate the light, neither come to the light, because their deeds are evil:—who are sincere unbelievers, because they sincerely do not *want* to believe. Do you need to be assured that toward one end of this scale there is a point where doubt, a failure to be fully satisfied with proof thus far adduced, ceases to be sin and begins to be a virtue?—where the heedless acceptance of unproved propositions would be sin? I hate the sweeping denunciation of the serious, earnest questionings of those who in all their doubt are only fulfilling the very teaching of him whom they have not yet learned to accept, and are treading the very path—the only path—which can bring them unto him. *They* are the real believers, who are not afraid patiently, fairly to inquire concerning Christ; for they have faith in God that he will lead the diligent seeker and bring him right. It is a comfortable thing, no doubt, to abide within the ship while all about the fluctuating billows of opinion are blown upon by gales of controversy; but he is the bravest in his faith, who dares leap out, even upon such a sea as that, to walk to Jesus on the waves. Let him not doubt but that God will be his Saviour, nor fear that he will cry in vain, "Lord, save me, I perish." *They* are the real infidels, who confess that they do not dare to question lest their faith should fail. When one says this, he need give himself no further anxiety about losing his faith. He has no faith to lose. He has made his confession of unbelief; and declared that his unbelief is so deep and fatal that it holds back his coward soul from taking the only step which can possibly lead him back to faith again.

In noting the gradations in the sin of unbelief, I have spoken, now, of two: Those who never having heard of Christ cannot believe in him of whom they have not heard, and are therefore not guilty on that count; and those who having heard of Christ have failed to be intellectually satisfied of the proofs of his divine mission; and the guilt of whose unbelief, mingled with more or less of ignorance or prejudice, ranges through the whole scale of human sinfulness, and can be gauged only by the eye of "the Judge of all the earth."

III. I ask you, finally, to consider the guilt of those who hearing the word of God by his Son Jesus Christ, convinced of his divine commission and authority to forgive and save, decline to commit themselves to his keeping and guidance. This is the willful, immitigable, crowning sin of human nature. Blessed are they who having seen do believe upon the Lord, committing unto him their hearts and ways. Thrice blessed they who not having seen do yet believe, reaching out the hand to him through the darkness to be led by him. But woe! woe to him who having seen does not believe! This is the will of God that we should trust in Jesus Christ whom he hath sent. Woe to that servant who knows his Lord's will and does it not! He shall be beaten with many stripes.

There comes to us an embassador from the King of all the earth, whom we have offended. There is no guilt for not receiving him, on their part to whom he comes not and who have not heard of him. Toward those who, in honest doubt, pause to examine his credentials, and with earnest diligence to understand his propositions, it is impossible that a merciful and patient King should bear anger for their reasonable delay. But what will he judge concerning those who have heard the message, who have understood its offers and promises, who have satisfied themselves of its royal authority, and who yet treat its questions with silent negligence? This it is to distrust the veracity of God. In the mutual dealings of men, this act of intimating a doubt of another's word is held to be the last intolerable act of insult. And you who by your professions and even boasts of sound knowledge have stripped yourselves of all apology, and stripped your act of every mitigation of its offensiveness, do, by every act of continued disobedience and persistent negligence, fling this uttermost insult into the face of Almighty God.

I have attempted, now, to enforce, in some of its most obvious applications, the doctrine of Jesus Christ concerning the Gradation of Guilt and Punishment. Are there any who will venture to accuse this doctrine of too great gentleness and mildness and of being toned to meet the acceptance of the human reason? I have yet to learn to entertain it as an objection to any doctrine of Christ that it is mild and gentle, and, even to human apprehension, just and fair. But are there those, peradventure, who will fear lest this preaching may weaken the power of the tremendous sanctions of the gospel,— this suggestion of possible mitigation of the terrors of God's justice to some, in consideration of human ignorance or error? I say again that it is nothing against the verity of Christ's word, though men pervert it never so much to their own destruction. But truly they are without excuse who so pervert the gentle, considerate justice of God. For he who would so comfort himself in his unbelief, does by that very act stultify himself. The moment one begins to consider in advance his claim of ignorance for mitigation of judgment in the great day, he does by that very act cancel and nullify his claim.

But whether or not this doctrine be severe and awful,— whether or not it be useful, it is God's word, and Christ's gospel. We are not God that we should make the word, but only prophets, to declare it. Our commission is only this, "Go preach the preaching that I bid thee." "What! comes the word of God out from us, or *unto* us only?"

And yet it is not to be disguised that upon us who preach the gospel this doctrine of Christ does cast a shadow of most solemn gloom. For it does seem to suggest to us that the faithful preaching of the gospel, just in proportion as it is faithful, and clear, and convincing, as it relieves perplexities and clears difficulties, is a peril, and may be a destruction: and that in our most earnest and effective labors we may be preparing for our hearers, disobedient still although convinced, a severer retribution. If it had been left to the church's judgment of expediency, who can tell whether, knowing the stubbornness of human hearts, it would have decided to deliver the story of salvation to all nations? Who can tell whether, if it had been left to men, we might not have hesitated to set wide the door which opens upon such an opportunity and yet on such a peril—the door which, once open, no power in earth or heaven can shut? Who knows but that holding in our hands that gospel which, to those who refuse it, is a savor of death unto death, we might have said to ourselves, "It is too awful a responsibility this of delivering the glad news to all the nations? Roll on, poor earth, and travail still in pain and sin, and yet in blessed ignorance, as until now! Pass on, ye generations, to your dark and hopeless graves! We will not speak to your froward hearts and your unbelieving ears the words which, if ye refuse, shall give swift witness against you in the judgment day, and sink you in a deeper hell! Fly on, ye cycles of remaining time, and let this sad, woeful tragedy of the human race be ended!"—who can tell what men would have done if it had been left to them to say? Thank God, who has left no such awful question for our decision. The command of his word is clear—"Speak my words unto them whether they will hear or whether they will forbear." And his comforting assurance is as clear—"Thou hast delivered thy soul." The ascended Lord still speaks to us the command he uttered as he rose, "Go preach the gospel to every creature." And still he speaks the promise—"Lo I am with you alway, even unto the end of the world. Amen."

XXV.

JACOB AND ESAU.

As it is written, Jacob have I loved, and Esau have I hated —Rom. ix. 13.

This quotation from the prophet Malachi (chap. i., 2, 3) is given here in Paul's Epistle to the Romans, as if it were meant to prove (so, at least, it looks to some students of the Scriptures) that God dealt toward these two brothers, and deals toward men in general, in the spirit of arbitrary and capricious favoritism—that excellence of human conduct and character may be a consequence of God's favor, but is not in any sense a condition of it. If you read the passage, it does look as if it meant so; if you look at it again, and think of it, you know it cannot mean so. In fact, instead of showing that God is arbitrary in his favor, it is quoted to show that God's favor is not bound by arbitrary rules, as of a line of pedigree or a law of primogeniture. In the case of these twin children, the law of primogeniture had been abrogated in advance, quite independently of any act of theirs, before they were so much as born into the world, by that divine declaration "the elder shall serve the younger." If now the language of the epistle seems to lead us further than this, and to impute to God arbitrariness, caprice, favoritism, instead of that equity with which the righteous Judge renders to every man according to his work,—we are bound to consider that so startling a suggestion is *meant* to startle us and put us on our guard. It writes up in bold letters, across the intricate lines of this apostolic argument, that warning that is interjected sometimes into the midst of the words of Christ, "He that hath ears to hear, let him hear,"—

"whoso readeth, let him understand." It is God's own invitation to us to put our best faculties on the stretch to search out the matter—to compare spiritual things with spiritual, and judge the apparent meaning of this scripture with the unmistakable meaning of other scriptures, and judge all scriptures by the standard of divine justice—and that is no other than the standard of human justice which he himself has written in our hearts. What is the standard to which God appeals, if it is not this, when he asks us to judge his ways, saying, "Hear, now; are not my ways equal?—are not your ways unequal?" It is not honoring God, to say, as some theologians and some preachers say, that whatever God does must be right, since there is no standard of right but in himself, and in his law. God claims a higher praise than this; implying that there is a standard of right eternal like himself, and that he is to be honored because he eternally conforms to it, and because his law is like it, being holy, just and good.

This is a great subject. But it is not the subject that I propose for this evening's study. I propose a study simpler and easier, perhaps,—certainly more immediately practical for ourselves. Since of these two men, these brothers, these twin brothers, whose lives run side by side, in close comparison and contrast, we are told expressly, and by the double authority of the Old Testament and the New, that God loved Jacob and hated Esau, what most weighty and profitable instruction there must be for us in scrutinizing these contrasted lives and characters with a view to discovering what in each was the object of the divine approval or displeasure! We shall not find it without study, and without the exercise of our own common sense and moral sense. To go blind and blundering through the history, and suppose that whatever we find in Jacob must therefore be right and acceptable to God, and whatever we see in Esau must therefore be the object of divine reprobation, would lead us into errors not less absurd, and a great deal more damaging and mischievous, than if we were to judge that God hated

Esau because he was ruddy, and loved Jacob because he was swarthy or fair. Reverently speaking, we must endeavor to put ourselves in God's place in judging of these two men, and see them as they should appear to one who sitteth in the circle of the heavens.

We trace the contrasted history of the brothers from the hour of their birth. The very aspect of the tiny infants was a contrast; and there were omens in their birth which led them to call the younger by the name of "the supplanter," Jacob,— one who would trip his rival by the heel and supersede him. They grew up side by side in the placid pastoral family of Isaac. The days of heroic Abraham, the brave, adventurous pioneer, with his martial household, every slave a soldier, were gone by; and in Isaac's time we hear of little but the quiet life of a prosperous herdsman, multiplying his wealth of flocks and cattle over those broad, unfenced acres in which private ownership was only here and there beginning to be recognized; and widening out, from year to year, the area of his movable village of black tents, and digging wells and cisterns at the various places of his customary encampment—these the only permanent memorial that he left of his uneventful life: he dug wells—good wells—and left the world better than he found it.

But that curious law of divergence in the human stock which gave to Abraham two such unlike sons as Ishmael and Isaac, was fulfilled again when under one tent and in one cradle there grew up together from their babyhood the twin children of Isaac and Rebekah. In the native traits of Esau we cannot but recognize the reappearance of some features of resemblance to his chivalrous and right royal grandfather; while Jacob was unmistakable own son to his mother—and such a mother! He was the home-boy always, and his mother's darling. He stayed by the tent, while young Esau grew up a skillful hunter and "a man of the field" or (as Dean Stanley felicitously translates it) "a son of the desert."

The first incident of their history is characteristic enough of both of them. Jacob is at home in his tent concocting a favorite and savory stew of red lentiles, when his brother staggers in, ready to drop with exhaustion from his day's hunting, and cries for some of "that red, that red," for he is faint. Jacob, not in the least discomposed, suggests that perhaps, in the circumstances, they might make a bargain that would be mutually advantageous; and succeeds in putting the matter so forcibly and opportunely that Esau sees the point in a moment: "I shall die if I cannot get something to eat," he says, "and then what good will this birthright do me?" Still Jacob is in no hurry to give his starving brother anything to eat until the bargain is clinched. He has a keen eye for business, and holds on with a terrible grip to the advantage he has got. "Swear to me this day," he says. "And Esau sware unto him; and he sold his birthright to Jacob. *Then* Jacob gave Esau bread and pottage; and he did eat and drink, and rose up, and went his way: thus Esau despised his birthright."

The next incident in the joint lives of the two brothers is very like the first, in the personal traits that it shows. Poor old blind Isaac! for all the favoritism of his wife toward Jacob, his heart goes out toward that rough, hasty, impulsive, eldest son. The one thing that he relishes on his sick-bed is a dish of the game which this cunning hunter loves to bring home from the desert when he goes abroad with his arrows and his bow. It is very touching to hear the blind old man call for Esau to bring him once more some of that savory meat that he loves, and then, when he feels a little refreshed, he will give him that solemn *ante-mortem* blessing which had, in that land and age, the force of a father's last will and testament. This is the moment for Rebekah to show her high qualities as a wife and mother, and she whispers to Jacob the pretty trick that she has contrived by which to defeat the will of her blind and helpless husband, and defraud her eldest son. It is a trick that we can hardly venture to call ingenious, for it was only to deceive a blind, dying old man by straightforward lying and perjury, supplemented by some trifling devices. It is a satisfaction to see that Jacob shrinks from the base proposition; but we discover in a moment that his sole scruple in the case is his fear that he may not succeed; and when his strong-minded mother assures him that she will take the responsibility, he enters into the plot with entire alacrity, and goes through his part in that revolting scene of imposture without missing a syllable.

An eminent theologian of the Church of England, commenting on the history, ventures to express himself in these bold terms concerning the conduct of Jacob and Rebekah: "I do not know whether it be justifiable in every particular. I suspect that it is not. There were several very good and laudable circumstances in what Jacob and Rebekah did; but I do not take upon me to acquit them of all blame."* Brave gentleman! Think to what a demoralized condition of conscience a man must have brought himself in his ignorant zeal for the Scriptures, when he is able to talk in such a tone of such a crime!

As for the defrauded brother, his conduct is characteristic of human nature, and not of the worst aspects of human nature, either. His first expression is of grief—"he cried with a great and exceeding bitter cry"—and then as he thinks of the outrage that has been perpetrated upon him, his grief settles down into indignation and a purpose of deadly revenge. It is high time for Jacob to provide for his own safety, and the woman who is the directing genius in the crime has an expedient all ready. These two Canaanite wives that Esau has brought home are "a grief of mind to Isaac and Rebekah." One more such would make her life a burden to her. Let Jacob be sent East across the Euphrates to find himself a wife—a *good* wife —among *her* relations. And so he sets out on this characteristic

---

* Dr. Waterland, quoted with approbation (!) by the Rev. W. T. Bullock, in Smith's Dictionary of the Bible, s. v. *Jacob*.

wooing and wedding expedition, which is made up of one part love and nine parts policy and terror. And it does make a strange impression upon a thoughtful mind, doesn't it? in reading the story, that almost at the outset of his flight there should come in among the uneasy dreams of this conscience-stricken and terror-stricken fugitive, a heavenly vision, a revelation of the grace of God, and a divine promise to him and to his seed after him. He does seem a strange subject for the special favor of a just and holy God, especially when in answer to the unlimited and unconditional bounty of the Lord's promise, he vows his characteristic and cautious vow, in which he stipulates expressly for the actual fulfillment of all his conditions before anything shall be due to the Lord from him.

Meanwhile, as if purposely to mark the contrast between the twin brothers, we have the picture of Esau starting off on a like expedition on his own account. He sees that his two ventures in matrimony have brought no comfort to the venerable old father whom he tenderly loves. It is certainly just like Esau, when he sees how the old man is laying it to heart, to do what he can to mend the matter by finding a third wife that shall be more to his father's mind. Nor can any one blame him, if in this new alliance he keeps to the father's side of the house rather than to the mother's.

Here, then, the two brothers part, and see nothing of each other again for more than twenty years. And Jacob grew rich and prosperous, and "had oxen and asses, flocks and men-servants and women-servants;" and especially was he rich in a great family of sons and daughters. Esau, too, who had established himself in the wild country to the east of the Jordan and the Dead Sea, had flourished and prospered; and if his possessions in pastoral wealth were not equal to those of his sharp and thrifty brother, he was strong in other ways, for as he moved about the country it was with a retinue of four hundred men, as if brave men were drawn by the prowess of this mighty hunter, and were glad to call him their chief. In such lordly style he ranged the Jordan valley, through which Jacob must needs pass with his family and all his possessions on his way back to his father's house.

It was an anxious time when Jacob, coming near to Esau's country (which is Edom), sent messengers to "my lord Esau, thy servant Jacob sends to tell my lord, that I may find grace in thy sight;" and they brought back word, "thy brother Esau is coming to meet thee,—*and four hundred men with him.*"*
When he remembered all his dealings toward his brother, when he thought of the just anger of that generous man toward himself, from which he had run away twenty years before, the thought of Esau's coming with four hundred men at his back was a terrible thought. No wonder that he "was greatly afraid and distressed." But he did the best that a coward could do in the case. He made such a disposition of his great caravan that if part of it should be swept off the other part might be saved. And then he took to praying. And oh, how he prayed! "Deliver me, I pray thee, from the hand of my brother, from the hand of Esau; for I fear him." And then by way of paying a heavy war insurance on all the rest, he made up five droves of his splendid Mesopotamian stock, a present fit for a king,—sheep, goats, camels, cattle, asses,—and then sent them forward across the ford, ordering a space to be left between drove and drove; and whenever Esau should meet them, each driver was to say, in turn, "These be thy servant Jacob's; it is a present unto my lord Esau." So he sent forward over the ford—first his cattle, and then his wives and children, and last of all, he crossed over himself. And then by and by he looked up, and behold! there was this terrible brother and his four hundred men. And once more he made his dispositions, putting the most precious of his family in the place of least exposure—the two hand-maids and their children in front, then Leah and her children, and finally Rachel and her one

---

*Genesis, chap. xxxii, xxxiii.

child. Then, at last, nerving himself to meet the possible vengeance that he had evaded for twenty years, he went forward cringing at every step. Some men would have thought it better to meet their fate with head erect, like men, than to escape it by such craven humiliations. But Jacob was not at all of that way of thinking. He went forward and "bowed himself to the ground seven times until he came near to his brother."

"And Esau ran to meet him, and embraced him, and fell on his neck and kissed him: and they wept." And here, again, after further words and acts of generous love on Esau's part, and of pitiful deprecation, but no syllable of honorable, frank acknowledgment, on the part of Jacob, the twin brothers separate, and we never see them together again, till they meet, two old men, to bury their venerable father in the family tomb at Machpelah.

Such a man as this was Esau; and such a man was Jacob. And yet it is written as in the name of God, "Jacob have I loved, and Esau have I hated." What are we to learn from this?

One thing it is safe to say at the outset. There was no misapprehension in the mind of the primeval writer of these chapters in the book of Genesis, as to the comparative dignity of the two characters, Jacob and Esau.

It would be as reasonable to suppose that Shakspeare was unconscious of the difference between Iago and Othello, as to suppose that the writer of this most dramatic history imagined that he was drawing a noble character in Jacob and a mean one in Esau. No reader could possibly miss the point and purpose of the narrative, except by reading it with the vail of a theological dogma on his heart. If we have ever been embarrassed by this difficulty, that here the Scriptures seem inadvertently to give approval to base conduct and disparagement to that which is noble, we may relieve ourselves entirely. There is no inadvertency about it. The writer understands himself and his subject perfectly; and goes on with his eyes open to portray

Jacob as a mean coward and Esau as a chivalrous gentleman. If any persons are able to discover in this story of Jacob the appearance of one of those myths by which nations love to decorate and glorify the heroes of their early history, I admire at their ingenuity and wish them joy of their theory. With astonishing deference to the sacredness of this record, the Hebrew nation accept this delineation of their founder, and the Christian peoples "surname themselves by the name of Israel." And this word of the Lord still standeth sure, which saith, "Jacob have I loved, and Esau have I hated." What can it mean?

This, plainly, if no more: that the judgment of God upon any man is not determined by the qualities of his natural disposition. Man's judgment is so determined. Society applauds or condemns, even rewards or punishes, sometimes, simply according as it is pleased or not with the instinctive outworking of the native character. God judges a more righteous and more merciful judgment. And when we look on this strange sight,— Jacob, the craven, the coward, the supplanter, enjoying the manifest favor and friendship of God, and Esau, brave, generous, impulsive, chivalrous, stamped with the mark of God's disapproval,—the inference is *not* that God prefers cowardice and intrigue to openness and generosity, nor that God is indifferent between types of character concerning which he has implanted in us the most ineradicable convictions of approval or disapproval. Not at all. We have no moral taste nor faculty of judgment that we do not get from God; and if our hearts despise the mean and admire the noble, God is greater than our hearts and knoweth all things. And the Judge of all the earth does right. The Father in heaven is a considerate Father. He does not cast out his crippled and deformed children to perish. He holds to a stricter and sterner responsibility the sons that are nobly endowed by birth and nature. He is not the gentleman's God, nor the Redeemer and Saviour of persons of fine culture and beautiful instincts. He is, and from the beginning has been, the Saviour of the lost. And by many a story as strange as this of Jacob and Esau, he has shown to the honorable and generous and high-minded that there is a possible way of ruin for them; and to those who know in their own sorrowful consciousness, and by the scornful words or looks of others, that they are not of noble or generous strain,—that there is a way by which such as they may find salvation and the eternal favor of God.

And further, we find in this same story the plain exhibition of that which it is the task of the Scriptures of both Testaments to make us know and understand—I mean, just what *is* this way of salvation. I am sure that this story of Jacob and Esau was needed to show it. If we had Abraham's story only, or Moses', we might suppose that the heroic adventurousness of faith, or its princely valor, or its sublime triumphs over sordid selfishness and vulgar clamor, were the conditions of God's friendship and covenant love. But, poor Jacob! when we come to him, there is no room for any such blunder as that. And when we set him side by side with his brother and ask how could God love Jacob and hate Esau, there is only one possible answer left to us. In the life of Jacob, the one redeeming trait in a character naturally low, weak and sordid was this vital thing that he believed in God. In Esau, it might almost be said that the only blemish in a grand and generous soul was that he was utterly destitute of faith. He *would not trust* in God, the God of Abraham and Isaac. From the beginning to the end, we look in vain for traces of any act or word or syllable on Esau's part, to indicate that he so much as believed there was a God, much less that he trusted in him. That divine promise given to Abraham and to his seed forever, to which his birthright entitled him, he treated as an unholy thing, and is handed down to all coming ages as "that profane person who for one morsel of meat sold his birthright." So that it is not more truly to be said of Abraham that he was the Father of Believers,—that he trusted in God and it was counted to him for righteousness,—than of

Esau that he is the father of all who trust in themselves that they are righteous, and who scorn God and perish.

Be of good comfort, all whose need of salvation is deepest and most inward. You shall be saved not only in spite of these shameful faults and infirmities which you abhor in yourself, and which God abhors. You shall not only be saved, blessed, loved, in spite of them;—you shall be saved *from* them—and that is a greater thing. Faith in God is the vital air of all true human nobleness. In this air the stunted germs of human virtue unfold and blossom. Without faith their fairest, strongest growths tend to shrivel and decay. For lack of faith in God, the noble gifts of Esau are of no avail. He shuts himself out, a willing stranger to the covenants of promise, having no hope, without God in the world. He moves, a wandering star, in a track without a centre, on toward blackness of darkness. By faith, the low nature of "that worm, Jacob," is by and by redeemed from the power of evil, and, transformed in character and in name, Jacob, the supplanter, is changed to Israel, the prince that hath power with God.

Be afraid, men of honor and generosity; be afraid, women of high impulse and delicate culture; lest for lack of trusting in the eternal God your souls shall perish, while those of a lower strain shall mount upward to glory and honor and immortality; lest the first be last and the last first.

XXVI.

HEROD PENITENT.

Herod did many things [*or*, was much perplexed] **and heard him gladly.**—
MARK vi. 20.

THE ordinary reader of the New Testament need not reproach himself very seriously if he finds himself at fault in distinguishing among the various *Herods* that are mentioned in the book. I have seen a volume of sermons by an eminent Presbyterian preacher, who fails to keep his head quite clear on this point, and connects Herod's being "eaten of worms" in the twelfth chapter of the Acts, with his remorse of conscience for what his uncle did with John the Baptist. This confusion is favored, not only by the identity of name, but by a strong family likeness in character, as this comes out not only in the New Testament but in other writers. Take them jointly and severally, they are perhaps the most detestable family in human history. The bad blood of old Herod the Great tells in every individual of his posterity through three misbegotten generations of them. The family history is a record of intrigues, jealousies, incests, adulteries, conspiracies, murders, in amazing complication, enough to furnish plots for bloody tragedies to all the world's dramatists to the end of time.

The first of the Herods mentioned in the Bible is Herod the Great, founder of the family, who, at the birth of Christ, was a hoary old tyrant of nearly threescore years and ten; "a man," as Josephus says, "universally cruel and of ungovernable temper." He had already murdered two of his sons and the most beloved of his wives out of suspicion of rivalry for his throne. It was quite like him to order the execution of the children in Bethlehem for a similar reason. A little after this, while the child Jesus is still safe in Egypt, he falls deadly sick, orders another of his sons to be murdered in prison, shuts up the leading men of the Jewish nation with orders to execute them immediately upon his own death, lest otherwise there might be a lack of mourners at his funeral; and at last, while his affectionate subjects are contriving how they may poison him as they would a mad dog, he dies in horrible agonies, and that is the last we hear of that Herod.

The next one mentioned by the name is this man who is connected with the ministry of John the Baptist and of Jesus. He began his career, upon his father's death, by intriguing at the court of Rome to throw his brother Archelaus out of his inheritance of the kingdom of Judea; and afterward distinguished himself by repudiating his lawful wife, and seducing his niece and sister-in-law, the wife of his living brother Philip and the daughter of his dead brother Aristobulus. This was the man that had a great respect for John the Baptist, and ended with murdering him; and was much interested to see Jesus work a miracle, and concluded with insulting him and sending him to Pilate to be crucified. A few years later, he went on an intriguing expedition to Rome, again ("that fox," that he was) to undermine the prosperity of a young Herod, his own nephew, and the own brother of his niece, sister-in-law and paramour, Herodias. He failed in this; and was sent off to Lyons in Gaul, with the wretched Herodias, to die in disgrace. And that is the last that we hear of *him*.

It is a third Herod who appears to us in the twelfth chapter of the Acts, stretching forth his hands to vex certain of the church, and slaying an apostle with the sword. Still at the same bloody business of the slaughter of the innocent, showing the same traits of this infernal stock, but not the same Herod. This was the young man whom his uncle, the murderer of John the Baptist, had been trying to put out, but who put *him* out instead. He was smitten by God amid the blasphemous acclamations of the people at Cæsarea, "and was eaten of worms and gave up the ghost;" and that is the last of the *name* of Herod, in the Scriptures.

But this man left one son, a brilliant young man, a favorite of the emperor Claudius, who is called, in the book of Acts, by his surname, Agrippa, and who succeeded to the family dignities and virtues. To do him justice, he does not seem to have been quite worthy, in point of atrocious cruelty, of his father, and great-uncle, and great-grandfather; but in other respects, no Herod of them all could out-Herod him. This was the "King Agrippa" before whom Paul was brought, and who remarked humorously to the apostle, "a little more, and you will be wanting to make a Christian of me." When this man's kingdom was wiped out at the destruction of Jerusalem, he went back to Rome, and spent the last of his days with his incestuous sister and wife Berenice. And (let the earth be glad thereof!) this is the last that history has to do with the Herod family; for God, in mercy to mankind, destroyed the last scion of the stock in the volcanic eruption that overwhelmed Pompeii.

To come back to our Herod of the text—Herod the Second. It is curious and instructive to observe that he is set before us here in the good points of his character—at least, in the best points that he had. It is in the Holy Gospels that one of the vilest wretches in human history is set before us in a somewhat amiable and interesting aspect. He feels a sincere respect for religion. He is not so far gone but that he knows honesty and faith and self-devotion when he sees them in another man. And he does not respect these the less, but a great deal the more, when the just and holy man does not spare his own sins, but denounces them to his face.

"Abashed he stands,
And feels how awful goodness is, and sees
Virtue in her shape how lovely."

Not only this, but he takes the preacher under his protection; and declares, doubtless with much hard swearing, when one and another of the courtiers propose to stop the prophet's insolence by taking his life, that no man shall hurt a hair of his head. That infamous creature, Herodias, was set with vindictive malignity, and withal, when she saw how Herod's mind was affected, with desperate fear of being cast out from her place at court, on silencing the preacher with a murder. But Herod was just as determined that, whatever else she did, she should not touch John the Baptist. And I have no doubt that he took enormous pride in it, too, as many a swearing, drinking, cheating reprobate nowadays will pride himself on hiring a pew in a most puritan church, where righteousness and temperance and judgment are faithfully preached to him, and will insist, with profuse expletives, that no man shall say a word against his minister. The case is common enough.

But we should do Herod injustice if we should suppose this to be all. Herod listened to the preacher of righteousness and repentance with a genuine personal and practical interest. He applied John's teachings to his own case—to his own sins and his own duties—so far as anything was left to his ingenuity in the matter of application, for John's teaching was sufficiently direct and pointed in itself. Herod did lay the word of the Lord to heart with reference to his own amendment, and did obviously begin to make such a difference in his course of life as to give Herodias reason to fear that he would not make an end of reforming until he had reformed her and her devil's imp of a daughter out of the palace altogether.

"He did many things" in consequence of John's preaching—many just and upright things such as were strange enough to hear of in the vice-regal court of Palestine; beneficent and public-spirited things, making his reign, for the time, a less unmitigated curse to that afflicted country; merciful things, using his princely wealth and power for the relief of the distressed. What a thing to give thanks for was even this partial repentance of Herod, for the good it did, for the pain and outrage that it saved! Let no one think that the preaching of God's kingdom is a total waste, even when no man yields to it his unreserved submission. The whole work of Christ's gospel in any community is not to be summed up in the net number of converts or communicants. How many a soul is saved from being just such an abandoned wretch as Herod was; how many a decent home from being such a sty of uncleanness as Herod's palace was; how many a State from being defiled with blood and turbulent with wrong, just through some men's standing in awe before the holiness of Christ, and hearing him gladly, and being willing to " do many things!"

There are some who, as they read, will say that after all, these many good things that Herod did at John's preaching were done solely out of policy, to conciliate the people, or out of superstitious fear, or out of some other base motive. I do not think it. It does not agree with this story in Mark, though when we compare the other gospels it seems likely that there was a mingling of lower motive in his good conduct, as there is so apt to be in yours and mine.

But the story is a capital specimen of the Bible's fair, impartial way—God's way—of dealing with human nature, giving every man full credit for all the good there is in him. They were not very strong in systematic theology, these four evangelists, or we might have had a very different story about Herod. But there is nothing more marvelous about the Bible than its constancy in dealing with human nature just as it is—nothing extenuating, setting down naught in malice. If there was any man toward whom the evangelist might have been justified in judging harsh judgments, whether as patriotic Jew or as Christian, it was Herod. If there was any point on which the facts ought to be so put as to bring out sound doctrine, it should be that fundamental point of the total depravity of man by nature. But neither passion nor the spirit of system is suffered to sway the evangelist's pen to the right hand or to the left in describing even the character of Herod. Here we might have had the portrait of a black villain, without a mitigating feature of his character; but we have instead the delineation of a man of like passions with ourselves, in one of his better moods, when he is seriously pondering questions of duty, and almost inclined to do altogether right. Evidently we are dealing here with historians of a very peculiar type. They are men of strong feelings, most religious men, earnest partisans of a new doctrine; but it is their sole care to give the facts just as they are. This is the wonder of the four gospels. There never were four such absolutely honest, truth-telling histories, before or since. In some respects they are nowise miraculous. They are not miracles of grammar and rhetoric. They are not miracles of pettifogging precision. They are not miracles of scientific chronology. But they are a *moral* miracle. Here are four men peculiarly subject to the two influences by which the truth of history is most often perverted—personal feeling and religious or partisan zeal. They are conscious of a great religious mission. Their hearts are sore with personal bereavement at the accomplishment of a bloody tragedy, the details of which men of distant races and generations are unable to read with composure. And yet in writing the very text-books of their religion, they are able to speak of the very agents in the murder of their dearest friend, their adored Lord and Teacher, with a simplicity of truth-telling in which we at this distance find it hard to follow them. Here we find Pilate represented as a gentleman, and an amiable and well-meaning gentleman, too; and Annas and Caiaphas as a pair of earnest and zealous clergymen, rather too much possessed of what we call, nowadays, a "denominational spirit"; and this Herod in the attitude of one who takes an earnest interest in religion, and is taking some serious steps of reformation. These people do not fare so well in our books when we write the story over. How many of our numberless *Lives of Christ* do not, just in this way, miss the very point of the gospel history,—that the crucifixion of the Lord of glory was the work of ordinary, average human nature, of common-place weaknesses and vulgar every-day faults, combined with an infusion of the ecclesiastical virtues? There is something divine in the way in which these four men have told their story. They had received "power from on high to become witnesses."*

But what can we make of this case of Herod, in a theological sense? How can we reconcile this account of a man of many good and honorable feelings, who is touched and perplexed in his conscience, and hears the word of God gladly, and is willing to do many things, with our doctrines of total depravity and the sinfulness of unregenerate doings? This is the sort of question that we often ask, or hear asked, without the slightest consciousness that there is anything absurd in it. But would it not be better, as a general rule, when there seems to be a falling out between our theology and the facts of the Scriptures, to reconcile our theology to the facts, instead of reconciling the facts to our theology? If you have a doctrine of total depravity which fails to correspond with the plain facts of human nature, both in the Bible and out of it, all the worse for your doctrine. The Christian doctrine of human nature, the doctrine of intelligent theologians generally, is only a summary of the facts. The only defense it needs is a fair statement before an honest conscience. The only attack it need fear is that which it suffers under a false name. For it is a false name, as language is now used, which theologians persist in applying to the true and reasonable doctrine of human nature, when they call it by the name of Total Depravity.

But what *are* the facts in Herod's case, as they appear to an honest conscience?

1. First, that in all his doing of right things, Herod does nothing right; for in all that he does he is Herod. The things that he does in obedience to John's preaching are right *in the abstract*, considered independently of the man that does them.

* Acts i. 8.

But as a matter of fact, these actions in the abstract never get done in actual life. We can think about them, and reason about them; but we never really see or know of an action that is not done by somebody. The action is *the man acting*. Strictly speaking, it is not actions that are right or wrong; it is men. And when the question is, Did the man do right? we have to look at the man as well as the deed. And the honest conscience has no doubt on this point: No man is right in his doing, so long as he is cherishing a fixed, conscious purpose to do wrong, or not to do altogether right. This is a rule that does not work both ways. The hidden thought of the heart is like the morsel hidden in the garment, of which Haggai spoke:* it can pollute a good act, it cannot sanctify an evil act.

Here is Herod resolutely protecting the sternest of God's prophets, eagerly listening to him, heeding him, obeying him in many things, but standing out obstinately in his incestuous and adulterous love against that word of the Lord, "It is not lawful for thee to have her." How does the case stand with him, just now? It was right, wasn't it? for Herod to "do many things" at the preaching of John the Baptist. He was a pretty good man for the time being, wasn't he? Wasn't it quite like heroism—moral heroism—backed up by political caution, when he stubbornly refused to permit the killing of John the Baptist, and said to Herodias, "No! I will not! I will agree to lock him up in prison, but not one step further will I go"? Was he not rather the pattern of what we should call a good member of society—a man with a sincere respect for religion, and a great interest in the church, and a strong attachment to his favorite minister;—a man who is willing to subscribe handsomely, and do many things, and deny himself many things, but of course, not *every* thing?

It was right for Pilate—wasn't it?—to refuse to crucify Jesus of Nazareth, and to make that long parley with the

---

* Haggai ii. 10-14.

Jerusalem mob, at the peril of his popularity and of his office, just to save the life of an honest man. Pilate was a good man,—was he not?—as long as it lasted, when he went out and faced the mob, boldly declaring, "I find no cause of death in him;"—when he went again, and said, "I will release him unto you—your King;" and, as his words were flung back into his face with that awful clamor, Crucify! crucify!—when he, the Roman, pleaded with their Jewish pride, saying, "Shall I crucify your King?"—when he stoutly refused their bloody cry—"No! I'll not crucify him! I'll—I'll—I'll scourge him and let him go!" Did not Pilate, as well as Herod, "do many things"? And was he not a pretty fair sort of man, as the world goes? And was not the Lord of glory crucified by pretty good men as the world goes? And is he not crucified afresh to-day by pretty good men as the world goes? And are you content to be a pretty good man as the world goes?

Now I do not find that the Gospel has any dealings with this kind of goodness. It does not appear that Jesus Christ has any advice or encouragement for those who would like to be rid of a part of their sins. He is not a specialist in spiritual maladies; he is a great Physician. It is not worth your while to go to him with a request for partial and local treatment—to hold up before him your infected, swollen limb, and say, "There! give me something for that! Don't touch the rest of me. I am all right. I only want that arm cured." He will not treat the case on any such terms. Your case is constitutional, not local. If you are not prepared to put the case unreservedly into his hands, and consent to all his prescriptions, why come to him with it? Take it to the cancer-doctor, and let him treat it with his salves and poultices. But if you would have the help of Jesus Christ, you must surrender the case to him, and prepare for thorough treatment, perhaps for sharp surgery.

It comes hard, sometimes, to have to say this thing. One rings at my door, and asks, in a business-like tone, "Can I see you by yourself for a few minutes?"—and then, when the study door is locked, the voice breaks down and the awful secret comes out mixed with sobs and tears—" Oh, sir, I have got into an awful habit. I have got to drinking, and I cannot stop. Can't you help me? For my poor mother's sake, for my wife's sake, for my little boy's sake, do help me!" It is hard to say to him, "No; if that is all you want—if that is all you are willing to have done—don't come to us. Go to the Rechabites —go to the Good Templars—go to Mr. Murphy. But if you want Christ's help, it must be in Christ's way—to be made a new man in Christ Jesus—to be healed and kept through and through—and this, through God's grace, you can have if you will receive it.

2. For this marks the wisdom of God's way of dealing with sin, that it is the enduring and stable way. We have seen, in the first place, that there is no real worth in Herod's repentance or in Pilate's goodness. We recognize now that in them is no continuance, and that when they have passed away, the last state of those men is worse than the first. Herod begins,—oh, how hopefully, as many may have thought!—with defending John the Baptist, and with "doing many things" in obedience to his preaching; and ends with cutting off his head to please a harlot. Pilate begins with a warm and sincere effort to save the life of Jesus; and ends with scourging him and delivering him to be crucified.

It is an old tradition that while Herod (as we know) was sent to pass his latter days of disgrace and exile at Lyons in Gaul, Pilate, in like manner was banished to the closely neighboring town of Vienne. It is no wild conjecture to imagine them coming together, in their sad and disappointed old age, and talking over the days when they used to be in politics together in that strange land at the further end of the Mediterranean. If we can conceive such men honestly unvailing their hearts to themselves and to each other, shall we have Herod boasting to Pilate of his brave fidelity to right at the preaching of the stern prophet of the wilderness; and Pilate speaking in turn with complacency of his gallant struggle with the mob to save the life of Jesus of Nazareth? Or rather will they point each other back, these joyless, hopeless old men, as the fatal crises from which their lives turned down to ruin,—the one to the eve of that fatal debauch, when he was heeding the prophet's word and "doing many things"; the other to that hour of struggle and vacillation, when he drew near with reverence to the King of heaven, asking, What is truth?—"and would not stay for an answer"?

XXVII.

THE FALL AND RISING AGAIN OF SIMON PETER.

I say also unto thee that thou art Peter, and upon this rock I will build my church. . . .
But he turned and said unto Peter, Get thee behind me, Satan; thou art an offense unto me.—MATT. xvi. 18, 23.

A PRETTY sudden and violent variation of language—does it not seem?—to be uttered by the lips of one who is declared to be "the same, yesterday, to-day and forever," and addressed to the same person! Does the Lord mean that he will build his church on a devil? or (if we adopt the Roman argument) are we to infer that all the popes are to be successors to a Satan? The language of our Lord might be puzzling if it stood alone, but is made clear enough by the story in which it stands. The opposites in his dealing fit precisely into the opposites of character in the man with whom he deals. They are made consistent by these inconsistencies. The constancy of the Lord never shines with such "true-fixed and restful quality" as when his varying words accommodate themselves to various exigencies; just as God's unchanging love is never so manifest as when, according to our changeful need, it passes through all the moods of providence. Such typical weaknesses of human nature are conspicuous in this man Simon, such oscillations of will, such swervings of judgment, such caprices of affection, that they illustrate, as nothing else could, the unvarying love, wisdom and patience of the Christ; so that, studying Simon, we learn not only something of human nature, but something of the glory of God. Therefore it is in the light of Christ's countenance that I propose to study the character of his chief apostle, noting,—

I. The Infirmities and the Fall of Simon as illustrating the Magnanimity and Patience of Christ;

II. The Worthiness of Simon and the Promotion of him to the foremost place in the kingdom of heaven, as illustrating the Wisdom and redemptive Power of Christ.

I. I know it will seem to many to be an ungracious work, this of emphasizing, in the first place, the faults that mar so grand a figure as that of the chief apostle; and that it would be far more reverent and becoming, and every way more edifying, if we should pass these over, and give our attention rather to studying and imitating his virtues. This is a mistaken notion. The way to be instructed by the Scriptures is to take their whole teaching—not to pick out the parts you like the best and skip the rest. Very likely these points to which you give the go-by as not edifying are the very parts which you need, to correct your one-sided blunders—those favorite blunders of yours which you are very sure about and do not wish to have corrected. It is a curious paradox, which seems nevertheless to be true, that the people who talk most zealously about the infallible authority of the Bible are most apt to mean their favorite systems of proof-texts or other preferred parts of the Bible. There is no way in which such people have done more to empty the Bible of much of its most wholesome meaning, and to make it an actual means of demoralization, so turning a precious corner-stone into a stone of stumbling and a rock of offense, than by resolutely blinking the faults of the Bible saints, and aggravating the faults and carping at the virtues of the Bible sinners. I always look, when I find an expositor bent on foisting into a text something edifying which does not belong there, to see him miss the very instruction which stares him in the face.

Is there any reason why we, as Christians, should look with favor on those faults and follies of this chosen man, by which

FALL AND RISING AGAIN OF SIMON PETER. 301

his Master and ours was daily grieved and wounded? Ought we for Peter's sake to hide the things which Peter himself denounced with bitter shame and weeping? Let Peter himself be our example. There is nothing more nobly characteristic of him in all his history, than that his own gospel, written (as we may reasonably believe) under his own eye and counsel by the pen of Mark, should be the one which records with inexorable minuteness the most humiliating incidents of his life.

The most obvious of the faults of Simon's natural disposition —that of hasty, presumptuous egotism, showing itself in self-assertion and arrogant officiousness—is a fault peculiarly damaging to the personal dignity of one who is subject to it. Perhaps we hold it in the more dislike and contempt, for the fact that we do not feel free to bestow upon it a very serious indignation and abhorrence. It is hardly like that settled and principled selfishness that takes hold of the deeper roots of character. Being more superficial, it is more constantly in view. Whatever dignity is in repose, in modest self-respect, in worthy deference to the wise and the great, is a dignity which is incompatible with this trait of character. The possessor of it is a standing impertinence, wherever he goes. Advising everybody, reproving everybody, high or low, putting in his word at every turn, answering before he is asked, and running before he is sent, he thinks nothing done unless he does it himself. He cannot wait even for himself, but whatever crude notion comes into his mind he must needs blurt it out at once, for (let us acknowledge this in its favor) this fault is no hypocrite. It does not know how to hide, but shows itself at full length, with all its deformities, at every turn.

I have said that it is damaging to one's dignity. Let me add, now, that if it is associated (as it truly was in Peter's case) with any sense of duty, or honor, or fitness, it is destructive to one's peace of mind. Every hasty, irrevocable word or act drags after it its after-clap of mortification: and when the man or boy begins to know himself, his life becomes pervaded with a sense of folly, a self-contempt that keeps up an uneasy conflict with this overweening self-assertion, and ought to restrain it,— but does not.

This is not all. This infirmity of character makes one not only ridiculous to the general eye and unhappy in himself, but odious to his associates. Whether by design or by perverse instinct, such an one is always elbowing himself forward to the front. Whatever company he may be in, he must needs be captain and spokesman. If he has, underneath it all, such true magnanimity and unselfishness as characterized Simon Bar Jona, he may commonly escape the mean vices of jealousy and envy. But even then, if there is a strife as to who shall be greatest, you may be pretty sure that Simon is mixed up in it. And even in his most chastened hours, when, by the Lake of Galilee, he is receiving from his risen Master a last token of restoration to his love and favor, you need not be surprised to see him pointing to a fellow-disciple and inquiring what is to be done about John; and to hear from the Lord the sharp, withering admonition to him to attend to his own duties and to keep meddlesome questions to himself.

For I beg you to notice, finally, concerning this infirmity of Peter's, that, absurd as it was, grievous to himself, odious to his associates, it was still more offensive and insulting to the great Teacher and Lord whom he had promised to follow and serve. Can we easily imagine any one more unfit to be the constant companion of this wonderful, serene and majestic Teacher, before whose calm words the rabbis bowed themselves, and the Roman soldiers retired as from one who spake as never man spake, not venturing to molest him, and before whose very silence the Roman proconsul trembled, although backed by all the power of Cæsar's legions,—any more unfit companion, I say, than this malapert, pushing, self-asserting pupil, who takes the words out of the Teacher's mouth to amend and suggest, and even takes him in hand to administer a deliberate rebuke to him. Said we not well that the lesson of Peter's character is a lesson of the bound-

FALL AND RISING AGAIN OF SIMON PETER. 303

less patience of Jesus Christ with human infirmity? It is our growing wonder, as we read, that the Lord did not a score of times, instead of once, bid him get out of his sight, because he was an offense. What words are those which we hear amid the exceeding brightness of the holy mount, when a celestial light came down upon them so that they were sore afraid, and the august presence of glorified prophets did obeisance to the Son of Man, and words of awful moment passed between them touching the decease which he should accomplish? Whose adventurous lip shall dare to break in upon the council-chamber of the King of heaven? This Galilee fisherman, forsooth, has a few suggestions to make, and talk he must, at the first impulse, though "he wist not what he said." Oh, what a patient Master, that was content to bear so gently, so forgivingly, so magnanimously, with such an infirm, halting disciple as this Simon of Galilee! What can we say of the loving kindness which retained this one in his nearest confidence, which placed him at the foremost point of honor and responsibility in the kingdom of heaven, which adorned him with such a name as God himself had been wont to assume as expressing his own unchangeable glory, surnaming him the Rock, as making him the foundation of the everlasting Church, the holder of the keys of the kingdom of heaven! Do you see what a friend this is to whom we commend you all, O men—this patient Jesus Christ—the same yesterday, to-day, and forever? Do you see him, O strugglers with temptation, O standers in slippery places, O oftentimes cast down and discouraged? Do you behold him, O mortified and self-ashamed? And can you fear to trust him? He knows your folly, yea, better than you know yourself. He hates—despises—all the pettiness and meanness which you abhor in your own heart. But withal he sees and honors every good and honorable thought and feeling, even those that men do not see, and that you yourself hardly know. He knows the work of his own hands, and under the wreck which you have made of yourself he recognizes the noble thing which he meant you to be,—which you ought to be, and which you may yet become. I beg you to look again, and take the full sense and impression of the follies and faults of this great apostle, and then, in moments of discouragement, ask yourself whether the love which bore with Simon Peter may not bear with you, and in moments of wavering, when you hear and almost obey his invitation, "Come unto me," decide if it be not safe for you altogether to take him at his word.

II. I have left myself brief time to speak of that more obvious and welcome topic, the Virtues of Peter as illustrating the Wisdom of Christ who called him to his chief apostleship, and the Power of Christ who qualified him for that great work. And indeed, after what has been said of his faults, there is the less need; for his faults were (to use the phrase of a wise French proverb) *les défauts de ses qualités*, "the faults of his virtues." His virtues were these same faults of his, restrained and corrected by the wisdom of Christ and the spirit of a living faith. It is no recondite observation that every vice is a virtue perverted and diabolized. And conversely, our Christian graces are often our morbid growths of character that have been healed and vitalized by healthful currents from the Heart and Life of the church. Shame is modesty corrupted; and cowardice is caution emptied of duty; and avarice is thrift and self-denial gone to decay; and arrogant presumption is the travesty of a noble boldness. And a loving heart, that looks out benignantly on human nature, can see, by the transfiguring light that is in itself, the noble possibilities of humanity shining through the outward blotches and blemishes which alone appear to the common eye. To a beautiful, loving, hopeful heart, the world of fallen, corrupt, depraved humanity grows beautiful. A great preacher, Frederick Robertson, reasoning from the loneliness of those who, living amid the multitude, are yet separated from those about them by wide chasms of moral difference, has spoken instructively of the solitude of Christ. And we are often bidden think of the daily disgust and pain that our Lord must have suffered from the daily contact of a character so base, so sordid, so revolting as that of Judas. But there is another aspect of all this; and I love rather to think of the grace and loveliness which Jesus could see, where other men saw nothing but deformity. There is no human face so ugly but that an artist can discern in it the suggestions of a type of beauty. There is no face so fair and perfect but that one who seeks can find in it the elements of caricature. In his daily random contact with the world, in markets and street-cars, one may, according to the temper of his own mind, dwell habitually, like Raphael, amid forms of beauty, or like Hogarth and Cruikshank, amid uncouth and repulsive shapes;—may "make a heaven of hell, a hell of heaven." It is no presumptuous guess, it has warrant of Holy Scripture, if we conceive that Jesus had before him, during those toils and sorrows that wrought out our salvation, the glorious vision, behind the deformities of men as they were, of men as they might be, as they were to be, as he was to make them. Here was a joy set before him for which it was good to endure the cross and despise the shame. Here was comfort amid the grievances and annoyances which his righteous soul endured from the faults of his disciples. These offenses that grieved him day by day, could they but be purged of the sin that was in them and chastened by divine love, should become the mould of apostolic virtue. The skeptic hesitancy of Thomas, the arrogant boldness of Peter, even the calculating utilitarianism of Judas, under the discipline of Christ, might furnish just the diverse material needed for the organization of the kingdom of heaven. Do you suppose that it was by accident or blunder that the Lord took Judas, with all his sordid narrowness of mind, and made him treasurer of the family? This man might have become, perhaps, the organizing and regulating mind of the infant church. And if Christ could bear with these frail, blundering, wandering disciples, cannot we bear with other such? And if he can be so patient as he is with us, can we not for his sake be patient with one another? Can we not be patient with children, and with absurdities and extravagances in youthful character, considering what may yet be done with such, through a divine nurture? Nay, can we not sometimes be a little more patient with ourselves, with the patience of hope?

Why not? Is it wrong to have long patience with yourself, and steadfast hope? Perhaps you feel that the way to honor Christ is to lose all hope, and doubt whether so holy and pure a being can have any kindness toward you. Perhaps it seems to you a mark of grace to be able to write a beautiful diary full of religious despondency, like so many of the dear saints in the religious biographies—as if the Christian graces were fear, despondency and misery, instead of faith, joy, hope. It is in order that we may have better and happier thoughts of Christ and his salvation, that we have written for our comfort and instruction those later chapters in the life of Simon Peter: his shameful apostasy, which was the consequence and summing up of all his sins, faults and weaknesses; and his rehabilitation and uplifting to be the chief and captain of the apostles, thus exhibiting the saving power and glory of God in Christ, which out of such material could build to himself so glorious a church; which could take "that worm, Jacob," the supplanter, and giving to him the new name of Israel, could raise him up to be a prince and prevailer with God; that could choose, for his own glory, the arrogant, unfaithful, cowardly Simon, and out of him create the Rock on which to build his church. The highest achievement of human culture is this—that taking for itself the choicest elements of manhood, it can finely temper them, and compact and build them together into such massive strength that they shall be a very tower and refuge to humanity,—

"Standing four-square to every wind that blows."

Out of stuff like this, of patriotism, self-sacrifice, trained obedience, imperial virtues all compact, are heroes made. Even in their budding youth men read the promise of their greatness; and when the crisis comes to which they are foreappointed, they step forward to their fit place of glorious peril, and men cling round them and gather strength from their immovable firmness. Such a man, one awful day, when the fate of our country seemed long to tremble in an even balance, and at last the capricious tide seemed to be setting hopelessly toward disaster and defeat,—such a man breasted his way forward to the rough edge of battle, and planted himself like a standard round which the wavering and breaking lines should rally and form again, and so saved the day. And there went up a great shout the wide land over, and men surnamed him the Rock—the Rock of Chickamauga.

But how much greater the glory of Jesus Christ which could take such an one as poor Simon Barjona, and create him captain and leader of his apostolic band, and foundation and bedrock on which his church should be builded up! See him, this Simon, "following Jesus afar off," skulking at the heels of that rabble-rout that follows the captive Saviour deserted of his friends, from the garden by the brookside to the high-priest's house! And is *this* the man, only these seven weeks later, whom we see standing forth upon the day of Pentecost, amid the crowd of mockers and unbelievers, and saying, "Jesus of Nazareth, a man approved of God among you by miracles and wonders and signs which God did by him in the midst of you, as ye also do know,—him have ye taken, and by wicked hands have crucified and slain. Let all the house of Israel know assuredly that God hath made that same Jesus whom ye have crucified, both Lord and Christ"?

Look at him, Simon of Galilee, creeping to the fire in the high-priest's palace to warm his trembling hands on that chill midnight,—hiding, shrinking, blushing, forswearing himself, denying his Lord, before the recognition of a servant-girl. What change is this, when, before high-priest and scribes and all the potentates of his people, Peter, filled with the Holy

Ghost, says unto them, "Be it known to you all, and to all the people of Israel, that in the name of Jesus Christ of Nazareth, whom ye crucified, whom God raised from the dead, even in him doth this man stand here before you whole. This is the stone, set at nought by you builders, which is made the head of the corner. In none other is salvation!"

Look, gaze on this amazing change, and take courage? See what the Holy Ghost can do! Learn, in your uttermost discouragement, your deepest conscious unworthiness, to commit yourself to the new-creating power of God, who is able to keep you from falling, and to present you *faultless* before the presence of his glory with exceeding joy.

XXVIII.

THE JUDGMENT OF JUDAS ISCARIOT.

That thou doest, do quickly.—JOHN xiii. 27.

No one knew what they referred to—these words of the Master to Judas. We are distinctly assured of this by the evangelist: "No man at the table knew for what intent he spake this unto him."

It was not strange. How should they have known? Had not Judas been with them regularly and faithfully from the beginning? Had he not occupied a position of trust in the little community? Had he not always shown great zeal in behalf of the poor? And when to the strange and dreadful announcement, "Verily, I say unto you that one of you shall betray me," the disciples looked around on one another and asked, "Is it I?"—had not Judas in his turn asked, "Lord, is it I?" as distinctly and affectionately as any one of the twelve? How *should* they know to what intent the words were spoken? Here was this active and well-known disciple of Christ; how could they guess that "Satan had entered into him," and that under that decent and respectable exterior was a heart already charring and smouldering with the fire of hell? As he disappeared from that upper room, doubtless with brotherly salutations from all but that beloved disciple to whom the Lord had whispered the secret, no wonder that they said one to another "he has gone to make some further arrangements for this passover festival," or "he has been sent by the Master with some message of charity or bounty to the poor."

But all the time the Lord knew the mind and purpose of

his treacherous disciple better than Judas himself knew it. Through the disguise of glozing words and specious looks,—through the pretenses and excuses with which the traitor heart was deceiving itself, and through the vail which was hiding the future from the minds of all the rest, that calm, patient eye was piercing, and seeing, undisturbed except with exceeding sorrow, the crime and the consequences which when Judas himself saw he went out in a passion of remorse and hanged himself.

And yet, knowing all these things, the Lord spoke to the traitor, and spoke in a tone so calm and so cheerful that the disciples all supposed that he was merely sending Judas on some errand of business or charity. "No man at the table" understood it.

None of them understood it. Are you sure that you even now understand fully the intent with which our Lord spoke these words to Judas? It is worth your understanding, if you will study it; for you may find that there is some word here for you as well as for Judas. And you may miss it, as I suspect that Judas did.

For the drift of the whole story indicates that this Judas was a man who habitually imposed upon his own mind with self-deceptions. His little hypocrisies—his zeal to give the price of the ointment to the poor—his "Lord, is it I?" in the upper chamber—his kiss in the garden—he kept them up to the end, long after they had ceased to impose on anybody but himself. And the horrible tragedy of his suicide in an agony of remorse seems to prove that the depth of his own sin and shame were not fully disclosed to his own soul, entangled in its self-deceits and perverting even the words of Christ to his own destruction, until in the light of its results "his iniquity was found to be hateful."

It is not difficult to guess at the construction he may have been trying to put on the Master's last words to him, as he picked his way by night through the narrow streets of Jerusalem, toward the place of his traitorous rendezvous. "'What thou doest, do quickly,' says the Lord; and the Lord, who knows men's hearts, must have known what I was about to do; he tells me to do it, doesn't he? he authorizes or permits it for some good end; or it is included in some comprehensive plan of Providence; or it is predestined, and I am only a helpless instrument in the hands of fate; I am not responsible, or at least I am not very much to blame. He said, 'Do it quickly;' the Lord said so; I am doing what the Lord said." We need not doubt that it was some such talk as this that Judas kept saying over to his own heart when he went out from the company of the disciples. It takes a great deal of sophistry, a great deal of make-believe, and a deep-seated purpose of wrong-doing, to use any command of Christ as a pretext for dishonoring and betraying him. But it can be done; and I do not doubt that Judas did it "in that night," as many have done it since. But it is needless to say that this was no part of the intent of Jesus Christ.

We can think of three considerations which may have entered into "the intent with which he spake these words":

1. It may have been the Saviour's wish to secure privacy from the presence of the traitor. Hitherto, it had not seemed to be of the highest importance to have the little company of disciples purified from hypocrites and unworthy ones. Even among these chosen and intimate companions of the Lord, the tares and the wheat had been let grow together, as it was to be in the church thereafter. He who knew what was in men's hearts had been patient with this man Judas, while his iniquity was hidden in his heart, and had been willing to extend the time of his pupilage if so be he yet might trust, and obey, and live. The man was deadly sick with his own selfishness and meanness—leprously, loathsomely sick; but this great Physician never deemed that that was a good reason why one should not come to him and be with him; and so Judas had been suffered to stay.

But now the case was changing. The Master was coming to those last tender words of love and farewell with his true disciples, with which it was not meet that the stranger should intermeddle. Withal he was about to appoint that festival of the Holy Supper, the feast of the union of the branches in the vine; and there was no right that the traitor should be there as a spot on this feast of charity. Let him begone, even on his foul and bloody business, rather than linger there to eat and drink judgment against himself. The sacred hour when the Lord, manifesting himself in the breaking of the bread, gives peace not as the world giveth, is no place for one who, with settled purpose, is planning treachery to the Master of the feast. Let him go, go quickly, from among the faithful disciples, that the world may see that he was not of them.

2. We cannot surely say that there may not have been expressed in these words of the suffering Saviour, something of

> the noble flame
> That burned within his breast,
> When, hasting to Jerusalem,
> He marched "before the rest."

Perhaps—who can tell?—there was here something of that eagerness to suffer with which he pressed forward and reached forth to that uttermost anguish from which his prostrate and bleeding frame recoiled. Perhaps in that moment when, as the traitor made ready to depart, the shame and agony were vividly set before him, there was set before him, too, that *joy* for which he despised them both. Perhaps with the foretaste of his dying pangs, he tasted also the glory that should follow. He may have greeted with prophetic exultation that multitude that should look unto him from the ends of the earth and be saved; and, with such love as a mother's "when she feels for the first time her first-born's breath," may have seen of the travail of his soul and been satisfied. "Then saith he, Lo, I come; in the volume of the book it is written of me, I delight to do thy will, O my God."

There are many things in the whole history of our Lord's passion that are given to us to make it manifest that he was a voluntary, consenting sufferer—not taken as a bird in the snare of the fowler, entrapped by a secret conspiracy whose machinations he had not suspected, whose toils he could not break; but knowing the hearts of his enemies, and having power over his own life to lay it down and to take it again, he went forward to accomplish what was given him to do, while Jew and heathen, open enemy and secret traitor, thinking only to execute their own malice and selfishness, with wicked hands prepared to do whatsoever the hand and counsel of the Father had before determined to be done. It seems to me, as I read, that there is something of this meaning, as signifying the free and willing consent, the joy of self-sacrifice, with which he went forward to the suffering of death, in this word to Judas, "What thou doest, do quickly."

3. But a more obvious reason, and the chief reason from one who never spake without reason,—the reason worthiest of him all whose words had their origin and end in love, would seem to be this: that they might perhaps reach the heart and conscience of Judas himself, to whom they were spoken. That wretched man, the son of perdition, had been hiding iniquity in his heart. Hiding it, I say. No man, in his progress toward some very great and unaccustomed crime is wont to carry the purpose of it about with him distinctly acknowledged in his consciousness. He *hides* it in his heart. He buries it in those deceitful depths, among broken resolutions, and neglected vows, and disappointed plans of good, and slighted admonitions of conscience, and there it germinates, and unfolds, and grows strong, and at last shoots forth and shows itself in action. And the hope for such a man is that he may be forced to look himself in the face—to see and understand his own heart—may be compelled to take up the question which he is continually postponing and avoiding, and decide it, consciously, deliberately. Or the hope is that even when he has gone and stricken cov-

enant with sin and death, and joined hands with deadly temptation, he may be brought to himself long enough to look upon his deed and its consequences, and so to snatch away his hand as out of a blazing fire. This word of the Lord to Judas is not so far unlike the word he has spoken to you or me sometimes in our moments of peril and crisis—a word salutary, full of blessing and salvation when we have listened to it as he meant it. For note well what he said to this recreant disciple, when he leaned toward him across the passover table. He did not give any commission or authority to execute treason against the Master; he did not say to him, "Go, betray me to my enemies." He said only, "What thou doest, do quickly." Whatever it be, go and do it at once. No more dallying with temptation,—no more plying to and fro between conscience and sin,—no more drifting along on the current of a concealed and unacknowledged purpose. The matter must be settled now and settled forever. That thou doest, do quickly. Even yet it is not too late. O wretched Judas! If he would but turn this moment he should be saved; and then all the forewarnings of the prophets, and the exceeding sorrowful words of Christ himself, would prove to be as warnings that had issued in repentance, as prophecies that had wrought against their own fulfillment. See, he rises from the passover table! Will he not turn and live? He looks once more on the face of his Lord. Will he not bow himself at those gracious feet, and confess the awful thoughts of his heart, and implore that forgiveness that never yet was refused to the penitent sinner? His hand is on the door. Do we not see him hesitate, and almost pause? No, no! He is gone. He is on his way to the treacherous assignation. He has decided for himself the question of his everlasting destiny. They will never see him again but twice,—at the betrayal in the garden; and at the Judgment Day, when he shall look upon Him whom he had pierced.

"That thou doest, do quickly." Christ speaks these words—has spoken them over and over, is speaking them now—to many a recreant disciple besides Judas. Here you are hesitating, going to and fro, dallying with temptation, saying to yourself you will go so far, but not much farther; saying to yourself that you will make up your mind by and by; and behold! there comes to you a voice still and small, which no one perhaps can hear but yourself, but which speaks to your conscience as if in tones of articulate thunder, "No! not by and by! You must make up your mind *now!* What thou doest, do quickly." You shrink from the voice. You do not want to quit your cherished sin. You do not want to renounce forever the love of Christ, the fear of God, the hope of heaven. You want to postpone the issue. But Christ is better to you than your own heart. He knows that the only hope for you is that you should be compelled to meet the issue, not postpone it; and so he forces your hand. "Quickly," he says, "do it quickly, if you would do it at all." He speaks to you in the clear utterance of events which set before you the necessity of choosing. The two ways part before your feet; and you cannot stand still, and you must go one way or the other. Your sin finds you out; it *is* found out by others, perhaps; the world is gazing at it, and what others know you can no longer pretend to keep a secret from yourself. The devil who has seduced you begins to betray you; and you abhor and lament over the exposure that is the most kind word of Jesus entreating and commanding you to decide your own destiny with your own free will and judgment, while yet it remains to be decided. Perhaps Christ speaks to you by the voice of his faithful church, reinforcing the voice of his providence, and saying, "Do it quickly, whatever you do! our Master has charged us that we require this of you. Choose, between the fellowship of the disciples of Jesus, and the company of the corrupt and the corrupting; between Christ and Belial; between the cup of blessing and the cup of devils. Choose. Choose now. You cannot have these both. What thou doest, do quickly."

You think it hard. It is hard. It is awful. But it is infinitely kind in its severity. It gives you the one remaining chance of safety. You think it is unwise, inexpedient for the interests of the church, for its quiet and peace, for its numbers and respectability. You say to yourself that for you to depart from your accustomed place would invite injurious comment and remark, and be no service to the church but an injury; that it is better to let things go on quietly as heretofore, to let them drift along, and never turn the eye to see whither they are drifting. No! no! be honest, at least, in your wickedness. Look your conscience in the face. Renounce your perjured vows; stand before the world and the church in your true light. Blot away the sign of baptism from your brow. Leave here the cup of thanksgiving and away to your drink-offering of blood. That thou hast resolved to do—and oh, is it resolved? Is there no going back? Does this last appeal of your dying Saviour have no power to turn your heart?—that thou doest, do quickly! It is better, for the reasonableness of the thing, that this case should come to trial on its merits, not go by default. It is going; the last moments of repentance are oozing drop by drop away, and the case is settling itself. If it settles itself, it will be settled wrong. And Christ, who has spoken to you in many an awakening summons of Providence, in many a monition of the lapse of time, in many an ending up of opportunity, in many a last thing and last time, speaks to you again at this hour, in this word of his from his seat by the passover-table, and says That thou doest, do quickly.

And what he saith to one, he saith to all. This word which is spoken to Judas, is a word which zealous Peter and loving John may lay to heart. Have they some word of love and faith that they would say to the Lord their Master, some tender utterance of regret for hasty and unworthy words that they have spoken, it were well they should speak them quickly, for soon the Shepherd will be smitten and the sheep be scattered abroad.

Is there not something here for every one of us? My dear friends, with whom I have counseled and labored together these twelve months, it is now the evening of the year, and the shadows have grown long, and there are many signs that the night is coming in which no man can work. I would fain that the opportunities of the year should not wholly pass without some visible record of larger good accomplished and sealed. In about one month from now is the last communion of the year. Is there no fruit to be gathered from all this year's sowing of seed? Among your children, your friends, your Sunday-scholars, is there not some one, or more than one, who might be and should be brought to the intelligent and conscious determination of the pending questions between the soul and God—to the act of consecration and communion with the church? They are passing, and we are passing, and the years are passing, and what we do must be done quickly.

And, O my friend, my unhappy friend, hovering still on the verge of duty, and yet poised on the brink of disobedience and despair, how can I let you go without one word more of love and farewell? Do you find comfort and peace in this wretched life? Have you a good conscience in once more turning away from the company of Christ's disciples as they gather about his table? If you meditate giving yourself over to the fellowship of those who neglect and scorn the Saviour who died for you, and exchanging for this the joy and hope of the Christian believer, then do it quickly! If Baal be God, away and follow him. But if indeed it is your purpose to put yourself among the avowed disciples of Christ, then do it quickly. Give no slumber to your eyelids, until, with faith and prayer, you have made covenant with the Lord who loves you. And let not another communion season pass away without finding you seated with the friends of Jesus, beside his table. Quickly, for the night cometh!—the night cometh!

XXIX.

GOD INDWELLING.

Thus saith the high and lofty One that inhabiteth eternity, whose name is Holy: I dwell in the high and holy place, with him also that is of a contrite and humble spirit, to revive the spirit of the humble, and to revive the heart of the contrite ones.—ISAIAH lvii. 15.

INHABITING eternity; yet making his abode within a broken heart! It seems as if we might apprehend either of these things singly; but both together—how can it be? The distresses, the wants, the fears, of life, make us long that indeed it were so. Our soul crieth out for God, for the living God.

We cry; but there seems no answer; only an awful silence. We look upon the outward facts of life and death, and see the steady, unswerving march of law—the unbroken, irrefragable chain of causes and effects—never yielding nor bending to all our needs, to all our prayers. And God seems so far, so far away! We turn the pages of our knowledge from the physical to the metaphysical, and we come no nearer. Our philosophical, our theological, yes, our *religious* meditations upon the nature and attributes of the infinite One—the omniscient, the eternal, the unchangeable—set him more and more beyond the reach of our fellowship and prayer. But all the time, one thing testifies to us of a heavenly Father that hears and loves and answers, and that is our ineradicable need. The cravings of our nature cannot be rebuked by scientific observation of the constancy of law, nor by philosophic meditation of the properties of absolute and infinite being. We need, we must have, a Father. Our heart and flesh, our soul, crieth out for the living God.

GOD INDWELLING. 319

In such a strait, there is true comfort in this word of the Lord by his prophet, in which the full measure of the difficulty is set forth, and the solution of it is found in faith.

It has seemed to me that we need not seek in vain in the created works of God for helps to that faith by which we know that the infinite and eternal God can have fellowship with us and can dwell within the narrow precincts of a human heart.

That sight in visible nature which gives to us the highest sense of vastness,—the aptest suggestion of infinity,—is doubtless the aspect of the starry heavens;—to all of us, ignorant or learned, poetic or unimaginative. It needs no diagrams nor distances from a book of astronomy to tell the lessons of the firmament. "Their sound is gone out into all the earth, and their words to the end of the world."

And yet it is when we come to study the dimensions of this creation in detail, that the sense of its vastness grows upon us and overpowers us. David never could have felt, as we can feel, the force of his own words:—

> When I consider thy heavens, the work of thy fingers,
> The moon and the stars which thou hast ordained,
> What is man that thou art mindful of him,
> And the son of man that thou visitest him?

They are like the chariot of Ezekiel's vision, "so high that it was dreadful." It seems a fearful thing to have to do with such magnitudes; and when we hear of scholars in their observatories measuring the distances among the stars, it overcomes us with a giddy feeling, as when we see men clambering on church spires, or crossing the East River on a strand of wire. A row of figures on a slate does seem such a frail support on which to go marching through the starry spaces! We almost shudder when we see human science springing clear of the narrow boundaries of the earth, and on such attenuated threads of calculation venturing boldly forth to other planets, and thence over chasms of space so vast that it is easiest to call them infinite, until he reaches the fixed stars. No longer content with numbering and naming the host of heaven, and marshalling them in constellations, this tiny creature must take upon himself to scrutinize their constitution, must weigh their floating bulk, must

> "Speed his flight from star to star,
> From world to luminous world, as far
> As the universe rears his flaming wall,"

and, as if bearing in this amazing flight the measuring-rod which once the prophet saw in an angel's hand, must measure the paths along which the planets travel, and tell in human language the distances on the chart of heaven.

And how human language staggers under the burden thus laid upon it! We begin with attempting to state the least of these distances in numbers of a unit of earthly distance, but, when we speak of some of our near neighbors in celestial space as being twenty trillions of English miles away, the words will not hold the meaning—they carry no conception to the mind. They are good to cipher with, but that is all they are good for. We try to invent a new form of speech, and for our unit we take the distance which a cannon-ball, if retaining the velocity with which it leaves the gun, would travel in twenty-four hours, and say that, at this rate of speed, it would take so many months, and years, and centuries, to reach such and such of the nearer stars. But this, too, is a clumsy failure; and we resort, at last, to the heavens themselves for a standard of measurement, and find it in the velocity of light. It shoots from the sun to the earth, a distance of ninety-two millions of miles, in eight minutes and seven seconds. And we attempt to represent the distance of certain of the stars by stating how many years, how many hundred years, how many thousand years, it takes a ray of their light to reach the earth. But it is all in vain. We commonly speak of imagination as outstripping, in its speed, the

GOD INDWELLING. 321

slow-paced reason; but here it is the reason that has outrun the imagination. From these unspeakable tracts of space, over which the reason of man has not hesitated to go,

> "Sounding along its dim and perilous way,"

the imagination shrinks back and refuses to follow. We *know* things which we cannot *conceive*. In presence of such stupendous magnitudes,

> "Imagination's utmost stretch
> In wonder dies away."

We can only bow with awe in the presence of things which the calmest computations have revealed, and seizing the words kindled on the lips of inspiration, sing aloud in worship:—

> "O Lord, how great are thy works!
> In wisdom hast thou made them all!"

I have showed you what is wonderful. Come now, and I will show you what is more wonderful. For I will show you these infinite spaces of the sky, and the glory of them, and the innumerable host of starry worlds, gathered up in a moment of time, within the tiny pupil of a human eye. It is wonderful that the heavens and the host of them should be so great; but that, being so great, they should be able to become so infinitely little,—this passes all wonder. The shepherd stretched upon the ground amid his sheep, gazes up into the starry depths, and finds them wonderful; but never thinks how far more wonderful than the heavens which he beholds is himself beholding them. As he lies gazing, long lines of light, from planet and star and constellation, come stretching on through the infinite void spaces, to centre on the lenses of his drowsy eye. Side by side, and all at once, yet never twisted nor confused, these ten thousand rays of different light enter the little aperture in the centre of the eye which we call the pupil.

There they cross, in a point which has no dimensions, and separate again, and paint in microscopic miniature upon the little surface of the retina, behind the eye-ball, the inverted *fac-simile* of the visible heavens. There, in the ante-chamber of the brain, marches Orion, with his shining baldric and his jeweled sword; there glow Arcturus and Sirius, and the steadfast North Star; there pass the planets to and fro; and the far-off nebulæ are painted there with suffused and gentle radiance—all the heavens and the glory of them gathered in that slender filament of light, threaded through that tiny aperture, painted by their own rays upon that little patch of nervous network, apprehended, felt, known through and through by that finite human mind. How far stranger and sublimer a thing is this than the mere brute bulk of the worlds, or the mere chasms of void space in which they hang weltering!

By this sublime fact in God's visible creation, we are led on to apprehend and feel the sublimest of the glories of God himself, set forth in the prophet's words,—that he whose lifetime is infinite duration, whose dwelling-place is infinite space, —he who before the earth and the world were made was no younger, neither will be older when they are all consumed,— whose presence reaches out to the farthest fixed star that eye or telescope has ever descried floating upon the far verge of the universe, and occupies beyond in all the orbits of worlds yet undiscovered, and still beyond in the regions of space where is naught but the possibility of future worlds, and fills all this immensity to repletion,—that this "high and lofty One that inhabiteth eternity" should enter into some poor, crushed and broken human spirit, that trembles at the very whisper of his voice, and should make the narrow recesses of that heart his abode, his home. This is the mystery and glory of the Godhead,—not alone that he should be infinite, eternal, immortal, invisible, but that being all these, he should yet be apprehended by the little mind of a man, and call himself that man's Friend and Comforter and Father.

For it is not more evident that the tiny pupil of the human eye can take in the expanses and abysses of the heavens, than it is that the little soul of man can receive into itself the infinite God:—

I. By the Intellect;
II. By the Affections;
III. By Spiritual Communion.

I. Man receives God into himself by the intellect. We trifle with the facts of our own consciousness, if we suffer the theological description of God as *incomprehensible* to divert us from the fact that our minds are made for nothing more expressly than for this, that they should receive God. The lowest rudiments of the knowledge of the simplest forms of matter are the beginnings of the knowledge of God. If we could remember, you and I, now that we are grown, all that came to us in infancy—the first struggles of the childish mind with the questions that we are not done with yet, we should see how soon the knowledge of God comes to the little one. Beyond the cradle in which it wakes up to the wonders of a new day is the nursery, and beyond the nursery is the house, and beyond the house is the garden, and beyond the garden there lies all the world, and beyond the world shuts down the sky with its stars, and beyond the sky—what? "Tell me, father—tell me, mother, what is there beyond the sky?" And, according to your knowledge or your ignorance, your faith or your unbelief, you may tell the little questioner of heaven, or of infinities of other worlds, or of infinite waste room and empty space, and he will believe you. But attempt to tell him that beyond is nothing, and not even room for anything, and he will not believe you. He may seem to believe you, but it is impossible that he really should believe. The infant mind—*any* mind—rejects it as impossible. It cannot think the thought. The mind cannot live in anything less than infinite space. It stifles. It leaps up and beats its wings against any bars with which you would cage it in, but that it will break through and take possession of its inheritance.

And, as with infinite extent, so with infinite duration. How well I remember, as a very little child, when men were talking of the end of the world, and the great comet stretched amain across the sky, and men's hearts were failing them for fear, how the thought of infinite duration pressed in, inexorably, on my soul! Come judgment day, come final conflagration, come end of all material things, come cessation and extinction of all angels, all souls, all sentient creatures, still this could not be the end. Eternity must needs go on and on, though there were never an event or thought to mark its movement. There cannot be an end.

They err, not measuring the import of their own arguments, who tell us, in that pride of not-knowing which is so high uplifted beyond any pride of knowledge, that the very form of the word *infinite* marks it as the sign of a thing inconceivable, being a mere negation. Nay, verily, it is the word *end, limit, cessation*, that is the negative word, having no meaning except as the negation of continuance; and *infinite* is the negation of this negation—a thing positive, affirmative, real.

So, then, it is not the idea of infinity to which the human mind is unfitted. The mind is so made that it cannot help receiving that. The incredible, inconceivable idea is the idea of absolute end. So far is the idea of infinity from being inconceivable, that it is just impossible to thrust the conception out of the mind. And with the conception of eternity, there rushes into the thoughtful spirit at once, the awful and lovely conception of "that high and lofty One who *inhabiteth* eternity, whose name is Holy." By such a wonder of creation is it, that he who made the little ball of the human eye so that it can take in the heavens and the earth, has made the petty intellect of man so that it can take in the knowledge of the infinite God.

II. But, secondly, it is even a greater wonder than this, that the infinite God, whom the intellect has conceived, draws near for a more intimate society with his creature, and enters the heart of man through the gateway of his *affections*. I say a greater wonder; for it must be confessed that this ideal of the intellect, this centre in which all infinite attributes inhere, does by his very majesty so overawe the heart that we shrink away from him. By every new perfection of his nature, that grows upon our apprehension; by his awful power as the Almighty; by his perfect knowledge as the All-wise; by his unswerving steadfastness as the Faithful and True—the Immutable; by the very infinitude of his nature, he is withdrawn farther and farther from the possibility of being counted among those humble objects on which the tendrils of a human heart are able to lay hold. How, for instance, shall this Inhabitant of eternity, whose name is *Holy*, be well-pleased with his petty creature who has dared withstand his perfect law, and looks shrinking toward the throne of infinite Majesty, fearing and crying, "Unclean! unclean!" How shall any prayer that we can frame bring arguments to bear upon the Mind that knows the end from the beginning, and to whom there is not a word upon our lips, but lo! he knoweth it altogether? How can any pitiful plight into which we may fall move the compassion of him who is Immutable, and under whose benign government even the pains and severities that befall his creatures are wrought into a plan of common beneficence to the whole? These are questions which the awe-struck intellect, gazing upward at the infinite attributes that adorn the Name which is Holy, puts to the yearning heart, which, with all the craving of its love, with all the outreaching of its need, gropes after a God to worship, to love, to pray to, if haply it may find him. And the heart cannot answer back the intellect with arguments of language. But love contains more reason than many arguments; and the strong instincts of affection and devotion with which the humble and contrite heart reaches out after the love and personal friendship of an infinite Creator are themselves an argument that God will not refuse himself to the affections which he has himself implanted. The hunger and thirst of our hearts for God are a promise from him that they shall be filled. He cannot deny himself.

The very arguments by which we climb to the knowledge of the infinite Spirit are like mountains that separate us from any relation with him of childlike prayer and mutual love. But a trustful confidence can say to these mountains, "Be ye removed and be ye cast into the sea," and it shall be done.

Have you ever pondered that dark mystery of human nature, the origin of the frightful idolatries of India? It seems to be proved that they had their beginning, not (as the prepossessions of modern science would suggest) through development from some form of fetishism baser and coarser still, but by degradation from the most refined and abstract speculations on the infinity, the spirituality, and the immutability of God. No subtler metaphysics is taught to-day in the lecture-rooms of Yale and Princeton, than was taught long centuries ago by Hindoo sages, enthroning their supreme divinity in the everlasting, impassive repose of the unconditioned, far beyond the reach of affection, sympathy or prayer, until the needy millions cried out, stifling, famishing, "Give us a God to love, to worship, to pray to!" and, for lack of answer, betook them to the forest or the quarry or the mine, to the carver and the smith, and made them gods that were no gods. So little can argument and reason hold us back in times when the stress of life comes down upon us, and the cravings of the soul grow strong!

I am bringing to the altar of God my offering—my poor little offering of thankfulness and prayer. Here have I my little bundle of anxieties, cares, troubles,—it may be the concerns of a nation in fear and perplexity; it may be the distress and terror of some sorely afflicted little household; it may be the secret bitterness of some humble and contrite spirit; in any case, a matter how infinitely small when measured by the scale of immensity and eternity; but oh, how great a thing to me! And there meets me, in the way, a philosopher. "And what, forsooth, have you there? Show it me, now." And I unroll before him my little bundle of griefs, of cares, of pains, of sicknesses, of fears, of forebodings,—here a handful of myrrh from a troubled heart, and there a sprig of frankincense from a grateful spirit. "And *this*, then, is what you would bring to lay before the Infinite, the Eternal, the Omniscient, the Unchangeable God!" And each great title smites upon my heart with discouragement and dismay. "*This* is what you would bring to him in prayer and deprecation! But do you not know that all this is part of a perfect system?—that it is all fixed by laws of nature, which no prayer can change or suspend without upsetting the constitution of the universe? You would lay before God your wretched plight to move his pity? Tush! did he not know it all a hundred thousand ages ago, or ever the earth was?" And I cannot gainsay him, and I cannot cease to pray. But by and by the philosopher himself comes face to face with some of the overwhelming things in human life and human death. He hangs with tears and wringing of hands over some cradleful of childish anguish, and shrinks from what the laws of nature, the system of the universe, are doing there—so pitiless, so deaf to prayer, so blind to agony; and he looks away, and looks up, and cries, "My God, my God!" And his reason is not one whit the less true, because now, at last, his love and faith are also true and strong. The awful wonder of God's unchangeable infinity abides; but out of cloud and darkness breaks forth, oh, what light of fatherly love! And the bewildered soul sings:—

> And can this mighty King
> Of glory condescend?
> And will he write his name
> My Father, and my Friend?
> I love his name! I love his word!
> Join all my powers and praise the Lord!

And now behold a mystery—the mystery of godliness, without controversy great, manifest in the flesh! That he may come over these mountains of hopeless separation, that we may be helped to know, to love, to trust that which is far too vast for the reach of our clinging affections to clasp, what wonders of condescending tenderness will not our Father do! There draweth near to us one having the likeness of man, but glorious with an unearthly glory, as of the only-begotten of the Father, full of grace and truth. He stands beside us in our daily cares, our household joys and griefs, our business troubles and anxieties, our national fears and sorrows. He shares our temptations. He is touched with the feeling of our infirmities. He carries our sorrows. He bears our sicknesses. He dies our death. How easy to love him, to come near to him, to trust him! Being lifted up, how doth he draw all men unto him! And what mean those wonderful words of his, telling of his intimacy, his sonship, his oneness with the invisible and eternal God? Could it be, perhaps, that such an one might bring us nearer to the inaccessible Light—might help us to draw nigh as seeing him who is invisible? O Master, show us the Father and it sufficeth us! And hear now his gracious words: "He that believeth on me believeth on him that sent me." "He that hath seen me hath seen the Father also." Thus the high and lofty One, who hath wonderfully entered into our narrow understanding, cometh also into our heart, and draweth us to his own bosom "with the chords of love, with the bands of a man."

III. Finally, with a true spiritual intercourse and converse, which no man can define, which is as the viewless wind that men know although they see it not, and feel its quickening and refreshment, although they cannot tell whence it cometh nor whither it goeth, God entereth into our spirits, "not to sojourn, but abide with us," and we become the temples of the Holy Ghost.

XXX.

CHURCH, SECT AND CONGREGATION.

SERMON TO THE WOODLAND CHURCH, MAY 25, 1884, ON OCCASION OF AN INVITATION TO BE INSTALLED AS PASTOR.

That thou mayest know how thou oughtest to behave thyself in the house of God, which is the church of the living God, the pillar and ground of the truth.—1 TIMOTHY iii. 15.

MY DEAR FRIENDS AND BRETHREN OF THE WOODLAND CHURCH:—Although I have thus announced to you, according to the ancient tradition of pulpit discourse, a verse of holy Scripture, it is not my purpose to comment on it, nor to illustrate it, otherwise than incidentally in the course of an answer which I owe to that invitation with which you have honored me, to continue permanently with you in the work of the ministry. It is a beautiful law of the kingdom of heaven, that even the business affairs of God's house, undertaken in a worthy spirit, should be part of a Christian's joy, and a means of his edification; and I am not afraid that you will reckon it other than a good and profitable use of holy time if I take so much of this hour of worship as may be needful, to set before you, without any reserve, what seems to be my duty as a minister of Jesus Christ, in view of your invitation.

I am thankful to divine providence that no room is left me for hesitation. I have no right to refuse to do the work of the ministry, whenever the opportunity is given me. And I have no opportunity except this. If there were any other demand for my service, I should be compelled to hesitate and compare. But there is no other. I am led in a plain path, and I am glad of it. It is my clear duty to go forward with the work of the gospel here as my permanent work, and I accept it.

But, indeed, you have made it very easy and pleasant for me to consent. I knew, when I came here, that I was coming to a difficult and doubtful work, involving labor, expense and self-denial on the part of whoever should enter into it. But the labor has been lightened and cheered by your faithful and willing co-operation. The growth of the congregation has been rapid beyond my hopes; the very serious pecuniary burdens of the church have been taken up by you with an honorable self-denial; and you have shown a care for my wants, according to your ability, which assures me that I was right in leaving that matter wholly to you. And, what is better than this, there has been no sign of dissension among you, such as I had been led to fear, but, on the contrary, as cordial a spirit of mutual kindness, and as willing a mind to serve each other and the church, as I have ever known in any congregation. Withal, there have been unmistakable signs of an earnest interest in the teaching of this pulpit, which encourage me to hope for something much better than outward prosperity and growth. Let me add one more reason of the great content with which I look forward to continuing my work here: the very cordial welcome that has been shown me, outside of this congregation, by Christian ministers and people of this community, without distinction or exception. Take it altogether, I do not count it any self-denial at all, but a privilege for which I am truly thankful, to continue to share with you the burdens of this work.

Let us not misunderstand each other as to what we mean by my *permanence* in this work. In my own mind and purpose, it means this: that so long as I am wanted here in the Woodland Church, I shall not look for any other work. I shall not leave this church of my own motion. If it should happen that some other work came seeking me, of course I could not escape from the duty of considering the claims of it. But you may be quite easy on this score. I have never been troubled by any eager competition for my services. The opposite contingency is much more probable. Your mind is much more likely to change than mine is. Notwithstanding this unanimous good-will which is now so apparent, and so grateful to my heart, the time will doubtless come when there will be two minds among this people about me and my ministry. Be assured that I am not more fully purposed in my heart to abide with you while you are agreed in desiring it, than to withdraw myself whenever it shall clearly appear to me that such withdrawal is better for you, or is desired by any considerable part of the congregation. I do not in the least doubt the sincerity of your present kindness. But I bear in mind what the situation is, and what it is likely to be. This is now a feeble church, to which I am able to give the very best of my strength. I hope it will soon be a strong church; and it is certain that I must soon be not so strong; it is certain also that if I have grace to be faithful, there will by and by be some to be offended in me. It is not without learning something that I have read the Epistle to the Galatians, and have had personal and painful experience of the changefulness of popular feeling in a congregation. Whenever the day shall come that it shall seem to some of you that the church has outgrown its minister, I only ask to be let go in peace, and to be kept in your kindly remembrance, as one who never refused any work which was asked of him, and who counted it joy to sow where other men should reap.

Let me speak now of the title and tenure under which I may remain in this charge. It has been urged in the kindest manner, both by members of this congregation, and by neighboring pastors, that I be installed here as pastor, according to the Presbyterian Order of Government. I might be excused, perhaps, from answering this proposal until it should be officially and responsibly tendered to me; and yet the suggestion comes so near as to require me thoroughly to ponder it; and it seems to me best on all accounts to give you frankly and without reserve, the clear and definite results to which I have been led, and the reasons for them.

In favor of the proposed formal and public installation are some slight considerations of convenience in administration; and the strong disposition which I have to respond, with deference and unreserved adhesion, to the truly fraternal welcome that is proffered me here by men who have so strong a claim on my love and veneration. I might add, the modicum of advantage which would accrue to the church from the formal and public advertisement of the newly established pastorate. I do not know that there is any other reason that could be named. But the reasons to the contrary are to my mind entirely conclusive.

I. The first reason is a negative one. A formal installation as pastor would add nothing to the real permanence of my relation to you. No installing authority has any power to hold a pastor in his place who has made up his mind to leave it; and if it sometimes helps to keep a man in his place after the people are willing to part with him, that is just the help which I do not want. I am willing to bind myself to labor here until plain duty calls me away. But I am not willing to bind *you*, otherwise than by "the chords of love" and hearty approval.

II. I am not disposed to ally myself to any one of the Christian sects of Philadelphia in its competitions and antagonisms toward the other sects.

There are persons who do not understand how one can be a good citizen without belonging to an organized political party. And there are those who do not see how one can be a good Christian without belonging to an organized sect or (as it is the American fashion to call it) to a "denomination." There is no need, at this time, for me to argue with those (if there are such) who hold that the organization of a community of Christian people into competing sects is the right, normal, apostolic way of organization. Neither need I argue with those who hold that even if it is not quite right, it is quite unavoidable; and that the best thing for each one to do is to join that sect which pleases him best, and push it all he can, on the principle that competition is the life of business; who consider that "emulations" are not, as Paul used to think, among "the works of the flesh." I am not here arguing against other people's views; I am only defining my own. If there are any that think thus, it is enough to say that I do not agree with them; and that among these various competitors, I quite decline to take sides with any sect as against the rest. My interest in the Woodland Church is not as being Presbyterian, but simply as being Christian; and outside of the Woodland Church, my fellowship, so long as I remain here, shall be with the whole commonwealth of Christ's faithful people and ministers in this city, and not distinctively with one sect of them.

What then, it may be asked, is your position? Are you a Congregationalist? I answer, No. I do not accept that theory of the Church; I do not belong to the sect which some men are now trying to organize under that name. I am held in fraternal fellowship as a minister of the gospel by the General Association of Connecticut pastors, most of whom are Congregationalists; but who, in accordance with their characteristic catholicity and liberality, willingly hold me in their valued fellowship, notwithstanding my known dissent from their views. But I am no more a Congregationalist than I am a Presbyterian. If it be asked, then, "What are you?" I answer that as I do not hold with Congregationalists that a *congregation* of Christians is a church; neither do I hold with Presbyterians, Episcopalians and others that a *sect* of Christians, seperated from their brethren on some basis of doctrine or polity, is a church; but only a schism. I acknowledge one Holy Catholic Church, the communion of saints. To my mind, and to the affections of my heart, the Church of Christ in Philadelphia is the whole commonwealth of Christian believers and ministers here; and if it is to be my privilege to labor here, I shall seek every opportunity of manifesting that my love for all good men is not in the least affected by sectarian lines.

Let me guard myself from one easy misconception. My love for the whole commonwealth of Christian people as constituting together the one Church, the body of Christ, does not depend on any disparaging or belittling of the importance of questions on which Christians differ; nor on my being content to hold in a vague way nothing but those points on which all Christians agree—if there are any such points. I have not a particle of sympathy with that Tract Society and Evangelical Alliance basis of fellowship. My love for all Christians is perfectly consistent with the most sharp and decided objections to the errors which some Christians hold, and with a positive and definite adhesion to important truths which some Christians reject. Undoubtedly the Holy Catholic Church, the communion of saints, includes some erratic, some most imperfect Christians; but for all that I love the Holy Catholic Church, the whole of it; and I cannot take part in confirming the divisions by which it is sundered.

What would be the practical bearing of these views of duty of mine on my proposed ministry here? I will try to answer:—

(1) I should hold myself bound by obligations of honor, more stringent than the letter of any canonical obligation, that this church should be distinguished by exemplary fidelity to its constitutional duties in that order of government under which it is placed;—strict in its constitutional duties, but also strenuous for its constitutional liberties, and using them with a free and wise discretion. I find the *internal* organization and regulation of a Presbyterian parish to be admirable and excellent—quite superior to what I have been accustomed to in the usages of Congregational churches; and in its external relations it would be my ardent desire and my confident hope to retain that fraternal confidence which has been generously extended to me by the ministers of the Presbyterian as of other denominations here.

(2) While I should wish, thus, that in the faithful conduct of its affairs according to the prescribed rules, this should be loyally *a Presbyterian Church*, it would be the constant tendency of my ministry that it would not be *a church for Presbyterians*, but should become more and more "a house of prayer for all people." Far from promoting among you a spirit of sectarian vaunting and competition, it would be my earnest effort to lead you in the direction of a larger fellowship. I should be careful not to encourage in you a foolish and vain complacency in the characteristics of your own sect as being better than anything to be found elsewhere, in doctrine, in organization, in usages of worship, and I should study to teach you the Christian duty taught by the apostle Paul, to "look not on your own things, but on the things of others,"—to be prompt to recognize an excellence in other Christians, and ready in acknowledging points of inferiority in yourselves. Especially in the matter of your charitable gifts, I should seek to exercise you in that charity which "seeketh not her own," so that you should learn to take especial delight in the sort of giving which does *not* inure to the advantage or the glorification of "our side," or "our party," or "our church." As much as in me lies, I would draw you to think less of "the glory of Presbyterianism" (to quote an expression that has grown familiar to me of late) and more of the glory of God.

III. It is a further reason with me for declining to be installed as a member of the Presbytery, that I am unwilling to give assent, in the usual form, to the doctrinal standards of the Presbyterian Church; and this, not so much because I dissent from them (for I have purposely refrained from studying them with reference to this question) as because I do not like this way of expressing my opinions. What my theological convictions are, is no secret from any man or body of men interested to inquire about them. It is the business of my life to declare them. I am eager to give account of them on every fit occasion. I would be glad to have the Presbytery examine me on every topic in theology; and *the Presbytery* may say, if it likes, whether my views are sufficiently in conformity with the church standards; but on that question *I* decline to pronounce. When asked for my solemn assent to certain ancient documents the exact meaning of which has been for generations under a dispute which is still pending, insomuch that at times one-half of the Presbyterian Church has been denouncing the other half as unfaithful to them,—it is impossible to give a categorical answer that shall not be an ambiguous one. One cannot say either Yes or No, without being misunderstood by somebody. Therefore I prefer not to put myself in a position in which such an answer will be expected of me. I judge no man who decides otherwise. I know that the "constitutional question" is framed with intentional vagueness and looseness. I know there are volumes of plausible casuistry about the *animus imponentis*—the right of giving assent to such documents in the sense understood by the body requiring it. But there is another right which is clearer still,—the right of giving no assent at all; and this is the right which I prefer to exercise.

"But in view of the vagueness of the required assent, in view of the acknowledged variety of sentiment that exists without objection among the Presbyterian clergy, and in view of the important interests involved, is it not best to concede this point?"

I think not. What the times call for—these perilous but hopeful times of the advancement of Christian truth amid conflicts with falsehood old and new,—what the times call for is not vagueness, and a spirit of concession in personal convictions; but the most conscientious definiteness in the statement of truth, on the part of every man, both as to what he will say, and as to what he won't say. And what the Presbyterian Church needs is, not a few more accessions from New England of men who do not quite agree with your standards of doctrine and polity, but who are willing, in view of important interests, to say, in a vague way, that they partly do; but more and more men, no matter where they come from, who, in spite of all interests, personal or ecclesiastical, insist that they will "swear in the words of no master," but that in answering all questions, "constitutional" or other, they will be fully, definitely, unreservedly understood, as to what they do believe, and what they do not believe, and what they have not made up their minds about.

From a wide and valued personal acquaintance with Presbyterian clergymen, and still wider acquaintance with their writings, I judge that I agree with them on points of theology as far as they agree with one another. You who have heard me here, these few months, are witnesses whether I preach "any gospel other than that which ye received." But if my teaching is found to be in agreement with "the standards," it is not because I have tried to make it so. I have not tried to humor your prejudices or traditions, but only to know and declare the truth. The orthodoxy that comes of trying to be orthodox is very little better than heresy. If the results of one's sincere personal study in the school of Jesus Christ and his apostles are found to be accordant with the results reached by other earnest and devout men, in various lands and ages, it is a thing to be recognized with satisfaction. But to take the tenets of a certain school of theologians and set them up as a "standard," and then (not without pressure from considerations of interest and convenience) to strive to work oneself into conformity thereto, or the semblance of conformity, this would be a shameful thing, as all will confess. The "standards" elaborated by the theologians who met in the Jerusalem Chamber two hundred and fifty years ago, are confessedly noble compositions. But they are not standards for me; and I cannot be guilty of the insincerity of affecting to regard them with any greater deference than that which is due to other attempted statements of Christian truth which have been widely approved by wise and good men.*

---

*Since this sermon was preached, the necessity has twice been laid upon me, of submitting to the Presbytery under whose government the

The tenure, then, on which I propose to remain with you in the ministry of the gospel, so long as my services shall be required, is simply that of an agreement continuing in force until dissolved by mutual consent. As to the details of the agreement, it will be easy to adjust them.

And now, my dear friends, that I have so unreservedly laid before you my inmost mind on the practical questions that have been raised before me by your most kind invitation, I beg you, first, very seriously to consider whether, in view of these statements, it is still your desire to have me for your minister; and in case you find, in what I have said, no reason to change your mind, then, secondly, to leave cheerfully to the Presbytery, which, under your polity, is charged with full power and responsibility in the case, the question whether, in view of the same, it shall permit the proposed arrangement. I gladly leave the matter in the hands of that body, knowing that there will be found in it no feeling toward me but one of personal kindness, and that it will have the warmest interest in your welfare.

Finally, brethren, I commend you to God, and to the word of his grace, which is able to build you up, and to give you an inheritance among all them that are sanctified. There let your confident trust abide. Beware of too much concern in the merely personal question who is to be your minister. It is

---

Woodland Church belongs, the question of admitting me to its membership. But the limitations with which I felt bound to qualify my assent to the ritual questions of initiation were held to be a bar to admission. I do not in the least complain of it; on the contrary, if we concede the right of Christians to organize themselves into mutually exclusive sects, we can hardly deny the duty of guarding the frontiers of the sect, and enforcing the rules of exclusion. It is without reflecting the slightest blame on any that I express the regret that these rules were deemed to involve my separation from a useful work and from a loving and beloved people. Great as the cost is, it is not too much to pay for the luxury of unreserved sincerity when the question is on the declaration of one's religious convictions.

unworthy of the dignity of your calling as children of God. In simplicity and godly sincerity, seek the kingdom of God and his righteousness, and all needful things shall be added unto you.

THE END.

www.ingramcontent.com/pod-product-compliance
Lightning Source LLC
Chambersburg PA
CBHW050333230426
43663CB00010B/1843